Growing Old in a New Age
Telecourse Study Guide

Growing Old in a New Age
Telecourse Study Guide
Fifth Edition

for

Hooyman and Kiyak

Social Gerontology
Seventh Edition

prepared by

Kathryn L. Braun
University of Hawai'i at Manoa

Michael Cheang
University of Hawai'i at Manoa

From
The Annenberg/CPB Project

PEARSON

Boston   New York   San Francisco
Mexico City   Montreal   Toronto   London   Madrid   Munich   Paris
Hong Kong   Singapore   Tokyo   Cape Town   Sydney

This guide was developed for use with GROWING OLD IN A NEW AGE, an introductory, college-level telecourse on aging. The telecourse consists of 13 one-hour television programs, a text, a Faculty Guide, and this Study Guide. The series was produced by the Center on Aging at the University of Hawai'i. Major funding was provided by The Annenberg/CPB Project. GROWING OLD IN A NEW AGE is closed-captioned for the hearing impaired.

ISBN 0-205-44597-7

Printed in the United States of America

10 9 8 7 6 5 4 3 2 1   07 06 05 04

GROWING OLD IN A NEW AGE

PROJECT PARTICIPANTS (1993)

Series Narrator

Susan Stamberg
Broadcast Journalist
National Public Radio
Washington, DC

Telecourse Project Staff

Anthony M. Lenzer, Ph.D.
Project Director/Executive Producer
Center on Aging
University of Hawaii at Manoa
Honolulu, HI

Joan Pabst Dubanoski, Ph.D.
Associate Project Director/Senior Producer
Center on Aging
University of Hawaii at Manoa
Honolulu, HI

Rebecca J. Goodman, M.S.
Project Coordinator/Writer
Center on Aging
University of Hawaii at Manoa
Honolulu, HI

Jay Curlee
Writer/Director
Pacific Focus, Inc.
Honolulu, HI

Kathryn L. Braun, Dr.P.H.
Student and Faculty Guides Writer
School of Public Health
University of Hawaii at Manoa
Honolulu, HI

Ellen Roberts, M.P.H.
Field Evaluator
University of Hawaii at Hilo
Hilo, HI

Floriana Cofman, M.L.S.
Researcher
Public Library System, State of Hawaii
Honolulu, HI

Senior Project Officer

Hilda Moskowitz, Ph.D.
The Annenberg/CPB Project
Washington, DC

Advisors

Nancy R. Hooyman, Ph.D.
Dean
School of Social Work
University of Washington
Seattle, WA

Thomas MacLachlan, M.A., M.Div.
Academic Gerontology Coordinator
North Shore Community College
Beverly, MA

Ancil H. Payne
Former President, NBC's Affiliates Board
Retired President/CEO, King Broadcasting
Company Seattle, WA

David A. Peterson, Ph.D.
Director, Leonard Davis School of Gerontology
Associate Dean, Andrus Gerontology Center
University of Southern California
Los Angeles, CA

K. Warner Schaie, Ph.D.
Evan Pugh Professor of
Human Development and Psychology
Director of the Gerontology Center
Pennsylvania State University
University Park, PA

Jeanette C. Takamura, Ph.D.
Director
Executive Office on Aging, State of Hawaii
Honolulu, HI

GROWING OLD IN A NEW AGE STUDY GUIDE

TABLE OF CONTENTS

INTRODUCTION TO THE COURSE

Welcome to GROWING OLD IN A NEW AGE. We are pleased that you have elected to take this course. This *Study Guide* is designed to make the subject more understandable and enjoyable.

What Is a Telecourse?

If this is your first telecourse, you will find it somewhat different from traditional on-campus courses you have taken. Therefore, the first question is, what is a telecourse? As defined by Gripp (1977), a telecourse is:

> "[an] integrated learning system that employs television and various print materials ...specifically designed...to forge a complete education unit available to the student in the convenience of his [or her] own home. [It] is not a correspondence course with pictures, nor is it a televised lecture with supplementary readings. It is an examination and presentation of a body of knowledge and information through the use of sight, sound, color, movement, and print...to stimulate, clarify, and quantify... designed to take maximum advantage of the strengths of each component to lead the student through a "success-oriented" experience."

GROWING OLD IN A NEW AGE introduces you to gerontology, the study of aging. Components of the telecourse include thirteen one-hour video programs, a text titled *Social Gerontology: A Multidisciplinary Perspective* (*Seventh Edition*) by Nancy R. Hooyman and H. Asuman Kiyak, this *Study Guide*, and assignments provided by your instructor. Each component is important; they all work together to provide a comprehensive picture of aging.

What Is Aging?

For some people, aging is perceived negatively, a time of decay, decline, or loss. In this course, aging is presented as an inevitable aspect of living, which is neither inherently good nor bad. Gerontologists, and your text, see aging in terms of four distinct, but interrelated, processes:

1) Chronological aging refers to the number of years we have lived.

2) Biological aging refers to the physical changes we experience as we age, primarily the reduced efficiency of our organ systems. This is also referred to as functional aging.

3) Psychological aging refers to the changes in our perceptions, mental functioning, personality, and motivation over the life course.

4) Social aging refers to the changing roles and relationships experienced over the life course.

These processes do not occur in isolation. For example, healthy lifestyle habits, a good attitude, adequate financial resources, and strong social supports throughout life can slow biological aging. In turn, healthier older adults have more options for social roles in old age.

Additionally, changes in one area can cause changes in another area. For example, a change in social status can affect one's psychological status, as in the case of a man who becomes depressed after the death of his wife. Psychological changes can affect him physiologically, as he may forget to eat, experience episodes of dizziness, fall, and break a hip. This change in physical health may precipitate another change in social status as this man moves in with his children who can help him recover from the hip fracture, the episode of malnutrition, and the death of his wife.

Thus, we are bio-psycho-social beings. To understand aging, we must understand the separate processes of biological, psychological, and social aging. In addition, we must learn how these aging processes interact with one another and with our environment.

Course Goals

The telecourse has two goals:

1) To provide you with a foundation for understanding the processes of aging and old age as a stage of life.

2) To help you understand the impact of aging on society.

Course Themes

GROWING OLD IN A NEW AGE provides an introduction to bio-psycho-social aging through six themes: 1) life span development; 2) person-environment interaction; 3) optimal quality of life; 4) cross-cultural considerations; 5) how aging is studied; and 6) access to resources in a new age. These six themes are emphasized throughout the course, although not every theme is addressed in each lesson.

Life Span Development

In the past, "development" referred to the growth processes in children and "aging" referred to the decline of older adults. Now, it is known that both processes occur simultaneously. Both start at birth and continue through childhood, adolescence, young adulthood, middle age, and old age. In this view, aging itself is neither favorable nor unfavorable. Instead, it is a process that continues throughout life. While experiencing growth and change, aging individuals also remain in some ways the same. Thus, stability and change are both part of life span development. A related concept is "active-aging" which views aging as a time of growth and productivity in spite of physical decline.

Person-Environment Interaction

The aging person is a biological, psychological, and social being who constantly interacts with the biological, psychological, and social environment. Older people both affect and are affected by their environment. By modifying the environment, older adults can help compensate for personal changes and make the environment better "fit" their needs. This view of aging indicates that adaptation is a complex, interactive process between the older adult and his or her environment.

Optimal Quality of Life

Quality of life in old age is rooted in the earlier years, when health habits are developed. Early attention to diet, stress-control, preventive health care, social supports, and activity patterns result in better functional ability and greater well-being in old age. Restorative programs, including rehabilitation after illness, can help adults regain function and result in improved quality of life in old age. A safe and supportive environment contributes to optimal quality of life for older adults.

Cross-Cultural Considerations

Similarities and differences exist among societies and among ethnic groups within societies. For example, societies differ in the ways in which old age is defined. Yet the rights and responsibilities of older adults across societies often are based similarly on productivity, control of resources, and possession of vital knowledge. Modernization, declining resources, and changing values can alter the position of older adults within a particular culture. The study of different cultures and ethnic groups provides an understanding of the universal and unique cultural forces that affect aging. Cultures have much to learn from one another as they cope with the changing age structure of society now taking place.

How Aging is Studied

Knowledge of aging is obtained in various ways. Animal and human studies both provide clues about age-related changes. Subjects are studied at several points in time to discover what changes occur with age (longitudinal studies). Other research provides a "snap-shot" of differences among age groups at one point in time (cross-sectional studies). Sequential designs combine the cross-sectional and longitudinal approaches to better clarify aging-related phenomena. When we know very little about an area of interest, we may use participant observation or focus groups prior to survey research. Each type of inquiry has its strengths and weaknesses. Therefore, research methodology must be considered when judging the certainty of knowledge in gerontology.

Access to Resources in a New Age

Urbanization, industrialization, and new technologies in communication, education, and health care have radically altered the world in which we live. In addition, the structure of populations is changing as birthrates drop, infant mortality declines, migration occurs, and more people survive into adulthood and old age. These shifts have significant implications for the world's future. The increasing proportion of older adults raises interesting questions about the allocation of resources, artificial prolongation of life, creative new roles for elders, intergenerational alliances, retirement age, caregiving patterns, and so forth.

HOW TO TAKE THIS TELECOURSE

Components of the Course

The Video Programs

Thirteen one-hour television programs present information on biological, psychological, and social aspects of aging. Experts in geriatrics and gerontology introduce facts, concepts, and theories of aging. Older adults provide examples of these concepts by sharing with us their personal experiences and views of aging. While each video stands alone, together they provide a comprehensive picture of aging and older adults.

The Text

The text for the course is *Social Gerontology: A Multidisciplinary Perspective* (*Seventh Edition*) by Nancy R. Hooyman and H. Asuman Kiyak. The text looks at gerontology, the science of aging, from a multidisciplinary perspective, i.e., from biological, psychological, and sociological points of view. It provides a framework for understanding the subject and helps illustrate concepts with interesting vignettes about older people. The text presents more factual information than the videos alone can convey.

The Study Guide

This *Study Guide* serves as a "road map" to the course. For each lesson, the *Study Guide* provides the learning objectives, an introduction to the video and text assignments, a summary of the key points presented in the video and text for each learning objective, self-study questions, and instructions for essay assignments that your instructor may require you to complete. This *Study Guide* also contains a glossary of key terms and concepts introduced in the text and video, along with an index of the participants in the video.

The Instructor

As in traditional on-campus courses, your instructor plays a key role. He/she will determine the exact content of the course, your homework, and your exams. The instructor is available to answer questions and provide guidance throughout the course.

Suggested Course Syllabus

The course is organized into thirteen program lessons. Each video program has a suggested assignment in the text and *Study Guide*, shown on pages 8 and 9. Your instructor may choose to provide you with a different syllabus.

What to Expect

Prior to the Start of the Course

After registration, but prior to the start of the course, you should receive information about campus services, including the library, computer lab, bookstore, academic counseling, health services, activities, parking, and ID cards. You should also receive information from your instructor about the telecourse syllabus, expectations for your performance, and instructions for interacting with the instructor.

Faculty-Student Interaction

Compared to an on-campus course, telecourse students have less scheduled contact with the course instructor and more opportunities for independent and self-directed learning. For example, most telecourses have only three scheduled class meetings, usually held at the beginning, middle, and end of the term. The first class provides orientation to the course while the other meetings usually include review and testing. Students, however, are encouraged to contact the professor as needed outside of the scheduled class time. Possible methods of contact include the postal service, electronic mail, phone, fax, and personal visits. The relevant addresses and numbers should be provided at the start of the semester.

The Student's Responsibility

Each component of the telecourse provides good information on the topic. But to meet the learning objectives for each lesson, materials from all the components are important and work together. It is your responsibility to absorb and integrate the materials, contacting the instructor for assistance as needed.

Weekly Instructions

• **Read** the *Study Guide* assignment.
• **Watch** the one-hour television program. Look for the terms and concepts the *Study Guide* has prepared you to see.
• **Read** the assigned pages in the course text, and go over the "points to ponder" for each chapter.
• **Reread** the *Study Guide*.
• **Answer** the self-study questions.
• **Write** down the questions that remain unanswered and contact your instructor for clarification.
• **Complete** and submit assignments as directed by the instructor.

General Instructions for Assignments

Your instructor has been provided with suggested assignments for each of the telecourse's lessons. General instructions for each type of assignment are provided below. Your instructor may choose to modify the instructions or provide you with alternative assignments altogether.

Reaction Paper

Your instructor may assign a Reaction Paper, in which you will be asked to write a paper describing: 1) new information you gained from watching the video, 2) how the experiences of the older adults in the video affected your personal view of aging, and 3) other comments to the instructor regarding the lesson or the course.

A good Reaction Paper is brief and to the point, documents the content of the video, and demonstrates your emotional response to the video. A Reaction Paper also serves as a personal and private communication between the student and the instructor. *Suggested length: two pages.*

Older-Adult Interview

Your instructor may assign you to interview an older adult, usually someone over the age of 60. Suggested interview questions are provided, along with questions for you to answer after completing your interview. The assignment requires you to write a paper about your interview and your analysis of it. *Suggested length: three to five pages.*

How do you locate an older adult willing to be interviewed? In our experience, most older adults enjoy being interviewed by students. It provides them with the opportunity to reflect on their lives and to share their experiences. You may find a willing participant in your family, in your neighborhood, at your church, or at a senior center. If you have difficulty finding someone to interview, your instructor may be able to identify an older adult for you.

Community Service Interview

Your instructor may assign you to interview an employee of a community service agency. In most cases, you will be provided with the name of the agency, or at least the type of agency, to learn more about. Suggested interview questions are provided. The assignment requires you to write a paper about your findings. *Suggested length: three to five pages.*

Research Paper

Your instructor may want you to research an area of gerontology introduced in the video or text. You may be assigned a single topic or you may be provided with a list of topics to choose from.

Read a book or five journal articles on the topic. A good place to start searching for reading material is in the reference section provided at the end of each text chapter. More current literature can be identified through print and computerized databases, described on pages 5 to 7 in the *Study Guide*.

The assignment requires you to write a research paper that describes the historical and current thinking on the topic. Identify things about the topic that are not yet resolved or may benefit from further study. *Suggested length: five to ten pages.*

Analyzing the Text Vignettes

Your instructor may ask you to read about the older adults featured in the vignettes that appear throughout the text and to write an essay in which you compare and contrast these adults on the concepts introduced in the lesson. *Suggested length: two to three pages.*

Future Trends

Your instructor may assign you to consider the current trends described in the video and text and to speculate about the future. For example, given that people are living longer, what new opportunities for work and leisure would you expect in the future? The assignment requires you to write a paper detailing the current trends and describing your vision of the future based on these trends. *Suggested length: 2-3 pages.*

In-Class Activities

Your instructor has been provided with suggestions for in-class activities. This category of assignments was developed primarily for instructors who use the telecourse materials in an on-campus course.

Tests

Your instructor has been provided with sample test questions. In preparing for quizzes, tests and exams, carefully review the *Study Guide* and your notes from the video and text.

How to Learn More About Aging

The video and text provide an introduction to gerontology. You may be interested in going beyond the text and video to learn more about the subject. What is the best way to do this? Here are two ways you can broaden your understanding of aging:

Meet Older Adults

You may be assigned to interview an older person. We suggest you go beyond the formal requirement of an interview to get a good understanding about the person's background and feelings. Or visit a senior center, nursing home, Elderhostel class, or another program for older adults in your community. Observe the activities, meet the participants, and ask questions. Older people have a lot to teach us about gerontology.

Additional Reading

References are provided at the end of each text chapter. One of the best and easiest ways to learn more about a particular subject is to consult the end-of-chapter list. Most of these references can be found via your campus library.

Journals. There are a growing number of scholarly journals devoted to disseminating research findings specifically about the aging process and older adults. Examples include:

Abstracts in Social Gerontology
Age and Ageing
Ageing and Society
Aging International
Aging and Work
Behavior, Health, and Aging
Canadian Journal on Aging
Clinical Gerontologist
Contemporary Long Term Care
Contemporary Gerontology
Death Studies
Education and Ageing
Educational Gerontology
Experimental Aging Research
Generations
Geriatric Nursing
Geriatrics
The Gerontologist
Gerontology and Geriatrics Education
Home Health Care Services Quarterly
Hospice Journal
International Journal of Aging and Human
    Development
International Journal of Geriatric Psychiatry
Journal of Aging and Ethnicity
Journal of Aging and Health
Journal of Aging and Physical Activities
Journal of Aging and Social Policy
Journal of Aging Studies
Journal of the American Geriatrics Society
Journal of Applied Gerontology
Journal of Cross Cultural Gerontology
Journal of Educational Gerontology
Journal of Elder Abuse and Neglect
Journal of Gay and Lesbian Social Services
Journal of Geriatric Drug Therapy
Journal of Geriatric Psychiatry
Journal of Gerontological Nursing
Journal of Gerontological Social Work
Journal of Health, Politics, Policy, and Law
Journal of Housing for the Elderly
Journal of Mental Health and Aging
Journal of Nutrition for the Elderly
Journal of Religious Gerontology
Journal of the American Geriatrics Society
Journal of Women and Aging
Journals of Gerontology
Omega: Journal of Death and Dying
Perspective on Aging
Physical and Occupational Therapy in Geriatrics
Psychology and Aging
Research on Aging
Topics in Geriatric Rehabilitation
Victimization of the Elderly and Disabled

In addition to these and other journals that focus on aging, journals in the fields of medicine, nursing, public health, and social work often carry articles of interest to gerontologists. A more detailed list of journals that address issues of aging can be found at the **AgeLine** website listed below.

Electronic Databases. Because reports of new developments in gerontology are published every day, the end-of-chapter list may not include the most recent literature on your topic of interest. Fortunately, much of the literature on aging is referenced in electronic databases accessible online, which can be searched by subject, author, title, or journal name or year. Some databases can be freely accessed. Other databases are supported through subscription and can be accessed only by subscribers. Many academic libraries subscribe directly to these databases or subscribe to an omnibus service such as **EBSCO** through which many databases can be accessed. Refer questions about specific databases to your campus librarian.

AgeLine is an online guide to books, reports, articles from journals and magazines, and videos related to issues of aging and life at age 50 and older. Links to complete publications on the web or to online ordering sources are provided. In addition to searching by subject, author, title, journal, or year, you can browse ready-made searches on high-interest topics using AgeLine's "Searches to Go" (for general-interest/consumer publications) or "Research to Go" (for research and policy publications) features. Publications are from 1978 to the present, with selected coverage from 1966-1977. This database is available free via AARP. http://research.aarp.org/ageline/home.html.

Aging from the **Annual Editions** series from Dushkin Online is a compilation of public press articles that address the most relevant and current problems in the area of aging. Articles are written by gerontologists, educators, researchers, and writers and present a variety of divergent views on the challenges of aging and ways to meet these challenges. The articles provide an effective and useful perspective on today's important topics in the study of aging. http://www.dushkin.com/online. It is available in print or online for a fee.

Cumulative Index to Nursing and Allied Health Literature (CINAHL) is a database including journal articles, books, dissertations, and reports relevant to nursing and allied health from 1982 to present. Although a bibliographic database, the CINAHL database includes selected full-text material from journals and newsletters, standards of practice, practice acts, government publications, research instruments, and patient education material. http://www.cinahl.com/. Available by subscription.

Educational Resources Information Center (ERIC) is a national information system funded by the U.S. Department of Education's Institute of Education Sciences. As the world's largest source of education information, ERIC contains more than 1 million abstracts of education-related documents and journal articles, including many full-text resources. http://www.eric.ed.gov.

PubMed is a free service of the National Library of Medicine that accesses **MEDLINE** (an important index to the medical literature) and additional life science journals. It includes more than over 14 million citations for biomedical articles back to the 1960's and includes links to many sites providing full-text articles in a few cases for free and other related resources. Check for your library's link to this database for access to full-text journals you're your library subscribes to. http://www.ncbi.nlm.nih.gov/PubMed/.

PsycINFO is an online database that provides abstracts and citations to the scholarly literature in the behavioral sciences and mental health. The database is maintained by the American Psychological Association and includes material of relevance to psychologists and professionals in related fields such as psychiatry, management, business, education, social science, neuroscience, law, medicine, and social work. http://www.apa.org/psycinfo/ Available by subscription.

Sociological Abstracts is an online database with abstracts of journal articles and citations to book reviews drawn from more than 1,800 serials publications, books, book chapters, dissertations, and conference papers relevant to sociology. Available by subscription. http://www.csa.com/csa/factsheets/socioabs.s html.

Social Sciences Citation Index and **Social SciSearch** provide access to current and retrospective bibliographic information, author abstracts, and cited references found in more than 1,700 of the world's leading scholarly social sciences and technology journals. Available by subscription. http://www.isinet.com/products/citation/ssci/.

Social Work Abstracts, produced by the National Association of Social Workers, Inc., contains citations spanning 1977 to the present from social work and other related journals. Available in print or online via subscription. http://www.naswpress.org/publications/journals/abstracts/swabintro.html.

Websites. Websites, e-mail discussion groups, chat rooms, and news groups devoted to aging are added to the Web every day. Sites for some key agencies and associations in aging are provided below. And many of these websites provide links to additional websites in aging.

http://www.aoa.gov/ - Administration on Aging, U.S. Department of Health and Human Services.

http://www.nih.gov/nia - National Institute on Aging

http://www.eldercare.gov/Eldercare/Public/Home.asp - An online directory of eldercare services in communities across the country, maintained by the U.S. Administration on Aging.

http://www.nia.nih.gov/resource/? - An online resource directory for older people, maintained by the Administration on Aging and the National Institute on Aging.

http://nihseniorhealth.gov/ - An online source of aging and health information for seniors and families, maintained by the National Institute on Aging and the National Library of Medicine.

http://www.asaging.org/ - American Society on Aging. You can link to other sites from http://www.asaging.org/peer-to-peer/natlinks.cfm

http://www.aarp.org/ - AARP. You can link to 700 of the best sites for people age 50+) at http://www.aarp.org/internetresources/.

http://www.aghe.org - Association for Gerontology in Higher Education

http://www.americangeriatrics.org/links/ - American Geriatrics Society Inc.

http://www.ncoa.org -National Council on Aging

http://www.geron.org/ - Gerontological Society of America. You can link to more online resources at http://www.geron.org/online.html.

http://www.hsclc.org - National Senior Citizens Law Center

http://www.caregiver.org/caregiver/jsp/home.jsp - An online resources for caregivers, maintained by the Family Caregiver Alliance.

Organizations Concerned about Older Women and Minorities. A number of other organizations are devoted to aging. Since the video and text bring up issues related to older women and minorities, it is appropriate to list a few of the organizations that advocate specifically for these populations. For more information on these and other organizations, visit this website: http://www.nia.nih.gov/resource/

> Gray Panthers
> Lesbian and Gay Aging Issues Network
> National Asian Pacific Center on Aging
> National Association for Hispanic Elderly
> National Caucus and Center on the Black Aged
> National Center on Minority Health and Health Disparities
> National Resource Center on Native American Aging
> National Hispanic Council on Aging
> National Indian Council on Aging
> Older Women's League

Growing Old in a New Age Website. A website specifically for this telecourse was developed by Joan Dubanoski as a meeting place for instructors, students, and other telecourse users.

It includes: 1) summaries of the Program Lessons; 2) answers to frequently-asked questions about the telecourse; 3) a discussion group; 4) links to national, international, and Hawai`i-based websites; 5) electronic survey and feedback forms which allow you to give comments about the telecourse videos, text, guides, and website; 6) tips on using telecourse materials in community and corporate settings; and 7) information on licensing the telecourse and ordering videos and print material; and 8) introductions to the telecourse team and our work with the telecourse. www.growingold.hawaii.edu/

Suggested Course Syllabus

Video	Text: *Social Gerontology: A Multidisciplinary Perspective, Seventh Edition*	Study Guide
1) Myths and Realities of Aging	Introduction to Part One Chapters 1 and 2	Lesson 1
Elders and experts examine the common myths surrounding aging compared with today's realities. The rapid growth of the elderly population is discussed, along with the impact of this growth on society.		
2) How the Body Ages	Introduction to Part Two Chapter 3	Lesson 2
Experts describe the universal physical changes that accompany aging and explain how other changes can be prevented. Researchers describe advances in cellular studies and the search for biomarkers of aging.		
3) Maximizing Physical Potential of Older Adults	Chapter 4, sections on Defining Health, Quality of Life, and Health Promotion with Older People Chapter 11, section on Person-Environment Theories of Aging Chapters 14 and 15	Lesson 3
Information is provided on ways to achieve one's physical potential while compensating for the effects of aging. Elders describe how lifestyle choices have helped them maintain an active, healthy life.		
4) Love, Intimacy, and Sexuality	Chapter 7	Lesson 4
Examines the sources of love and affection in old age and describes how aging may affect sexual and reproductive functioning. Older adults discuss their continuing need for companionship, intimacy, love, and sex.		
5) Learning, Memory, and Speed of Behavior	Introduction to Part Three Chapter 5	Lesson 5
This program explores what happens to our mental capacities as we age. Techniques used to maintain and augment mental functioning are examined. Elders explain why lifelong learning is crucial.		
6) Intellect, Personality, and Mental Health	Chapter 6	Lesson 6
Intellectual function and the nature of personality are examined. Gerontologists describe longitudinal and cross-sectional research designs to study intellect and personality. Elders discuss mental health and stress-reduction techniques.		
7) Social Roles and Relationships in Old Age	Introduction to Part Four Chapter 8 Chapter 12, sections on Leisure, Membership, Volunteer Work, Educational Programs, Religious Participation, and Political Participation	Lesson 7
This program looks at how family, friendship, work, and leisure roles evolve as we age. Elders discuss coping with role loss resulting from retirement or death of a loved one. The pioneering of new roles is explored.		

Video	Text: *Social Gerontology: A Multidisciplinary Perspective, Seventh Edition*	Study Guide
8) Family and Inter-generational Relationships	Chapters 9, 10 and 11	Lesson 8
This program profiles older people as spouses and grandparents and looks at how elders help sustain family traditions and culture. Older adults describe the satisfaction and stresses of caring for spouses and frail parents.		
9) Work, Retirement, and Economic Status	Chapter 12, sections on Retirement, Employment Status, Economic Status, and Poverty Among Old and Young Chapter 16, sections on Income Security Programs and Private Pensions and Income Tax Provisions	Lesson 9
Explored are labor force trends, retirement planning, and new job opportunities for older workers. Retirees describe community service and leisure activities, along with concerns about their financial security in retirement. Social Security and other income sources are discussed.		
10) Illness and Disability	Chapter 4, sections on Chronic and Acute Diseases, Causes of Death, Common Chronic Conditions, Falls, and Use of Physician Services Chapter 6, sections on Psychological Disorders Among Older People, Depression, Dementia, Alzheimer's Disease, Alcoholism, Paranoid Disorders and Schizophrenia, Anxiety, and Older Adults Who Are Chronically Mentally Ill	Lesson 10
This program examines chronic health problems and availability of supportive services. Older people discuss how they cope with physical and mental illness and face tough decisions regarding institutionalization and costs of long-term care.		
11) Dying, Death, and Bereavement	Chapter 13	Lesson 11
Discussed are the services older people need to deal with dying and death. Elders describe their views on widowhood and management of grief. Experts examine the ethical dilemmas posed by terminal illness.		
12) Societal and Political Aspects of Aging	Introduction to Part Five Chapters 16 and 17	Lesson 12
Reviewed are roles older adults play in the political process, major social and health programs affecting older Americans, and the policy issues surrounding long-term care.		
13) The Future of Aging	Sections on "Implications for the Future" at the end of Chapters 16 and 17	Lesson 13
The final program explores how demographic, health, and technological changes will impact families and society in the future. The video suggests that intergenerational coalitions can help us build a better future for people of all ages.		

What's Your Aging IQ?

National Institute on Aging (2003)

We all know someone "old."

It might be a grandparent, a neighbor, or maybe the person behind the counter at the dry cleaners. But do you really know what it means to be old? Do you know what older people are concerned about, how they can get the most out of the rest of their lives, and what normal aging really is?

Here are several very short stories, each followed by a few related questions. Scattered between these story/question combinations are more general questions about growing old. Some are multiple-choice, some are true/false (T/F), and some yes/no (Y/N).

Circle the answers you think are right.

Follow your instructor's directions to find the correct answers from your text or from other sources.

1. Which of the following age groups is one of the fastest growing segments of the American population?

    a.   babies and children under age 5
    b.   children ages 15 to 19
    c.   people over age 85

Let's look at some older people and see how much you know about aging.

Phyllis is 64. Recently, she had a DEXA-scan to check her bone density. The results showed she was at risk of a hip, wrist, or spine fracture because she was developing osteoporosis. Her doctor wants her to start doing weight-bearing exercise 3 or 4 times a week to increase the density of her bones. The doctor also suggested she get her husband to exercise with her to protect his bones. An exercise program of 30-minutes of moderate-level activity on most days of the week would also help prevent heart disease in both of them.

2. Is Phyllis too old to lift weights?

    Yes   No

3a. Should her husband worry about his bones?

    Yes   No

3b. Do men get osteoporosis also?

    Yes   No

4. I thought heart disease was a man's disease. Does Phyllis have to worry about that too?

    Yes   No

Sylvia is 75. She has smoked cigarettes since she was 20. Her children and grand-children all want her to quit. But several members of her family died of cancer in their old age, and she believes it's too late now.

5. Even if an older person has smoked tobacco his or her whole life, it still makes sense to quit.

    True   False

6. Screening for cancer is less important with each year of life since older people can't put up with aggressive treatment.

    True   False

7. After heart disease, the next most common cause of death after age 65 in 2000 was:

    a.   stroke and related diseases
    b.   chronic respiratory disease, such as chronic bronchitis, emphysema, and asthma
    c.   cancer

Harry is 80 and seems depressed lately. His wife has noticed a change in his mood around the house and is concerned. He has always loved to drive his car. But, lately, he's worried when he gets behind the wheel. His vision seems to be changing. Last week he almost hit a messenger on a bike. The eye doctor says he has a cataract in one eye and needs surgery.

8. Is cataract surgery really likely to help Harry see better?

 Yes   No

9. Will Harry still have to stop driving his car anyway, since he is 80?

Yes   No

10. Is depression normal at Harry's age?

Yes   No

Sam is 70. He can't understand why he is more tired than he used to be. He goes to bed and gets up at the same time he always has. He often takes a nap in the afternoon. Maybe it's because he has a lot on his mind right now. He's worried because he seems to be more forgetful than before - even a little confused some times. And his younger brother was just diagnosed with probable Alzheimer's disease. Does he have it too?

11. The older a person gets, the less he or she needs sleep.

True   False

12. Forgetfulness and even a little confusion are not necessarily signs of Alzheimer's disease.

True   False

13. Sam's brother having Alzheimer's disease means Sam will get it too.

True   False

Osteoporosis, heart disease, eye problems, trouble sleeping—just to name some of the things we've discussed. No wonder older people seem to take a lot of medicine!

14. Which age group uses the most prescription medicines?

　　a.　Under age 18
　　b.　Age 19 to 64
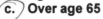　c.　Over age 65

Mary is 66. Her husband had a heart attack and died two years ago. She's gained weight in recent years although her eating habits haven't changed. This makes her wonder if she is still attractive. Last month George, a man she met in her local senior center asked her out. After a few dates, he suggested they become more intimate. Her husband had lost interest in having sex before he died, so Mary was surprised, but also pleased. George added to her surprise by asking if she had been with other men and suggested they use a condom to avoid HIV/AIDS.

15. Why might Mary be gaining weight?

　　a.　Her body needs less food as she gets older.
　　b.　She is not exercising as much as in the past.
　　c.　Both of the above
　　d.　Neither of the above

16. People begin to lose interest in sex around age 50.

True   False

17. What is George thinking? Do older people really have to worry about getting HIV/AIDS?

True   False

Jim, 82, lives alone on a pension. To save money in the winter he keeps his thermostat at 62, even when it's freezing outside. Now its summer and he refuses to buy a window air conditioner. When the weather report predicted 100° heat, his son Bob offered to pick Jim up and let him spend the day in Bob's cool house. Jim was grumpy and refused to leave his home.

18. Like Jim, most older people live alone.

True   False

19. Do people always get grumpy as they age?

Yes (No)

20. What about the heat? Can too much heat or cold be dangerous for older people?

(Yes) No

It seems like older people are always going to the doctor. Or, is that just another myth about the aging population? Let's see.

21. Americans are living longer, so they are sicker and more disabled.

True (False)

Harriet is 68. She is always on the go—busy doing things around her house. And she has always managed the finances for her husband and herself because he worked long hours and she was a homemaker. But, lately she has been bothered by urinary incontinence. Sometimes she can't make it to the bathroom in time. Then last month, while hurrying to the bathroom, she slipped on a throw rug in the hall, fell, and broke her hip. She spent almost a week in the hospital and then several weeks in a care facility getting therapy. Her husband had trouble at home finding what he needed to pay the bills.

22. Urinary accidents are a fact of life for older people.

True (False)

23. Older people can't help falling.

True (False)

24. Make sure someone you trust knows where all your important papers are.

(True) False

John, age 72, appears to be fairly healthy, but he takes several medicines regularly. There are pills for his high blood pressure, high cholesterol, and arthritis, plus a multi-vitamin. It's a little hard to keep track of them all. What he would really like is a "fountain of youth" pill. Maybe he'll try some of those dietary supplements. His daughter says exercise, eat well, and keep your mind active—you'll stay young at heart. She wants him to get a computer and learn how to email his grandchildren. He says, "You can't teach an old dog new tricks."

25. John should try a dietary supplement because we know they are natural, safe, and effective.

True (False)

26. John is right. Older people can't learn new things.

True (False)

27. Will there ever be a "fountain of youth" pill?

Likely (Unlikely)

So, since more Americans are living longer, will there be more people who are 100 or older in the future?

28. In 2002 there were an estimated 58,684 centenarians, people over the age of 100, in America. The estimated number of centenarians in the US in the year 2050 could be:

(a.) 112,000
b. 238,000
c. 1,095,00

PROGRAM LESSON 1
MYTHS AND REALITIES OF AGING

Learning Objectives

1) Explain how and why attitudes toward older people have changed over time.

2) Discuss the impact of the changing age structure of society.

3) Discuss the advantages and disadvantages of longitudinal and cross-sectional methods of studying aging.

4) Describe and "debunk" five common myths about aging and older adults.

Summary of the Video and Text

Video

The video has three segments. In the first segment, experts and older adults share with us their views on aging. Many older adults report positive experiences with aging. However, an individual's view of old age is influenced by health, income, culture, and family relationships. The second segment presents information on the increasing numbers of older people in the country and the world. These demographic changes will continue to impact all aspects of our society. For example, new family and work roles will emerge for older people; the timing of retirement may change; and citizens will demand more research on the problems of old age. The third segment identifies and "debunks" common myths of old age and discusses the impact of "ageism."

Experts on aging who appear in the video include: Msgr. Charles Fahey, Rabbi Earl Grollman, and Drs. Robert Atchley, Vern Bengtson, James Birren, Colette Browne, Kenneth Brummel-Smith, Gene Cohen, James Dator, Herman Feifel, Lou Glasse, Harvey Gochros, Leonard Hayflick, Nancy Hooyman, Asuman Kiyak, Theodore Koff, Linda Martin, Meredith Minkler, Marta Sotomayor, Richard Sprott, Percil Stanford, Robyn Stone, Richard Suzman, Jeanette Takamura, Joseph Tobin, and Fernando Torres-Gil. A number of older adults share their perceptions and experiences with us. They include: Ruth Dow, Celestine Eggleston, Robert Okura, Mollie Pier, David and Eleanor Reese, Leo and Lillian Salazar, Lois Swift, Virginia Templeton, Mildred Tuttle, and Roger and Mary Sue Wonson. Kristin Pollard, a young student, shares her perspective as well.

Text

Chapter 1, "The Growth of Social Gerontology," presents definitions for gerontology, social gerontology, and geriatrics and outlines the four types of aging: chronological, biological, psychological, and social. The book's major perspectives–diversity in aging, the active aging framework, and the importance of person-environment fit–are introduced. Next presented is information on the changes in life expectancy and life span, population age distributions and dependency ratios, and population trends among very old people and ethnic minorities. The chapter also introduces readers to the methods by which aging is studied and gives examples of some of the well-known research on aging and older adults. Specific problems of older adults as research subjects, of cross-sectional and longitudinal studies, are discussed.

Chapter 2, "Historical and Cross-Cultural Issues in Aging," summarizes how old age was viewed in prehistoric times, in Greek and Roman cultures, in Medieval Europe, and Colonial America. Modernization theory and alternatives to it are discussed. Different cultures assign different roles to their elders, often based on social position, control of property, or control over knowledge. Examples from Africa, Native American tribes, Pacific Island nations, and Asia illustrate these concepts.

Your instructor may provide additional readings for this lesson.

Key Points

Changing Attitudes Toward Older People

Attitudes toward aging and older people have changed over time and often differ by culture. Research suggests that in prehistoric times, few people lived to an advanced old age. Those who did were respected and honored and usually served as the society's historians and mediators. When old people became frail and unproductive, or when the "cost" of maintaining them outweighed their contributions, society encouraged them to die or leave the community. Chapter 2 of the text provides several examples of this practice, known as geronticide or senecide.

13

The text then traces the evolution of our views of old age through western history and from traditional to modern societies. Across time and culture, it appears that the status of older people corresponds to the amount of resources they control. Resources can include money, property, knowledge, religious power, and political power. Modernization theory suggests that older people lose political and social power as the society places increasing value on technology, mass education, urbanization, and nuclear (rather than extended) families. For example, when knowledge depends on experience, older people have the advantage and are respected in part because they control access to this knowledge. In more modern societies, young people often have more access to knowledge than older people, for example, through school and exposure to computer technology. Thus, the status of older people begins to decline.

Older adults in the video appear to view old age as a positive time. Most of them are healthy and continue to control resources; for example they have homes, cars, pensions, and experience. These resources command respect and allow them the freedom to fill meaningful roles in society. Mollie Pier, for example, realizes that old age is fun for her because she has good health, can still drive her car, and is secure financially.

Older adults who are not healthy or who have fewer resources may have a different experience of old age. David Reese didn't really feel old until he started having health problems and experiencing limitations on his activities. Different views of aging by ethnic group may also stem from differential access to resources. Dr. Vern Bengtson describes a study in which older Caucasian Americans and African Americans were asked to identify the best thing about growing old. The Caucasians in the study liked the increased opportunity to travel that came with retirement. The African Americans, on the other hand, had fewer resources throughout their lives and were just happy to have survived to old age. Research suggests that older women, minorities, those who live alone, and those over 85 years old are likely to experience old age as a hardship.

Many older adults continue to act as preservers of cultural heritage. For example, Leo Salazar describes the role his own grandfather played in introducing him to his Hispanic heritage. Mollie learned about Jewish culture from her grandparents. Celestine Eggleston feels responsible for explaining the family's African American heritage to her grandchildren and helps them rise above prejudice in their own lives.

But other roles and attitudes are changing. Several adults in the video say they resist societal pressures to "act their age." For example, Virginia Templeton resents societal notions that interest in sex stops at 39. Robert Okura is having trouble getting a job at age 62 and resents being seen as "too old to work." Ruth Dow occasionally shocks her children by taking off on adventures, such as sea plane rides.

Many changes stem from the fact that we have now, for the first time, large cohorts of people who are living into advanced old age. Who knows how a great-grandparent should act? We do not have adequate role models because so few people have ever been great-grandparents. The older adults who become great-grandparents in coming years will be pioneers of this relatively new role.

Dr. Gene Cohen tells us that medical schools only began adding geriatrics to the curriculum in the mid-1970s. Physicians and scientists who were interested in aging in the 1970s were pioneers in the field. Dr. Bengtson is glad he came into gerontology on the ground floor. He tells us it's "a wonderful time to be a gerontologist. We're just riding the crest of the first few waves of explanation, of understanding, of classification."

Despite the general enthusiasm for aging expressed in the video, some older adults and experts have experienced ageism. Ageism includes stereotyping and discrimination based on age. Reasons for ageism are discussed in the Chapter 1 of the text and include lack of knowledge about aging, a general fear of the aging process, and perceived competition for resources.

Statements like "all old people are forgetful" or "older people aren't interested in sex" are stereotypes, or generalized beliefs based on age. We will identify and debate several common stereotypes about aging later in this lesson.

Stereotyping can lead to discrimination. For example, Dr. Kenneth Brummel-Smith reminds us that calling older people names like "geezer" and "gomer" paints a negative picture of older people and isolates them from younger people. When negative feelings about older people become pervasive, we see a decline in society's respect for aging and a decline in the self-esteem of older people themselves. Experts have experienced discrimination too. Dr. Leonard Hayflick remembers when expressing an interest in studying aging was "professional suicide" for a researcher.

According to Dr. Robert Atchley, the experience of ageism is usually worse for people who already experience other kinds of discrimination, such as sexism and racism. For example, Lou Glasse tells us that most research studies on the diseases common in old age have excluded women. Ageist attitudes are apparent in the way buildings are constructed. Msgr. Charles Fahey has noticed that most churches and synagogues are poorly lit and inaccessible to people with disabilities.

As society ages, and as we age, we will continue to reshape our views of aging and older adults. It appears that older people will have more and more options for how they live, who they live with, and what they do in old age. Increased choices will lead to increased questioning and testing on the part of older people. Already, Dr. Jeanette Takamura notices that retired friends are asking questions like: "Who am I?" and "Who does society permit me to be?"

With so many more people living into their 80s and 90s, Msgr. Fahey suggests we institute a special ceremony that signals an individual's entry into the Third Age, the last 30 to 40 years of life. This ceremony would include a culturally sanctioned period of transition in which people could take the time to reflect on who they are and what they want to do in their remaining decades.

Changes in the Age Structure of Society

The size of the elderly population is growing rapidly. Much of its growth has occurred in the past century. For example, in 1900 only 4% of Americans were 65 years of age or older; in 1990, almost 13% were elderly. For people born in 1900, the average life expectancy in the U.S. was 47 years; people born in 1996 are expected to live to age 76. According to the text, life expectancy at birth is expected to increase to almost 78 years by 2005 and almost 83 years by 2050. The "oldest old," those 85 years and older, is the fastest-growing group; it has increased by 300% between 1960 and 1995. By the year 2050, about 19 million Americans are expected to be in the 85+ group.

Subgroup differences exist, however, in average life expectancy. For example, women live an average of seven years longer than men and will continue to do so well into the future. They also outnumber men in the older age groups. Figure 1.3 in the text shows that among people 85 years and older, there were only about 41 men per 100 women in 2000. Mildred Tuttle sees evidence of this trend in her retirement community, Leisure World, where the average age of residents is 77 years and almost 80% of the residents are female.

Ethnic differences exist as well. Compared to Caucasian Americans, the average life expectancy is 5.5 to 7.5 years less for African Americans and about eight years less for Native Americans. Thus, the Caucasian group has the greatest proportion of elderly today (see Figures 1.10 and 1.11 in the text). However, the number of older African, Hispanic, Asian, and Native Americans is growing rapidly, and in some cases more rapidly than Caucasians. Thus, the ethnic diversity of our "senior citizens" will increase in the future.

Demographers (scientists who study human populations) use a population pyramid to illustrate the changing age structure of society. In Figure 1.8 in the text the age distribution for the U.S. in 2000 looks somewhat like a pyramid. But by 2025, the age distribution is projected to look more like a rectangle.

Dr. Bengtson sees evidence of this in his own family structure. In the early part of the 20th century, his father's family contained one grandparent at the top of the pyramid and eleven children at the base. The Bengtson family now includes a great-grandparent, a grandparent, two parents, and three children...much more of a rectangle, or a bean pole, than a pyramid!

Present-day age pyramids for developing countries look like the U.S. age pyramids of 1900. However, as Dr. Linda Martin tells us, even countries with low proportions of elders today are experiencing increases in their number and proportion of older people. Japan, for example, has experienced a dramatic increase in its numbers of older adults; while Japanese families traditionally have cared for their elders at home, this demographic shift is causing caregiving patterns to change.

What accounts for the growth of the elderly population? Lower birthrates have resulted in a smaller proportion of children in the population. But advances in sanitation and immunization have allowed more children to survive infancy and grow to adulthood. Improved nutrition and lifestyles, high cure rates for infectious disease, and improved medical care for chronic conditions have allowed those who reach maturity to live longer. Most Americans now don't die until old age. Thus, mortality is "compressed" into the later years. This has resulted in the increased rectangularization of the survival curve (see Figure 1.4 in the text).

Another important U.S. phenomenon that affects the age structure of society is the Baby Boom, the nickname given to the large number of Americans born between 1946 and 1964. The Baby Boom generation has been likened to "a pig in a python" because it causes a huge, demographic bulge as it moves through time (see Figure 1.8). Due to its great size, this cohort has a big impact on society. For example, when the Baby Boomers were school-aged, more schools had to be built. Now we don't need as many schools and some have been closed. By 2025, one in 26 Baby Boomers will be living as centenarians! Dr. James Dator notes that the Baby Boomers have always been vocal and when they become senior citizens, he feels sure that they will continue working to win freedoms for their cohort.

Msgr. Fahey reminds us that we are among the first people in history who can look forward to a relatively long and certain life. Views of aging will change as members of the older generations continue to renegotiate old roles and try out new ones.

Methods of Studying Aging

In the past 25 years, scientists and researchers have paid increasing attention to studying age differences and age changes. Cross-sectional research is conducted at a single time point to look for differences among subjects of different ages. Longitudinal studies, on the other hand, follow the same group of people over time to look for changes that happen as people age.

Each type of study has its advantages and disadvantages. Cross-sectional studies are more common than longitudinal studies; they are usually easier and less expensive than longitudinal studies because the subjects are interviewed at a single time point. On the other hand, it is hard to know if differences among subjects are really due to age. They may be due to a cohort effect or a period effect, meaning that differences may be due to the fact that different generations are shaped by different cultural and historical conditions.

Longitudinal studies eliminate this problem, known as the cohort or period effect. However, longitudinal studies may be compromised by attrition, i.e., subjects dropping out over the course of the study. When attrition is selective (subjects with certain characteristics drop out while subjects with other characteristics stay in), research findings may be biased toward those who stayed in the study. In fact, research shows that older adults who drop out of longitudinal studies tend to be those who score lower on intelligence tests and are more socially isolated.

Sequential designs combine cross-sectional and longitudinal methods to examine age differences and age changes at the same time. Dr. James Birren gives an example of a Swedish study that used a sequential design. Subjects enter the study at age 70. Every five years, a new group of 70-year-old people enter the study. Data are collected on all subjects. Both age differences (among successive cohorts entered in the study) and age changes (in the subjects re-surveyed at regular intervals) are being measured. The findings to date suggest that each new cohort is healthier than the last.

Regardless of the type of design a researcher employs, he/she must pay attention to how representative the sample is. For example, if the researcher wants to learn something about older adults who live independently, studying older people living in a nursing home will not provide data that could be generalized to the well elder population. It would be better to select a sample from the pool of older adults who apply for bus passes or senior ID cards as they are more likely to be living independently. Other studies, and the methods used to conduct them, are described in Chapter 1 of the text.

Common Myths About Aging and Older Adults

A number of myths are presented and disputed in the video and in Chapter 1 of the text. Dr. Herman Feifel, in the video, scoffs at the myth that all older people are the same. He explains that there is great diversity among the aged. Dr. Atchley wonders how anyone can stereotype older adults. "Older adulthood" spans 40 years and is comprised of people of different races, genders, backgrounds, and experiences. How can we develop a general statement that captures the essence of all the people in these groups?

Another common myth is that older people cannot learn new things. But Dr. Takamura has firsthand evidence of older adults who have embraced and excelled at computer technology. David Reese learned to play the piano in retirement.

Do all older people want to retire? According to our experts, most older adults want options for work and leisure. In the past, mandatory retirement rules have limited older adults' options for working past the age of 65 or 70. But continued work may add structure and spice to life, without which, Rabbi Grollman tells us, you may find that your Wednesday haircut is the high point of your week.

It's a myth that all older people are conservative or religious. In fact, most people maintain their political and religious beliefs throughout life. In addition, Dr. Fernando Torres-Gil notes that many older people are receptive to new ideas and can change their minds when presented with new information and persuasive arguments.

Dr. Atchley notes that positive stereotypes (such as "all older people are wise") are as damaging as negative stereotypes. Again, we see a wide variance in how people age and we need to give older people the latitude to explore their own developmental paths.

Lou Glasse discusses our ideas about attractiveness. When the population was dominated by young people, beauty was equated with youth. But as the population ages, she bets we will begin thinking differently about who is and who isn't attractive. You can probably think of several older movie and television stars who are considered "sexy." And sex doesn't end at 39, as Virginia Templeton fears most young people believe. In fact, the desire for sexual intimacy and the ability to enjoy sex continues throughout life. Roger and Mary Sue Wonson tell us that their sexuality just "gets better with old age."

Nor are all older people infirm or irreversibly disabled. Only 5 percent of adults over age 65 reside in nursing homes at any one time and health providers have found that many conditions previously considered to be part of the aging process can actually be treated and reversed. For example, Dr. Theodore Koff tells how his clinic has reversed many cases of incontinence (loss of bowel or bladder control) in older adults. It is the hope of all gerontologists that research will help increase everyone's active life expectancy, that is, the number of years we can expect to live independently.

It's a myth that children abandon their parents. In fact, Dr. Robyn Stone tells us that 85 to 95 percent of long-term care needed by older adults is provided by family members. Dr. Martin notes, however, that while we have more opportunities to live together in multigenerational families compared to the past, few families actually choose to live together in a single household. As Ruth Dow tells us, she loves her independence and won't give it up until she has to. Although independent, older adults continue to play vital roles within the family. Dr. Meredith Minkler sees an increase in grandmothers caring for grandchildren.

Dr. Colette Browne closes the video with her wish for the future: that we begin to view aging not as a process of decline and decay but as a natural course of continued growth and development over the life span, filled with joys and challenges.

Key Terms and Concepts from the Text, Video, and *Study Guide*

Active Aging
Active Life Expectancy
Age Changes
Age Differences
Age Graded
Ageism
Ageist
Attrition
Baby Boomers
Baltimore Longitudinal Study on Aging
Biological Aging
Birth Cohort
Centenarians
Chronological Aging
Cohort
Cohort Effect
Competence Model
Compression of Morbidity
Compressed Mortality
Cross-Sectional Research Design
Demography
Dependency Ratio
Dependent Life Expectancy
Developing Nations
Elderly Support Ratio
Environmental Press
Ethnic Minority
Filial Piety
Functional Aging
Geriatrics
Geronticide
Gerontological Society of America

Gerontology
Individual Competence
Life Expectancy
Life Span
Longevity
Longitudinal Research Design
Maximum Life Span
Median Age
Modernization Theory
Old-Old
Oldest-Old
Pathological Aging
Period Effect
Person-Environment Perspective
Pig in a Python
Population Pyramid
Psychological Aging
Rectangularization of the Survival Curve
Representativeness of the Sample
Selective Dropout
Selective Survival
Senescence
Senecide
Senior Citizens
Sequential Research Design
Social Aging
Social Gerontology
Social Stratification
Stereotype
Terminal Drop
Third Age
Young-Old

Self-Study Questions

Instructions: Fill in the blank with the appropriate word or phrase from the list of Key Terms and Concepts.
Note: Only 38 of the 64 key terms and concepts can be used.

1) Sometimes, age groups are given nicknames. _____ is a popular nickname for the large group of individuals born between 1946 and 1964. Older adults are often called _____.

2) _____ refers to changes that occur in perceptual processes, mental functioning, personality, and coping as we grow older.

3) The age group comprised of people 85 and older is called the _____ while the age group comprised of people 65 to 74 is called the _____.

4) _____ refers to the physical changes that occur with age, including the reduced efficiency of organ systems. This is also referred to as _____.

5) _____ refers to changes in social roles and relationships over the life course.

6) The field of medicine that focuses on how to prevent and manage the diseases of aging is called _____. The study of the biological, psychological, and sociological aspects of aging is called _____.

7) A _____ is group of individuals of the same generation or a group of people sharing a trait such as age, socioeconomic status, or ethnicity.

8) _____ refers to ways that people normally change over time while _____ refers to ways that one generation differs from another.

9) A researcher who surveys different age groups at a single point in time is using a _____ design. A problem with this kind of design is that differences among generations may be due to a _____ or a _____, which means that differences may not be due to age but due to particular histories or characteristics of the different age groups.

10) A researcher who studies the same people at regular intervals over a period of months or years is using a _____ design. A limitation of this kind of design is that people may stop participating in the study after a while. This is called _____. When people leave the study due to poor health, this is called _____.

11) When researchers study a small group of people, they must be concerned about the _____ because otherwise they may not be able to draw valid conclusions and generalize results to the larger population.

12) An _____ society is one that assigns different roles, expectations, opportunities, status, and constraints to people of different ages.

13) Figure 1.4 It represents a trend toward _____, where more and more people die in old age, rather than in childhood or in adulthood.

14) _____ is the view that aging is a positive time of growth and experience in spite of any decline in physical health and ability.

15) _____ refers to the number of years individuals can expect to live independently. In contrast, _____ refers to the number of years individuals can expect to live when they need help from other people with day-to-day living.

16) One's _____ is the actual number of years one lives. The _____ refers to the maximum number of years a given species could expect to live if environmental hazards were eliminated, (115 to 120 years for humans). The average length of time members of a specific population can expect to live is called its

_____.

17) The theory that suggests that older people lose political and social power as society puts increasing value on technology, mass education, and nuclear, rather than extended, families is called the _____.

18) Societies that deliberately allow aged community members to die are committing _____ or _____.

19) An _____ is a small group of people of a particular race, ethnic group, or culture residing within a community dominated by a different culture.

20) If someone is _____, he/she has negative stereotypes of older people and may even discriminate against them.

21) A _____ is a standardized mental picture that is held in common by members of a group and represents an oversimplified opinion, attitude, or uncritical judgment.

22) The term used to describe the huge, demographic bulge made by the Baby Boomers over time is _____.

23) _____ describes the proportion of people who are dependent on others for support compared to the number who are employed. When referring only to dependent people who are elderly, the proportion is called the _____.

24) A name for the last third of one's life is the _____. Some gerontologists feel we should create ceremonies to honor people's entry into this period of life.

Use the Glossary at the end of the Study Guide to check your answers.

Topics for Discussion

1) Various cohorts are influenced by various historical and cultural factors. Think of two cohorts of people: those that are aged 60 to 75 and those that are aged 20 to 35. Which historical events and cultural expectations impacted each group? How much do these factors explain differences that you see between these two cohorts?

2) Discuss the consequences of the continuing growth of the older population in terms of the "active aging" framework. What implications does this trend have for life-long learning and employment in the US?

3) Discuss the usefulness and dangers of stereotypes for those who work with the elderly.

4) To what extent can older people maintain power in a social system through control of knowledge and property? Describe any gender and cultural differences that may arise in this ability to control resources.

5) A researcher wants to study stereotypes about aging among different age groups. If the researcher used a cross-sectional design, what would he/she be able to find out? If the researcher used a longitudinal design, what would he/she be able to find out? In each case, how would the researcher find a representative sample? Compare the strengths and weaknesses of the two designs.

Website Challenge

Visit the following websites that can provide more information on the telecourse and Internet resources in aging. Bookmark the sites for easy access in the future.

1) GROWING OLD IN A NEW AGE at http://www.growingold.hawaii.edu/

2) AARP's "Guide to Internet Resources on Aging" at http://www.aarp.org/internetresources/

"What's Your Aging I.Q.?" Open-Book Test

Use your text to find the answers to the quiz, "What's Your Aging I.Q.?" which appears on pages 10 - 12 of the *Study Guide*. Explain each answer in your own words. Include the page number of the text where you find each answer.

Written Assignments

Your instructor may ask you to complete one or more of the following written assignments.

Reaction Paper: New Knowledge and Feelings Stimulated by the Video

Write a two-page paper describing: 1) new information you gained from the video; 2) how the experiences of the older adults in the video affected your personal view of aging; and 3) other comments to the instructor regarding this lesson or the course.

Older-Adult Interview

Arrange to spend an hour or two with a person who is 60 or older. Make sure the older adult understands that you will be discussing some questions about aging and sharing your perceptions about it.

1) Before the meeting, take "What's Your Aging I.Q.?" Compare your answers with those provided to you by your instructor.

2) During the meeting, have the interviewee review "What's Your Aging I.Q.?" Consider each question together and discuss the correct answer. Take your textbook in case either of you wants to read more about the topic. If either or both of you answered a question incorrectly, discuss what events or beliefs may have led you to this incorrect answer.

3) After the meeting, write a three- to five-page paper on how well each of you did on the quiz and what might account for any differences in your answers. Use the questions below as a guide. Include in your paper the page number in the text where each topic is addressed.

a) Which questions did both of you answer correctly? How did you know the answers to these questions?

b) Which questions did both of you answer incorrectly? What is the right answer and why? What discussion did these questions stimulate between the two of you?

c) Which questions did you answer differently? Which events or beliefs led you to answer this way? What discussion ensued between the two of you?

d) How has this interview affected your personal view of aging and older adults?

Research Paper

Select one of the topics below for in-depth study. Read a book or five journal articles on the topic. A good place to start searching for reading material is in the reference section provided at the end of each text chapter. Write a five- to ten-page research paper that describes the historical and current thinking on the topic. Identify things about the topic that are not yet resolved or may benefit from further study.

1) How do ageist attitudes and stereotypes affect the type of care a health professional provides to older adults? Describe in detail a study that tested an intervention that tried to change attitudes of health care providers. Was it successful? Why or why not?

2) Read publications by Dr. Erdman Palmore on the Facts on Aging quizzes he developed. Why did he develop them? Which populations have they been tested on? What are the common findings? Is there any evidence that age-related stereotypes have changed over time?

3) How are older people depicted in the media? What are common roles for older people on television, in magazines, and in children's stories? Have images of older adults changed over time? If so, in what ways? How do these depictions compare with what we know about the reality of old age?

4) Review past issues of the *Journal of Cross-Cultural Gerontology* (Kluwer Academic Press). Read articles about aging in two separate countries or two separate cultures. Compare and contrast their attitudes toward and treatment of older adults.

Community Interview

Two types of government agencies operate in each state to study your community's population of older adults and coordinate services to meet their needs—a State Unit on Aging and local Area Agencies on Aging (AAA).

Work with your instructor to identify a contact at one of these agencies. Interview an employee who knows about your community's population of older adults, asking the questions below. Write a three- to five-page paper on your findings.

If you are interviewing someone at your State Unit on Aging, ask questions about the state. If you are interviewing someone at an Area Agency on Aging, apply these questions to the census tracts covered by the agency. Because you are asking for specific numbers and percentages, you may want to mail or fax these questions to the agency prior to the interview.

Interview Questions

1) What is the population of the state/area? What percentage of the population is 60 or older? Is the older population growing? Why or why not? Are older adults concentrated in certain areas of the state/area or spread evenly throughout the state/area?

2) What are the characteristics of older adults in the state/area? What are the proportions of women and men? What are the proportions that are married, widowed, divorced, and never married? How many live below the poverty level? How many are illiterate? What is the ethnic composition of older adults in the state/area? How many have a first language other than English?

3) What proportion of people over 60 years of age live independently? How many older adults in the state/area are disabled and need help with daily activities? Of these, how many live with family, how many live in nursing or care homes, and how many live alone?

4) Which services are provided for older adults in the state/area? Which services are needed but not provided? Who decides which services to offer older adults?

5) How does this office find the answers to questions like the ones above? What other questions is the office asking? How do the answers to these questions affect this office?

Student Questions

1) Are you surprised by anything you learned about your community's elderly population?

2) Why or why not?

Learning Objectives

1) Describe how the biological changes that occur with aging affect appearance, strength, stamina, and resistance to disease.

2) Discuss environmental and programmed theories of biological aging.

3) Describe two directions for future research in the biology of aging.

Summary of the Video and Text

Video

The video has four segments. The first segment introduces us to the changes in appearance that occur with age, for example in our skin, hair, muscle strength, and body composition. The second segment presents information on theories of biological aging. A major class of theories sees the environment as the main cause of aging while another class of theories points to the importance of genetic determinants. We are introduced to the concept of biomarkers in aging and the potential impact of caloric restriction on the aging process. The Baltimore Longitudinal Study of Aging is described. The third segment presents information on organ system changes in aging, including the cardiovascular system, the immune system, and the brain. The final segment introduces some of the promising avenues for research on biological aging, particularly in the areas of cell aging, cell death, genetic mapping, and genetic replacement therapy.

Experts who appear in the video include Robert Harootyan and Drs. William Adler, Gene Cohen, Michael Crow, Leonard Hayflick, Edward Lakatta, Linda Martin, Jeffrey Metter, Antonino Passaniti, and Richard Sprott. Several older adults describe how they view their own biological aging and their hopes for research, including Ilse Darling, Donald McClure, Mollie Pier, David Reese, Leo Salazar, and Roger Wonson.

Text

"The Biological and Physiological Context of Social Aging" serves as an introduction to Chapters 3 and 4, which are concerned with biological aging and its effects on older adults. This section also includes two vignettes that illustrate variations in health status among elderly people.

Chapter 3, "The Social Consequences of Physical Aging," presents information on the biological theories of aging, major research studies on physiological aging, and on the normal age changes that occur in the: body composition, skin, hair, musculo-skeletal system, kinesthetic systems, respiratory system, cardiovascular system and the effects of exercise, urinary system, gastrointestinal system, endocrine system, nervous system, sleep patterns and in the five major senses.

Your instructor may assign additional readings for this lesson.

Key Points

Biological Changes in Aging

Chapter 3 in the text presents details on the biological changes that occur with age. The most overt signs of biological aging, or senescence, are in our appearance. Skin wrinkles over time because cell replacement in the epidermis (outer most layer of skin) decreases with age and the collagen (connective tissue) that makes up the dermis (second layer of skin) loses elasticity. With exposure to skin-damaging sun and wind, the skin can darken, dry, or become cancerous. In the video, David Reese discusses his experience with skin cancer; he hopes to prevent its recurrence by wearing sunscreen and a hat whenever he goes outside. In addition, the deepest layers of skin (known as subcutaneous layers) lose fat and water, making it more difficult for older people to regulate their internal temperature. Ilse Darling reports that she has become more sensitive to cold over the years. Wound healing also slows with age.

As our levels of estrogen and testosterone decrease over the years, the rate of hair replacement decreases as well. Hair follicles shrink in diameter with age and lose pigment, so that our hair thins and grays. While disguising skin and hair changes has generated a huge cosmetics industry in modern societies, age does have its advantages. Dr. Gene Cohen reports that Bertrand Russell appreciated looking older; he noticed that the whiter his hair became, the more likely people were to believe what he had to say!

Changes also occur in the musculo-skeletal system. Maximum body size and strength generally reach a peak at age 25. After that, size and strength start to decline. In time, the spine may become more curved and the shoulders may stoop. Bone loss can also occur in the jawbone of people who have no teeth. Loss of cartilage in the joints can cause arthritic stiffness. Body composition changes, with decreased proportions of water and lean muscle and an increased proportion of fat (see Figure 3.1 in the text).

Figure 3.2 in the text displays graphically how normal aging results in declines in metabolism, cardiac function, lung capacity, and kidney function. Specifically, breathing capacity decreases as the muscles that operate the lungs lose elasticity. The number of cilia (hairlike structures) in the airways is also reduced, and this makes it harder to remove pollutants and irritants from the air we breathe. The heart and blood vessels also lose elasticity, the muscle in the heart is replaced with fat, and blood vessel walls line with lipids (fat). Blood pressure tends to increase with age (see Figure 3.3 in the text). Dr. Edward Lakatta and Dr. Michael Crow discuss cardiovascular changes in the video.

Changes in the kidneys result in a slower rate at which impurities are filtered from the blood and a decreased capacity to absorb glucose (sugar). Bladder capacity is reduced and the sensation of needing to urinate becomes delayed. The gastro-intestinal system slows as muscle function and enzyme levels decline. Changes to the reproductive organs also occur; these are elaborated upon in Program Lesson 4, "Love, Intimacy, and Sexuality in Old Age."

Brain cells die as we age, but because we have an enormous reserve of neurons (nerve cells), mental ability does not decline with normal aging. Brain cells that remain develop new extensions, or synapses, so that communication between areas of the brain is maintained, although transmission tends to slow with age. Reaction time and reflexes also decline. Fine motor control is also reduced as noted by Ilse Darling who has seen declines in the handwriting skills of her peers.

Several older adults in the video notice that they have a reduced capacity for activities requiring physical strength and stamina. For example, Ilse Darling says she can no longer plant bushes in her garden, is a lot slower at Ping-Pong, swims fewer laps in the pool, and is stiffer after her swim compared to when she was younger. Roger Wonson and Donald McClure find they are slower at tennis.

Many of the experts in the video, however, cite scientific evidence that these declines are delayed in people who engage in regular physical activity and watch their diets. In fact, Dr. Lakatta notes that arteries do not stiffen in individuals in non-industrialized societies who maintain high levels of activity and consume very small amounts of sodium chloride (salt).

Although research has found patterns of physical decline in normal aging, we see a great variance in the rate of aging among older adults. Dr. Richard Sprott illustrates this when he compares Aunt Maude, who is active and healthy in her 60s, with a person in his/her 50s who has slowed down considerably. The experts concur that individual aging is based in genetic inheritance but is greatly influenced by lifestyle and environment. Ways in which lifestyle and environment can help maximize physical potential are discussed further in Program Lesson 3, "Maximizing Physical Potential of Older Adults."

As Mollie Pier says, "getting older is not a disease." And, in fact, most normal age changes do not threaten health. But some age changes put older adults at higher risk of disease. Dr. William Adler tells us that a decline in lymphocyte function over the life course makes the immune system less effective at protecting us from illness or helping us recover.

He notes that the incidence of respiratory illnesses among adults over age 65 is as high as among children under five years of age (these two groups are most susceptible to disease), but that the mortality, or death rate, is 30 times higher in the older group. Knowing this, Dr. Adler is disturbed by the fact that less than 20% of older adults take advantage of vaccines that can help them avoid contracting influenza and pneumonia. These and other common diseases of old age are covered in Program Lesson 10, "Illness and Disability."

Theories of Biological Aging

Two themes emerge when biological theories of aging are discussed. A group of theories centers around the idea that life span and the aging process are genetically programmed or governed by some biological clock. Dr. Sprott notes that, from biblical times, the maximum human life span has not appeared to exceed 115 to 120 years. Another class of theories link aging with the damaging effects of the environment and poor lifestyle.

The text provides an overview of five theories of biological aging; each helps us understand the biology of aging but none totally explains what causes aging. The Wear and Tear Theory purports that each species ages at a genetically determined rate within a genetically determined life span. This, compounded by environmental stress and poor lifestyle, leads to the deterioration of cells, and to frailty and death. The Autoimmune Theory suggests that, as the body's immune system declines with age, it becomes defective and attacks itself. The Cross-Linkage Theory associates aging with the loss of collagen (connective tissue) in the skin, blood vessels, muscles, eyes, and other organs. This process makes tissue less pliable and more susceptible to damage. The Free Radical Theory links aging with the destructive effects of free radicals, highly reactive chemical compounds with an unpaired electron. It is hypothesized that increasing intake of antioxidants, like vitamin E and beta carotene, can inhibit free radical damage. The Cellular Aging Theory is based on Dr. Leonard Hayflick's finding that cells are mortal.

Dr. Sprott feels that "many of the differences between individuals within a species are genetically programmed, but that interaction with the environment is very, very significant." Because of this belief, he jogs four times a week.

As Dr. Cohen explains, longitudinal studies, those in which a group of people is followed for several decades, help researchers differentiate between biological changes associated with normal aging and changes associated with disease. Longitudinal studies have also provided clues about the effects of lifestyle on life span. For example, findings from the Baltimore Longitudinal Study of Aging (BLSA) suggest that obesity cuts years from the life span while "not smoking" adds years to life.

Donald McClure, a participant in the BLSA, explains that the study provides him with a complete physical examination every few years and then compares his biological status to his baseline profile. He learns of any abnormalities and follows up with his personal physician. Dr. Jeffrey Metter notes that, on the average, male participants in the study have lived eight years longer than men in the general population. This may be because the study attracted people who were already interested in health, because the study raised participant awareness about health and health promotion (as expressed by Donald McClure), or because of selective attrition (the less healthy participants dropped out over time). Although the study was initially restricted to men, Ilse Darling, and other women, joined the study in 1978.

Future Research in the Biology of Aging

The video introduces some of the promising avenues for research on biological aging, particularly in the areas of cell aging, cell death, genetic mapping, genetic replacement therapy, and biomarkers of aging. Robert Harootyan and Drs. Hayflick, Sprott, Antonino Passaniti, and Cohen discuss scientific explorations in these areas.

Dr. Hayflick says that the overt signs of aging, such as wrinkles and gray hair, "are very simple reflections of an enormous number of changes that occur at much more sophisticated levels of biology," i.e., at the cell level, at the organ level, and at the tissue level.

He has spent his career studying cell mortality. A central question in aging research is "why do cells stop dividing?" On the other hand, why do cancer cells divide out of control? Dr. Passaniti and Dr. Cohen see these as two sides of the same question and support more research in this area.

The Human Genome Project is attempting to identify the position and function of every gene on every human chromosome. The first two chromosomes were fully mapped in 1992 and Robert Harootyan believes all will be mapped by 2005. (Check this website for the latest on the Genome Project at http://www.nhgri.nih.gov/).

Video experts explain how this project may help us add quality to life; if we understand the hormones needed for genetic function, we can replace depleted hormones through injection and reverse aspects of the aging process. For example, growth hormone injections in animals have been associated with increased muscle mass, reduced fat, and improved activity levels. We could also alter, correct, or replace defective genes that speed aging or cause disease. An example would be in people with progeria, a rare condition in which the aging process is speeded up and death occurs at age 15 or 20. If the genes that control this process were replaced, would the person with progeria age at a more normal rate? Dr. Passaniti describes efforts in which defective immune system genes are replaced in humans.

In the video, Dr. Sprott is very excited about using genetic engineering, as this process is called, for tackling problems at the somatic cell level (tissue and organs are composed of somatic cells) as described in the preceding paragraph. He stresses that, in the context of gerontological research, genetic engineering does not refer to the manipulation of genes at the germ cell (egg and sperm) level to create "politically acceptable" people.

Researchers also continue to search for human biomarkers of aging. Dr. Sprott explains that a biomarker is a scientific measure that allows us to judge the rate at which an individual is aging.

It is important to identify biomarkers so that when we intervene to change one's rate of aging, we will know whether we have succeeded or not. In other words, we would hope that our intervention would delay appearance of the biomarkers.

Dr. Sprott gives us an example from research with mice. By feeding mice an adequately nutritious but low-calorie diet (the intervention), researchers noticed significant delay in the appearance of laboratory-induced tumors (the biomarker). These experiments also suggested that caloric restriction with adequate nutrition extended the average mouse life span by 35%.

But how long do older adults want to live? Mollie Pier notes that the definition of "long life" has changed from 53 years old in her grandmother's time to 90 or 100 years old now. David Reese would like to live to see 100, providing he can still see, hear, and move around. Leo Salazar would like to live life to its fullest and then die quickly in his sleep.

Dr. Sprott agrees that biological research should concentrate on improving the quality of the terminal third, or last one-third, of one's life span. Dr. Cohen suggests that biological researchers do not want to replicate the experience of mythical Tithanus, to whom Zeus granted immortality but not eternal youth; according to mythology, Tithanus lives to this day, growing more and more frail.

Mollie Pier summarizes for experts and elders alike by hoping that, "whatever research is going on now will not just prolong life, but give [it] a very, very good quality."

While recent anti-aging research findings are encouraging and may lead to important discoveries that can slow the aging process, most genetic research focused on single cell or simple organisms. Hence, it will take many more years of research to move beyond single cell and simple organisms to human beings.

According to the text, there seems to be a shift in emphasis as the 20th century unfolds— biological aging research will move away from the treatment of disease and genetic disorders to their prevention.

Key Terms and Concepts from the Text, Video, and *Study Guide*

Aerobic Exercise
Age Spots
Antiaging medicine
Antioxidants
Arthritis
Atherosclerosis
Baltimore Longitudinal Study of Aging
Biomarker of Aging
Body Composition
Caloric Restriction
Cellular Aging Theory
Cilia
Collagen
Cross-Linkage Theory
Cross-Sectional Research Design
Dehydroepiandrosterone (DHEA)
Dermis
Epidermis
Free Radical Theory
Free Radicals
Functional Capacity
Genetic Engineering
Genetic Replacement Therapy

Germ Cells
Human Genome Project
Human Growth Hormone
Immunosenescence
Hypothermia
Kinesthetic System
Lipids
Lipofuscin
Liver Spots
Longitudinal Research Design
Lymphocytes
Melanin
Neurons
Photoaging
Progeria
Sarcopenia
Sebaceous Glands
Somatic Cells
Subcutaneous
Synapse
Telomerase
Vital Capacity
Wear and Tear Theory

Self-Study Questions

*Instructions: Fill in the blank with the appropriate word or phrase from the list of Key Terms and Concepts.
Note: Only 31 of the 45 key terms and concepts can be used.*

1) _____ refers to the normal process of biological changes in the body and its components as we age.

2) Dark skin pigmentation produced by the body to protect it from ultraviolet rays is called _____. Concentrations of dark skin pigmentation are called _____ or _____.

3) _____ refers to the proportions of lean muscle, water, and fat in the body. Humans tend to experience an increase in fat and decreases in water and lean muscle as they age.

4) _____ is an important element in a fitness regime because it increases the heart rate and increases oxygen consumption.

5) A _____ is a junction between any two _____ in the brain.

6) _____ refers to the maximum amount of oxygen that can be brought into the lungs with a deep breath.

7) _____ is a general term to describe the 100 different conditions of inflammation and degenerative changes in bones and joints.

8) The skin has three layers. The _____ is the deepest layer. The middle layer is called the _____. The outer most layer is called the _____. The _____ in the skin produce oil.

9) _____ is the connective tissue found in most organ systems that helps maintain elasticity.

10) Another word for fats is _____.

11) A _____ is a scientific measure that allows us to judge the rate at which an individual is aging.

12) The _____ is a study funded by the federal government in which a large group of healthy middle-aged and older individuals living in the community are being assessed regularly to describe normal changes that occur with aging. When the study began in 1958, it was limited to male participants; women were included in the sample in 1978.

13) Cells at the egg and sperm level are called _____ while cells that make up tissue and organs are called _____. Cells that include the cellular mediators of immunity are called _____.

14) The _____ is a research program that is identifying the location and function of every gene on every chromosome.

15) According to the theory called the _____, cells are mortal and aging occurs as cells slow their number of replications.

16) _____ are highly reactive chemical compounds with an unpaired electron. According to the theory called the _____, increasing your intake of _____, like Vitamin E, may help slow the aging process.

17) The hormone that stimulates growth and may help reverse aging is called _____.

18) _____ and _____ refer to the manipulation or replacement of genes at the somatic level to correct deficiencies or slow the aging process, thus prolonging the quality of life and perhaps life span.

19) _____ is a rare condition in which aging is accelerated and death may occur by age 15 or 20.

20) _____ refers to the idea that aging results in a significant decline in the immune system, increasing the older person's susceptibility to infectious disease and risk of death.

Use the Glossary at the end of the Study Guide to check your answers.

Topics for Discussion

1) How could specific changes in body composition with aging influence an older person's reactions to medications and alcohol?

2) If maximum body size and strength peak at age 25, many adults that you know are already experiencing physiological declines. Which physiological aging changes have you noticed and how have these adults adapted to the changes?

3) Discuss how diet and exercise can slow the physiological aging process.

4) What suggestions can be made for improving the person-environment fit for persons experiencing changes in their vision as they get older?

Website Challenge

Visit the following websites that can provide more information on this lesson's topics. Bookmark them for easy access in the future.

1) American Geriatrics Society at http://americangeriatrics.org

2) SeniorHealth at http://nihseniorhealth.gov/

3) MedLine Plus at http://www.nlm.nih.gov/medlineplus/seniorshealthissues.html

4) National Human Genome Research Institute at http://www.nhgri.nih.gov/

Written Assignments

Your instructor may ask you to complete one or more of the written assignments that follow.

Reaction Paper: New Knowledge and Feelings Stimulated by the Video

Write a two-page paper describing: 1) new information you gained from watching the video; 2) how the experiences of the older adults in the video affected your personal view of aging; and 3) other comments to the instructor regarding this lesson or the course.

Older-Adult Interview

Interview a person 65 years of age or older about physical changes they have noticed as they have aged, asking the questions below. Write a three- to five-page paper on your findings.

Interview Questions

1) Most people experience physical changes as they grow older. I'm interested to hear about physical changes in your:
   a) height and weight
   b) sleep patterns
   c) hair and skin
   d) eyesight and hearing
   e) bones and joints
   f) strength and stamina

2) Do you have more aches and pains now than you did when you were a young adult?

3) Have you noticed any other physical changes?

4) Have these changes been gradual or sudden? Have these changes affected your ability to do the things you like to do? If so, how have you been able to adjust to or compensate for these changes?

5) How have these changes affected your self-image? How have they affected your outlook on life?

6) How old are you? How old do you feel? Which age is the "best age" to be? Explain.

Student Questions

1) How does the interviewee's experience with physical aging compare with the information provided in the text? Explain.

2) How has this interview affected your personal view of aging and older adults?

Research Paper

Select one of the topics below for in-depth study. Read a book or five journal articles on the topic. A good place to start searching for reading material is in the reference section provided at the end of each text chapter. Write a five- to ten-page research paper that describes the historical and current thinking on the topic. Identify things about the topic that are not yet resolved or may benefit from further study.

1) Read source documents on the Human Genome Project. What advances have been made in the past five years? Why are researchers excited about the project? Give specific examples of what has been accomplished and what researchers hope to accomplish in this project.

2) Read source documents on the Baltimore Longitudinal Study of Aging. Describe the methods used by the study to measure physical changes with age. How have the methods changed over time? Describe in detail some of the findings from the study. What limits generalizing the study's findings to other populations?

3) What research has been conducted that indicates that women live longer than men? What are the suggested reasons for gender differences in longevity? How do men differ from women in ways their bodies age?

4) Compare and contrast health status in three different ethnic groups or cultures. What differences exist in longevity and rates of aging among older adults in these ethnic groups or cultures? What reasons are suggested by the literature for these differences?

MAXIMIZING PHYSICAL POTENTIAL OF OLDER ADULTS

Learning Objectives

1) Explain the value of physical fitness and good nutrition over the life span.

2) Describe changes that occur with aging in vision, hearing, and sleep patterns.

3) Give three examples that illustrate the concept of person-environment interaction in aging.

4) Describe how gender and ethnicity affect health status in later life.

Summary of the Video and Text

Video

The video has five segments. The first segment presents the benefits of exercise and good nutrition for older adults. The second segment, on preventing illness, discusses the importance of early detection and treatment of real and potential health problems, for example, cancer, osteoporosis, diabetes, and adverse drug interactions. The third segment presents information on compensating for age changes in vision, hearing, and sleep.

The fourth segment focuses on the concept of person-environment interaction. Experts discuss the importance of environmental modifications, technological advancements, and social services in helping older adults compensate for physical, mental, and social losses that occur with age. The fifth and final segment of the video discusses societal effects on health. Experts discredit our tendency to "blame the victim" for poor health, citing evidence that gender, racial, and socio-economic status also affect health. In some cases, biases in health care and health research hinder the ability of some groups of older adults to optimize their health.

The following experts appear in this video: Marie-Louise Ansak, Lou Glasse, Rabbi Earl Grollman, William Narang, and Drs. Kenneth Brummel-Smith, Jerome Fleg, Michael Kaplan, H. Asuman Kiyak, Theodore Koff, George Martin, Meredith Minkler, Marta Sotomayor, E. Percil Stanford, George Williams, and Steven Zarit.

Older adults who share observations about their health include: Elizabeth Allen, Doris Birchander, Faye Cruse, Ilse Darling, Louise Di Virgilio, Mary Franggos, Hayward King, Donald McClure, Walter Morris, Pat Nickerson, Mollie Pier, Jane Potter, David and Eleanor Reese, Joseph Serrao, Robert Shaw, Samuel Stephens, Charles Stump, Betty Tuff, Mildred Tuttle, Blanche Woodbury, and members of the Danvers Walkers.

Text

New Readings. In Chapter 4, "Managing Chronic Diseases and Promoting Well-Being in Old Age," read the sections on Defining Health, Quality of Life in Health and Illness, Falls and their Prevention, and Health Promotion with Older People.

In Chapter 11, "Living Arrangement and Social Interactions," read the section on Person-Environment Theories of Aging.

Chapter 14, "The Resiliency of Elders of Color," provides information about the special conditions of older African Americans, Latino Americans, Native Americans, and Pacific Asian Americans. In general, older Americans of these ethnicities live fewer years and are at higher risk of poverty and poor health than are older Caucasian Americans. Read section on Ethnic Minorities in gerontology on page 531. Implications for service providers are presented.

Chapter 15, "The Resiliency of Older Women," presents information about the health, social, and economic status of older women. This group is of special interest because older women outnumber older men, especially among the old-old, and are at higher risk of poverty and poor health.

Review. In Chapter 1, "The Growth of Social Gerontology," review the section on A Person-Environment Perspective on Social Gerontology.

The introduction to Part Two, "The Biological and Physiological Context of Social Aging" provides a short overview of Chapters 3 and 4 in the text. Please review the two vignettes that provide examples of variation in the health status in older adults.

In Chapter 3, "The Social Consequences of Physical Aging," review the section on Changes in Sensory Functions.

Key Points

Physical Fitness and Good Nutrition Over the Life Span

Research suggests that physical fitness and good nutrition are important to the health of older people. In the video, Dr. Jerome Fleg says, "we think that regular exercise certainly puts more life in your years, and...that it may even put more years in your life." Specific benefits of physical fitness and aerobic exercise include improved muscle tone, increased oxygen consumption, reduced blood pressure, improved sugar and fat metabolism, weight control, and stress control. Members of the Danvers Walkers have noticed improvements since they began exercising; one says that exercise helps control her arthritis, another found that it helped her recover from a stroke, and a third says it helped her adjust after placing her husband in a nursing home. Jane Potter finds that a daily swim keeps her limber and makes her feel better.

Dr. Michael Kaplan reports that even people who begin exercise programs in later life show improvements in their life expectancy. Donald McClure began to take exercise more seriously when he learned that he had diabetes. Although he admits that it was tough to change his lifestyle, he was able to do so by increasing his association with people who were already involved in exercise programs. David Reese began to exercise after his heart bypass surgery and has progressed to walking three miles and doing 15 to 20 minutes of calisthenics a day. The text notes that even very frail elderly people can benefit from increased exercise, for example range-of-motion exercises for bed-bound adults who might otherwise experience contractures (the freezing of joints into rigid positions). Sedentary older adults who want to start exercising should have a thorough medical exam and get their physician's advice about type and amount of exercise. As Dr. Kaplan states, "It really isn't ever too late to begin an active exercise program."

What kind of exercise is best? Dr. Fleg recommends a program of cross-training with both aerobic and resistance activities; the aerobic activities improve cardio-pulmonary function and stamina while the resistance activities improve muscle tone and strength.

Adults should engage in sensible exercise on a regular basis (three to five times a week), rather than trying to make up for a month of no exercise with a strenuous game of racquetball. Some adults who have been active throughout life report that they need to modify their activities in later life. For example, Walter Morris had to reduce his tennis playing due to arthritis and aging changes in his knees; instead he does more swimming and walking. Jane Potter's physician tells her that it's not how fast she swims or the stroke she uses, but that she continues to swim throughout her life.

The basic principles of a good diet are similar for all adults: consume a variety of foods; increase consumption of fresh fruits, fresh vegetables, legumes and whole grains; and reduce intake of red meat, fat, and sugar. Dr. Kiyak notes that increased intake of antioxidants (found in fruits and vegetables) has been linked to increased longevity and delayed tumor growth. Findings from the Baltimore Longitudinal Study on Aging suggest that participants have made positive dietary changes over the past 30 years, as they now report consuming more fiber and fewer fats.

Older adults should also guard against excessive weight gain, which is associated with higher incidence of diabetes, heart disease, high blood pressure, and some types of cancer. Belonging to a support group called KOPS (Keep Off Pounds Sensibly) helps Mollie Pier maintain her ideal weight.

A number of age-related changes can affect nutritional status. For example, sensory changes in taste and smell may reduce enjoyment of food, resulting in loss of appetite or a tendency to over-salt meals. Loose teeth or poorly fitting dentures can lead to difficulty chewing, poor digestion, and low intake of food. Chronic illness and depression can reduce the appetite. For example, since his wife died Charles Stump has found that just walking in his kitchen makes him sad; he eats only in restaurants now.

High prices of food and poor access to stores and restaurants can negatively impact an older person's nutritional status. Knowing the importance of maintaining a good diet, most communities sponsor programs like community meal sites and meals-on-wheels. Nutrition programs must meet the needs of the specific community in which they are located; the video describes feeding programs for elderly people in rural areas and for elderly people of different cultural and ethnic backgrounds.

Physical fitness and good nutrition are two important components of most health promotion programs. Other components include stress management, injury and illness prevention, and early detection of disease. Good oral health (of teeth and gums) is important too. More information on these health promotion guidelines is provided in Chapter 4 of the text.

While the onset of many chronic diseases can be prevented or delayed by healthy lifestyle habits, remember that health status is also influenced by genetics and environmental exposures. When disease does occur, early detection is crucial. Older adults should have regular medical check-ups that include screening for hypertension, heart disease, breast cancer in women, prostate cancer in men, colon cancer, diabetes, glaucoma, and adverse drug interactions. These conditions, if caught early, can be cured or managed without severely curtailing longevity. For example, Doris Birchander's breast cancer was diagnosed and treated in an early stage and she can expect many years of productive living ahead. In contrast, Joseph Serrao's cancer was diagnosed in a late stage and he tells us that his prognosis is not good.

The text also points out that health can be improved by enacting broad social changes. Examples include increasing feeding and food stamp programs for low-income adults, expanding access to health care and disease screening, reimbursing for the costs of exercise programs, decreasing the amount of salt in processed food, and involving mass media in health education campaigns.

Age-Related Changes in Vision, Hearing, and Sleep

Figure 3.4 in the text shows the parts of the eye. Age-related changes in vision include a thickening and flattening of the surface of the cornea, a decrease in the size of the pupil, a slower shift from rods to cones, a reduced supply of oxygen to the retina, and a decrease in the response time of the pupil in changing light conditions. These changes may negatively impact an older adult's ability to function in low-light situations.

With age, the lens of the eye becomes less elastic and the muscles that control the lens deteriorate. These changes cause problems with close vision, which is easily corrected with glasses. This also interferes with the eye's "accommodation" ability, meaning that it takes the eye longer to adjust between looking at something very close to looking at something in the distance. The lens also becomes more opaque with age. Severely clouded lenses are called cataracts, most of which can be removed surgically with good results. Yellowing of the lens also occurs and this results in a decreased ability to discriminate among colors.

In addition, normal age changes can lead to reduced perception of depth and distance and reduced peripheral vision. The eye disease macular degeneration can cause poor central vision. If caught early, laser treatment may be effective. The eye disease glaucoma can result from inefficient drainage of, or excessive production of, aqueous humour. If caught early, glaucoma can be controlled with medications or surgery; in later stages, it can result in tunnel vision and blindness.

Figure 3.5 in the text presents a diagram of the ear. With advancing age, the supporting walls of the external auditory canals deteriorate, joints within the ear may become arthritic or fixed, and the cochlea undergoes structural changes. Occupational exposure to noise can also damage the ear. The result is decreased ability to hear.

With presbycusis (age-related hearing loss), one loses the ability to hear high-frequency sounds and to distinguish background noise from relevant information. The text notes that about 39% of the population age 65 and older in the U.S. has mild to moderate loss of hearing. Fortunately, hearing aids can help most older adults compensate for age-associated hearing loss. Tinnitus refers to a high-pitched ringing in the ears. Although it cannot be cured and can be distracting, this condition is not dangerous.

Many older adults also notice changes in their sleep patterns, e.g., that sleep is lighter, shorter, and more disrupted. Circadian rhythms may change from a two-phase pattern (awake in the day and asleep at night) to a multiphasic rhythm pattern (day-time napping and shorter periods of sleep at night).

Both Betty Tuff and David Reese find that they are awake for two to three hours in the night. David doesn't worry about it; he just reads a book until he feels sleepy again. Chapter 3 of the text notes that these sleep changes are not dangerous and that most older adults can adjust to these changes without resorting to medications. A few older adults have sleep apnea (interrupted breathing during sleep) or other serious sleep disorders that require medical attention and treatment.

Person-Environment Interaction

As noted in Chapter 1 of the text, "The Growth of Social Gerontology," the concept of person-environment interaction "suggests that the environment is not a static backdrop but changes continually as the older person takes from it what he/she needs, controls what can be manipulated, and adjusts to conditions that cannot be changed. Adaptation thus implies a dual process in which the individual adjusts to some characteristics of the social and physical environment...and brings about changes in others..." Person-environment fit or person-environment congruence refers to having obtained a good match between an individual's needs and his/her environment. More information on person-environment theories is provided in Chapter 11 of the text.

Many examples of person-environment interaction are provided in the text and video illustrating how older adults can manipulate the environment to help compensate for biological changes. Consider an older person whose vision has declined; in most cases, glasses or surgery will correct the problem. John Franggos, for example, remembers becoming very depressed when he developed cataracts. After successful cataract surgery, his vision was restored and his mental outlook improved.

Ilse Darling found that after cataract surgery, her vision was actually better than it had been in her youth. For Blanche Woodbury, glasses and surgery were not enough to perfect her sight. Instead, church members have volunteered to "be her eyes" and escort her to church. Other environmental modifications or services that help compensate for declines in vision include large-print books, bright lighting, computer scanning and voice reading, and seeing-eye dogs.

For David Reese, a hearing aid has helped him recover some of his hearing. Although he and his wife, Eleanor, have noticed a remarkable improvement, David needs to manipulate his environment in other ways in order to optimize the functioning of the hearing aid. For example, his hearing aid amplifies all the sounds around him so that he gets too much irrelevant background "noise" if he stands in the middle of a group. Instead, he stays at the edge of the group and concentrates his conversation on one or two people.

Physical changes can lead to serious deterioration in health and to complicated social problems. For example, consider an older woman who has lost some teeth. Because of chewing problems, she stopped eating a balanced diet and became weak and confused. One day she fell, broke her hip, and was hospitalized. Her family was not prepared to bring her home, and placed her in a nursing home. Along each step of this path to the nursing home, environmental modifications were possible that may have prevented the ultimate outcome. With good dental care, perhaps the teeth could have been saved. Once teeth were lost, the woman could have been fitted for dentures.

Once chewing problems were corrected, a meals program may have restored her nutritional balance and perhaps prevented her from falling. Once hospitalized, the family could have been taught the rehabilitation exercises their mother required. This example illustrates how easily age changes can impact well-being and how early assessment and intervention can compensate for loss.

Drs. Kaplan, Theodore Koff, and Kenneth Brummel-Smith discuss ways in which homes can be designed or modified to compensate for losses expected in old age. Shower grab-bars help older adults compensate for declines in strength and balance. Raised toilet seats with arm rests help older adults compensate for declines in lower and upper body strength. As vision, reaction time, and coordination decline, throw rugs become tripping hazards; gerontologists recommend removing them or tacking them down.

William Narang discusses three programs at Leisure World, a retirement community in Southern California, that help residents live independently despite losses. Leisure World provides health services on the premises, assisting in early detection and treatment of disease and disability. They provide opportunities for socialization, especially important for newly widowed adults. And third, they provide a lifeline system by which residents can push a button to summon immediate assistance in case of an emergency. Marie Louise Ansak describes how On Lok, a comprehensive program of health and social services in San Francisco, helps maintain frail elders in their homes. For example, the program helped client Samuel Stephens return home after a hip fracture. Workers visited him at home to bathe and dress him, delivered three meals a day, and supervised his rehabilitative exercises. The program will continue to monitor his health status to prevent any recurrences of isolation, excessive drinking, and depression. According to Samuel Stephens, On Lok services "fit" his needs.

Hayward King describes how his environment jeopardizes his health status; his neighbors have been beaten and many will walk the streets only with an escort. As a result, elderly people in his neighborhood easily become isolated.

Dr. Meredith Minkler describes a program in San Francisco's Tenderloin aimed at reducing social isolation; over the years, she has seen improvements in the mental and physical well-being of formerly isolated participants.

Dr. Kaplan describes some promising technology for people with speech loss. For example, devices are being developed that would translate small eye or finger movements into yes-no responses. He also is excited about research that shows that complex environments may increase synapses in the brain and lead to improvements in the abilities of brain-injured adults.

In the context of person-environment interaction, we can compensate for many of the changes that occur with aging and disease. Even in the face of disabling conditions, environmental modifications that fit our needs can help maximize our physical potential. As Dr. Brummel-Smith says, "there are no handicapped people, there are only handicapping societies."

Effects of Gender and Ethnicity on Health Status

Rabbi Earl Grollman is concerned about a tendency to blame sick people for their illnesses, a concept known as "blaming the victim." However, as we learned in Lesson 2, "How the Body Ages," the rate of aging and the onset of disease are affected by more than lifestyle. Health status is also influenced by genetics and environmental exposure. Variables that may predispose an individual to a particular disease include gender, ethnicity, and socio-economic status.

There are several gender differences in disease status. For example, men have higher rates of heart disease, chronic obstructive lung disease, and cancer than women. As noted in Chapter 15, "The Resiliency of Older Women," however, older women are more likely than men to experience arthritis, hypertension, stroke, diabetes, incontinence, more types of orthopedic problems (like arthritis and osteoporosis), cataracts, and depression. Breast cancer incidence is rising, now affecting one in nine American women. Lou Glasse notes that, in the past, most federally funded longitudinal health research has focused on men.

Given that older women form a fast-growing segment of society, that they live longer than men, and that they are more likely to face social problems, Lou Glasse insists that more studies of women's health issues are needed. In fact, in 1994 the National Institutes of Health funded a national Women's Health and Aging Study to look at the causes, prevention, management, and rehabilitation of disability in older women.

Ethnicity is also a factor in health status. For example, Dr. Percil Stanford notes that African American males are dying at much younger ages than other ethnicities. In addition, Chapter 14 of the text, "The Resiliency of Elders of Color," notes that African Americans are at higher risk of developing glaucoma, hypertension, stroke, obesity, and diabetes than are Caucasians.

On the other hand, African American women are less likely to develop osteoporosis than Caucasian women. Native Americans have a relatively short life span as well. Dr. Marta Sotomayor notes high rates of diabetes and cardiovascular disease among Hispanics, and that only one in four has health insurance.

Despite the fact that ethnic minority groups tend to have poorer health than Caucasian Americans, they use fewer health services. Some health care providers have speculated that minorities use fewer services because they have strong family networks and like to "take care of their own."

Chapter 14 outlines other reasons for differential access of services, however, including: 1) language barriers; 2) lack of services that are specifically oriented toward the ethnic group; 3) feelings of shame attached to using services, especially mental health services; 4) lack of knowledge about services; 5) geographic distance from services and lack of transportation; and 6) fear and/or distrust of Western service providers. The text suggests a number of ways services can be designed to increase their "cultural competence" and better "fit" the needs and expectations of ethnic minorities.

Research also suggests that health status is related to socio-economic factors. For example, higher rates of chronic disease are found in elders with low incomes and low educational attainment. Dr. Minkler points out that these factors limit access to health care. We will revisit the issue of differential access to health and social services in Lesson 10, "Illness and Disability."

Key Terms and Concepts from the Text, Video, and *Study Guide*

Accommodation
Acculturation
Activities of Daily Living (ADL)
Aerobic Exercise
Anti-miscegenation
Antioxidant
Arcus Senilis
B = f(P,E)
Blaming the Victim
Cataract
Circadian Rhythms
Cross-Over Effect
Cultural Competence
Differential Access
Disability
Double Jeopardy Hypothesis
Environmental Press
Ethnic Minority
Ethnogerontology
Frailty
Functional Health
Gendered Nature of the Life Course
Glaucoma
Health Care Disparities
Health Disparities
Health Promotion Guidelines

Health Status
Homogeneity
Hypokinesia
Indian Health Service
Interindividual Differences
Intraindividual Changes
Macular Degeneration
Myopia
Nocturnal myoclonus
Olfactory Sense
On Lok
Perception
Person-Environment Interaction
Polypharmacy
Presbycusis
Primogeniture, Law of
Range-of-Motion Exercises
Recognition Threshold
Resistance Exercise
Rural Elderly Enhancement Program
Sensation
Sensory Discrimination
Sensory Threshold
Sleep Apnea
Somesthetic
Tinnitus

Self-Study Questions

Instructions: Fill in the blank with the appropriate word or phrase from the list of Key Terms and Concepts.
Note: Only 23 of the 52 key terms and concepts can be used.

1) _____ refers to a dynamic process in which an individual's needs change over time and in which the individual constantly interacts with, adapts to, and changes the environment to meet these needs.

2) Within the concept of person-environment interaction, _____ refers to the demands that social and physical environments make on the individual to adapt, respond, or change.

3) An _____ is a nutrient or metabolite that can absorb the unpaired electron on free radicals and, it is speculated, delay aging.

4) An individual's cycle of sleeping and waking within a 24-hour period is referred to _____.

5) A five- to ten-second cessation of breathing during sleep is called _____.

6) _____ is a disease of the eye in which there is excessive production of or inefficient drainage of the aqueous humour.

7) A _____ is a severe clouding, or opacification, of the lens of the eye which impairs vision.

8) _____ is a disease of the eye in which the macula receives less oxygen than it needs, resulting in destruction of the existing nerve endings in this region and a loss of the central visual field.

9) _____ becomes more difficult with age as the lens of the eye lose elasticity; this delays our eye's ability to adjust from focusing on close items to looking at something in the distance.

10) Another word for near-sightedness is _____.

11) _____ is the severe limitations in activities of daily living

12) Age-related hearing loss is called _____.

13) _____ refers to ringing in the ears.

14) _____ is a program in Alabama that helps keep people in their own homes and improves their nutritional status through the use of home visitors who shop and help prepare meals.

15) _____ is a comprehensive program of health and social services provided to very frail adults residing in certain neighborhoods of San Francisco with a goal of preventing or delaying institutionalization by safely maintaining these adults in their homes.

16) Movements that help stretch and keep limber the arms, legs, hands, and other parts of the body are called _____.

17) _____ are specifications for good nutrition, exercise, stress control, injury prevention, and disease screening aimed at maximizing health and reducing the incidence of chronic disease.

18) The _____ refers to the sense of smell.

19) If you believe that an individual is personally responsible for all of his/her own misfortunes, you may be accused of _____.

20) Minority elders utilize fewer health and social services than do older Caucasian Americans. Barriers such as language, geographic location, and distrust of Western health care are partial causes of this _____.

21) A program that wants to attract clients from a specific ethnic minority group can increase its _____ by hiring workers who speak the same language and understand the customs of that ethnic minority group.

22) _____ refers to the subspecialty in gerontology that focuses on the causes, processes, and consequences of ethnicity and culture on individual and population aging.

23) The _____ is a hypothesis that suggests that a person who is both old and a minority or both old and female may be doubly discriminated against.

Use the Glossary at the end of the Study Guide to check your answers.

Topics for Discussion

1) Describe some communication techniques and environmental interventions that may be used by professionals working with older adults who have impaired vision and hearing.

2) You are hired by a senior program to find our why ethnic minority elders in your community are not joining in their health promotion programs. Why might ethnic minority elders not be participating? What would you do to increase their participation?

Website Challenge

Visit the following websites that can provide more information on this lesson's topics.

1) Living to 100 Health Span Calculator at http://www.livingto100.com/

2) National Institute on Aging's Senior Health website physical exercise for older adults at http://nihseniorhealth.gov/exercise/toc.html

3) National Institute on Aging's AgePage on good nutrition for older adults at http://www.niapublications.org/engagepages/nutrition.asp

4) Office of Minority Health at http://www.omhrc.gov/OMHRC/

Written Assignments

Your instructor may ask you to complete one or more of the essay assignments that follow.

Reaction Paper: New Knowledge and Feelings Stimulated by the Video

Write a two-page paper describing: 1) new information gained from watching the video; 2) how the experiences of the older adults in the video affected your personal view of aging; and 3) other comments to the instructor regarding this lesson or the course.

Research Paper

Select one of the topics below for in-depth study. Read a book or five journal articles on the topic. A good place to start searching the topic for reading material is in the reference section provided at the end of each text chapter. Write a five- to ten-page research paper that provides historical and current thinking on the topic. Identify things about the topic that are not yet resolved or may benefit from further study.

1) Read source documents on the Framingham Study. Describe the sample and methodology. What do the findings suggest about the relationship between lifestyle and the development of heart disease? Can the findings be generalized to all Americans?

2) What are Cardiac Risk Appraisal (CRA) and Health Risk Appraisal (HRA) instruments? Describe their rationale and history of their development. In what health settings are they likely to be used? What are their limitations, especially in their use with older adults?

3) Several studies have been conducted that have attempted to engage whole communities in health promotion activities. Examples include the Stanford Five-Cities Study, the North Karelia Study, and the Minnesota Heart Health Program. Read the source documents on one of these large health promotion programs. Describe the sample and methodology of the program. What do the findings suggest about the success of community-wide health promotion studies? What are the limitations?

4) Why are older adults prone to polypharmacy and adverse drug reactions? To what extent are health professionals aware of the prevalence and risks of polypharmacy and adverse drug reactions in older adults? What combinations of drugs are likely to cause these effects? What can be done about this problem?

5) Compare the methodologies and findings of studies conducted on older athletes. What do these studies suggest about the benefits of exercise for older adults?

6) Discuss the value of the congregate meals program funded by the Older Americans Act of 1965. In what ways does this nutrition program benefit older adults?

Older-Adult Interview

Arrange to interview a person 65 or older who works out regularly. You may find this person at a health club or through a cardiac rehabilitation program, a back health program, or an association of runners, bikers, swimmers, or hikers. Ask the questions below and write a three- to five-page paper about your findings.

Interview Questions

1) How many years have you been working out? Have the type and amount of exercise you do changed over the years? If so, what events triggered these changes?

2) What are the advantages and disadvantages of the type of activity you are involved in (compared to other types of exercise)? Would you recommend it to other people? If so, to whom?

3) Do you also follow a particular diet? If so, please describe it to me and tell me when and why you adopted this way of eating?

4) Do you smoke or drink? If so, how much? If not, why not?

5) Do you ever skip your workout or stray from your diet? Why or why not? If so, what happens?

6) What benefits do you experience from your diet and exercise regime? Does this behavior help reduce stress, increase your ability to sleep, or keep you from getting sick?

7) How old are you? How old do you feel? Which age is the "best age" to be? Explain.

Student Questions

1) How closely do your interviewee's diet and exercise patterns follow the health promotion guidelines noted in the text? Explain.

2) How has this interview affected your personal view of aging and older adults?

Community Interview

Listed below are examples of professionals and programs that help promote health in older adults or compensate for physical losses

Professionals:
Opticians/Ophthalmologists
Nutrition counselors
Health educators
Physical therapists
Audiologists

Programs:
Rehabilitation programs
Sleep disorders clinics
Stress management classes
Weight Watchers
Cardiac rehabilitation programs
Stop smoking programs
Senior day care/day health programs
Risk appraisal programs
Health maintenance organizations
Senior meal sites

Work with your instructor to identify a professional or program listed above that provides services to adults over 65 years of age. Arrange to interview a professional staff member who frequently works with older adults, asking the questions below. Write a three- to five-page paper on your findings.

Interview Questions

1) What is your name and job title? Do you work alone? If not, what job positions are held by your colleagues in the office?

2) What proportion of your clientele is over 50? over 60? over 70? How do older people hear about your service?

3) What kinds of concerns do your older clients have about health promotion or compensating for physical losses? Give examples.

4) What kind of assistance do you and your colleagues provide to older-adult clients? Give examples. How does it differ from assistance provided to younger adult clients?

5) What are the professional qualifications for your job? What are the professional qualifications for your colleagues?

6) How much does the service cost? Who pays?

7) What additional services are needed to assist older adults who have concerns about health promotion or who want to compensate for physical losses? Are they currently available? Explain.

Analyzing the Text Vignettes

Read the text vignettes about Mrs. Hill and Mr. Jones in the introduction to Part Two: "The Biological and Physiological Context of Social Aging" and Mrs. Wilson in Chapter 3, "The Social Consequences of Physical Aging." Write a two- to three-page paper in which you compare and contrast these three older adults, using the questions below as a guide:

1) Which sensory declines and physical problems are these older adults experiencing?

2) How have these changes impaired their abilities to function independently?

3) What modifications have they made to their lives and environments to help compensate for these losses?

4) How do the elders' experiences with disabilities and assistance illustrate the concept of person-environment interaction?

PROGRAM LESSON 4

LOVE, INTIMACY, AND SEXUALITY

Learning Objectives

1) Explain how common social beliefs and attitudes may affect the opportunity for sexual expression among older adults.

2) Describe the changes that take place in sexual functioning as males and females age.

3) Describe three avenues for affection and intimacy for older adults without spouses.

Summary of the Video and Text

Video

The video has three segments. The first segment explores attitudes toward sexuality in old age. The second segment presents information on the physiological changes to the reproductive systems. A number of older adults tell us how physiological and social changes have affected their expression of sexuality. The third and final segment discusses avenues for affection in later life. The married couples in the video report deepening friendship. Elders without spouses discuss how they receive affection from other family members, friends, and pets.

Experts appearing in the video include Drs. Vincent DeFeo, Harvey Gochros, Madeleine Goodman, Douglas Kimmel, and Barbara Payne. Older adults include Elizabeth Allen, Eric and Doris Birchander, Marian Cowan, Louise Di Virgilio, Oliver Francisco, John and Mary Franggos, Jean Jaworski, Pat Nickerson, Mollie Pier, Leo Salazar, and Betty and Lindsey Tuff.

Text

Chapter 7, "Love, Intimacy, and Sexuality in Old Age," presents information on prevalent attitudes and beliefs about love and sexuality among older adults, how the reproductive systems of men and women age, the effect of chronic illness on sexual functioning, gay and lesbian relationships, and factors that support or limit the ability of older adults to be involved in relationships of love and intimacy.

Your instructor may assign additional readings for this lesson.

Key Points

Attitudes Toward Sexual Expression in Older Adults

Examples of negative and inaccurate stereotypes of sexuality in old age can be seen in the media. Dr. Barbara Payne notes that the greeting card industry treats aging as an embarrassing event that should evoke sympathy. Dr. Harvey Gochros points out that most passionate relationships on television involve young people and that sexual feelings among older adults often are portrayed as silly or inappropriate.

Betty Tuff tells us that many older adults were raised during a time when sex was considered "nasty." Dr. Gochros feels society's attitudes stem from a belief that the sole purpose for sex is reproduction, not enjoyment or expression. Both ideas tend to discourage sexual activity in later life. Negative attitudes may lead older people to avoid discussing sexual concerns with partners and helping professionals. An older man may withdraw from social activity and relationships for fear of looking like a "dirty old man." An older woman may feel that sexual desires are inappropriate at her age.

At the same time, society offers few opportunities for sexual expression among older adults. For example, long-term care facilities rarely provide a place where couples can privately engage in sexual activities. Adult children may be embarrassed when their parents talk about their sexual needs and desires.

Society has misconceptions as well about the ability of older adults to engage in, and receive satisfaction from, sexual activity. These myths have been disproved by research, which suggests that the frequency of sexual intercourse and the level of sexual satisfaction do not necessarily decrease over the life span. Instead, it appears that frequency and satisfaction relate to the individual's lifelong pattern of sexual expression and the availability of partners.

Widowhood can curtail sexual desire as well as sexual activity, as noted by Louise Di Virgilio. This phenomenon has been called the widow's or widower's syndrome. Chronic illness and psychosocial factors that influence sexual activity in the elderly are discussed in the text.

For helping professionals who work with older adults, Dr. Madeleine Goodman and Dr. Gochros both stress the importance of addressing the concerns older adults may have about sexual functioning. Sexual expression is a natural and exciting aspect of our humanity; it can add spice to life over its entire course.

Physiological Changes in Sexual Functioning

Dr. Gochros reminds us that the body experiences as many changes between the ages of 45 and 60 as it does between the ages of 10 and 25. While we freely discuss adolescent changes and how they affect behavior, we rarely talk about the changes that occur in an older person's body. In later life, both men and women experience a decline in their levels of sex hormones, known as the climacteric, which affects the nature of sexual response.

The text and Dr. Goodman in the video describe the physiological changes in the sexual functioning of women in great detail. To summarize, between the ages of 40 and 60, women begin the process of menopause. The early stages are marked by a decline in ovarian function, a reduction in estrogen and progesterone levels, and an irregularity of menstrual periods. After 12 consecutive months of no menstrual flow, menopause is completed and the natural ability to reproduce is lost.

For some women, menopause can be very difficult. Some have severe physical symptoms. Others, who have built their identity around the ability to have children, may become depressed during menopause. But menopause can also be positive. According to Dr. Goodman, Palestinian women are accorded greater power and authority with menopause. For Mary Franggos and Jean Jaworski, menopause was just another life challenge; Mary says she now feels more free sexually and Jean thinks "menopause is great."

Regardless of how menopause is perceived, the sharp decline in female sex hormones can result in hot flashes, sleep disturbances, urogenital atrophy, and urinary tract changes. About 65% of older women experience only mild menopausal symptoms that require no medical intervention. For women with severe menopausal symptoms, hormone replacement therapy (HRT) may help alleviate or postpone these symptoms. In addition, HRT has been shown to lower risk of osteoporosis in older women. However, it is also associated with increased risk of endometrial and breast cancer. Dr. Goodman recommends that each woman weigh the risks and benefits (shown in Table 4.3) before starting a hormone replacement therapy.

Physiological changes to the reproductive organs do not reduce a woman's ability to fully engage in sexual activity. Satisfying orgasms are still obtainable, although the orgasmic phase may take longer to reach, be of shorter duration, and be less intense in older women than in younger women. Physical discomfort during sex appears lower in older women engaging in regular and consistent sexual activity, including masturbation. Lubricants and vaginal hormone creams are useful for women with vaginal dryness.

As explained by the text and by Drs. Vincent DeFeo and Douglas Kimmel in the video, men experience less dramatic changes in sexual functioning over the life span. While testosterone production is reduced, it does not stop entirely, and the decrease does not result in a loss of reproductive ability. Sexually, the aging process results in an increase in the time it takes to achieve an erection, a decrease in the erection's firmness, reduced intensity of orgasm, reduced force of ejaculation, and a longer refractory period. Some couples report that sex is better in old age because age changes in men decrease the likelihood of premature ejaculation.

Some older men experience impotence, which may result from a combination of physical, psychological, and social concerns. Men with impotence should work with health care professionals to identify and treat its cause. As in the case of women, normal physiological aging does not necessarily result in decreased sexual performance or enjoyment. A summary of normal, age-related physiological changes in genital function is provided in the box on page 263 in the text.

Sex education may help older adults distinguish between normal changes and unusual symptoms and may lead to increased attention to and treatment of sexual or erectile dysfunction.

Enlargement of the prostate, known as benign prostatic hypertrophy, occurs in more than 50% of men age 65 and older. While it can be painful and result in difficulties urinating, it usually can be treated with medication or surgery without impeding sexual performance.

Drug interactions and alcohol use can negatively affect sexual functioning, but their effects are usually reversible. In men, lifelong diabetes or uncontrolled diabetes may cause impotence. Radical treatment for prostate cancer, a prostatectomy, also may result in impotence. To treat irreversible impotence, Dr. DeFeo suggests penile implants and injections. Benefits of Viagra as the wonder drug for men have been empirically supported.

The link between sexual function and disease underscores the importance of seeking medical attention for unusual symptoms. At the same time, Drs. Gochros and Goodman encourage helping professionals to take seriously the health and sexual concerns of older adults. With baby boomers getting older in large numbers and proportions, it will not be surprising that they will expect health care providers to consider their sexual needs when prescribing medication and other treatments.

Avenues for Affection for Older Adults Without Spouses

The importance of affection does not appear to diminish with age. Affection and intimacy can include sexual activity, but sex is not essential for the expression of affection and intimacy.

Many older married couples, like the Franggos, the Birchanders, the Tuffs, and the Wonsons, report a deepening of regard and an increase in affection for each other over time. They tell us that sexual desire and activity are ongoing aspects of their relationships. In fact, research shows that 50% of married persons 75 years and older have sex about four times a month.

When sexual activity is defined more broadly, to encompass touching and caressing, about 60% of women and 80% of men can be considered sexually active. The Wonsons also note the importance of demonstrating affection for each other in front of their children to show them an example of a stable, loving, caring couple in these unstable times.

But many older adults do not have spouses, and demographic patterns suggest that we will continue seeing more than twice as many widows as widowers among older adults. What opportunities do non-married people have for affection and intimacy?

Dr. Gochros reports that 5% to 10% of men have homosexual feelings in early or mid-life and suggests that 5% to 10% of older men do as well. Some older gay people have been gay their entire adult lives and others, like Oliver Francisco, affirm their homosexuality in later life. Dr. Payne suggests that the imbalance in availability of older male partners may result in increased homosexuality among women and the practice of polygamy in the future.

Many older adults strengthen their relationships with children and grandchildren, as noted by Marian Cowan and Louise Di Virgilio. Older widows, like Mollie Pier, usually increase their circle of women friends. It often is harder for men to develop friendships outside of marriage. Leo Salazar, however, talks of his "compadre," a male friend with whom he shares secrets. Other older adults, like Elizabeth Allen, satisfy their needs for affection and intimacy through relationships with pets. Research suggests that having friends, confidants, pets, and close relationships with family members can enhance physical and mental health and extend longevity in older adults.

Dr. Gochros talks about our continued need for touch, which is accompanied by a reduced chance of being touched in old age. Betty Tuff reminds us that touch reassures people of their humanity; she sees it as an important part of her regular visits to nursing homes.

Key Terms and Concepts from the Text, Video, and *Study Guide*

Benign Prostatic Hypertrophy
Climacteric
Compadre
Cystitis
Ejaculation
Erectile Dysfunction
Erection
Estrogen
Estrogen Replacement Therapy
Gay
Heterosexual
Homosexuality
Hormone Replacement Therapy
Hot Flashes
Hysterectomy
Impotence
Incontinence
Intimacy
Lesbian
Love
Male Menopause
Mastectomy
Masturbation
Menopause

Monogamy
Mutuality
Nocturnal Penile Tumescence
Orgasm
Ovariectomy
Penile Implant
Polygamy
Postmenopause
Premenopause
Preorgasmic Plateau Phase
Progesterone
Prostate, Enlargement of
Radical Prostatectomy
Refractory Period
Serial Monogamy
Sex
Sexual Dysfunction
Sexuality
Testosterone
Two-Stage Orgasm
Urogenital Atrophy
Viropause
Widow(er) Syndrome

Self-Study Questions

Instructions. Fill in the blank with the appropriate word or phrase from the list of Key Terms and Concepts. Note: Only 30 of the 47 key terms and concepts can be used.

1) A _____ is a male's close male friend and confidant for whom he has great trust and mutual regard.

2) A _____ is someone who is sexually attracted to the opposite gender.

3) A _____ is someone who is sexually attracted to persons of the same gender.

4) The male sex hormone is called _____.

5) Two female sex hormones are _____ and _____.

6) If someone has a _____, it means that the uterus is surgically removed.

7) _____ refers to the inability to have or maintain an erection.

8) When entering menopause, some women may choose to start _____ or _____ to supplement decreasing hormone levels.

9) In men, the time between ejaculation and another erection is called the _____.

10) _____ refers to the time in women's and men's lives when the level of sex hormones decline and reproductive ability is either reduced (in men) or stopped (in women).

11) Many men experience _____ as they age, which can be painful and result in difficulties urinating. This is also called _____.

12) In men and women, the phase of love making prior to orgasm in which sexual tension is at its height is called the _____.

13) After menopause, a woman may experience _____, which refers to a reduction in the elasticity and lubricating abilities of the vagina.

14) When women stop having monthly periods, they are in _____.

15) When someone has an _____, both ovaries are surgically removed.

16) A common term for a homosexual male is _____; a female homosexual is often referred to as a _____.

17) _____ is a term coined by Masters and Johnson describing sexual dysfunction following a long period of abstinence due to a spouse's illness and/or death.

18) _____ and _____ are terms that suggest a significant change experienced by men as their production of testosterone decreases in later life. This is sometimes accompanied by testicular atrophy, prostate enlargement, and associated psychological doubts.

19) If someone has breast cancer, a doctor may recommend _____, which refers to the surgical removal of one or both breasts.

20) A _____ refers to the sense of ejaculation inevitably followed by actual semen expulsion as experienced by younger males.

21) The climax of sexual excitement is called an _____.

22) The surgical removal of the prostate, usually in treatment for prostate cancer, is called a _____.

23) A person who has a faithful relationship with another person is engaging in _____. If this person develops another faithful relationship after losing his/her first partner, this person is engaged in _____.

Use the Glossary at the end of the Study Guide to check your answers.

Topics for Discussion

1) How can professionals assist older men and women to adapt to age-related changes in their reproductive organs that will facilitate their experiences with intimacy and their sexual functioning and enjoyment?

2) In what ways do nursing homes deny the sexual needs of residents? What can nursing home staff do to respect the sexual needs of older residents?

Website Challenge

Visit the following websites that can provide more information on this lesson's topics. Bookmark them for easy access in the future:

1) Widownet at http://www.fortnet.org/widownet

2) Lesbian and Gay Aging Issues Network at http://www.asaging.org/networks/lgain/lgainmain.html

3) Women's Health Initiative at http://www.nhlbi.nih.gov/whi/

Written Assignments

Your instructor may ask you to complete one or more of the written assignments that follow.

Reaction Paper: New Knowledge and Feelings Stimulated by the Video

Write a two-page paper describing: 1) new information gained from watching the video; 2) how the experiences of the older adults in the video affected your personal view of aging; and 3) other comments to the instructor regarding this lesson or the course.

Older-Adult Interview

Interview a person who is 65 or older, asking the questions below. Write a three- to five-page paper on the responses.

Interview Questions

1) How many close friendships do you have at this time? How does this compare to when you were a young adult? Middle-aged?

2) Think about your close friendships over your life. Do your close friends have similar characteristics? For example, are they usually the same age or gender as you? Do they usually share the same ethnicity or religion with you? Are they usually neighbors or family members? What makes someone a best friend?

3) Can you describe for me one of the close friendships you have at this time? What things do you do together? What do you talk about? In what ways can you rely on each other?

4) Do you now, or have you ever, had a close friendship with someone much older or much younger than yourself? What things did you do together? What did you talk about? How did you both benefit from the relationship?

5) What are the advantages and disadvantages of close friendships in old age?

Student Questions

1) Intimacy is defined as feelings of deep mutual regard, trust, and affection, usually developed through long association. It is often found in relationships between close friends and between spouses. Did any of the friendships and close relationships described by the interviewee fit this definition? Why or why not?

2) How has this interview affected your personal view of aging and older adults?

Community Interview

Listed below are examples of professionals and services concerned with love, intimacy, and sexual activity.

Professionals
- Geriatricians
- Gynecologists
- Marriage counselors
- Psychiatrists
- Psychologists
- Sex therapists
- Social workers
- Urologists

Programs
- Humane Society (pets to nursing homes)
- Impotency clinic
- Lesbian, gay, transgender support group
- Sex education classes
- Widow's support group

Call one of the programs or professionals above to ask if they work with adults over age 50. If so, arrange to interview a professional staff member who frequently works with older adults, asking the questions below. Write a three- to five-page paper on your findings.

Interview Questions

1) Based on your estimates, about what proportion of your clientele is over age 50? over 60? over 70? How do your older clients hear about you?

2) What kinds of concerns do your older clients have about love, intimacy, or sexuality? Give examples.

3) What kinds of assistance do you provide older adults who have concerns about love, intimacy, or sexuality? Give examples.

4) What are the professional qualifications for your job?

5) How much does this service cost? Who pays?

6) What additional services are needed to assist older adults who have concerns about love, intimacy, or sexuality? Are they currently available? Explain.

Research Paper

Select one of the topics below for in-depth study. Read a book or five journal articles on the topic. A good place to start searching for reading material is in the reference section provided at the end of each text chapter. Write a five- to ten-page research paper that describes the historical and current thinking on the topic. Identify things about the topic that are not yet resolved or may benefit from further study.

1) How prevalent is homosexuality in older adults? What are the special concerns of older gay men and lesbians? How are these concerns different from those of younger gays? How are the concerns of older gay and lesbian adults similar to and/or different from the concerns of older heterosexuals?

2) Read the source documents on the Duke Longitudinal Study's findings regarding sexual activity in older adults. What limitations were seen in the 1954 methodology and initial analysis? Why were the data reanalyzed in the late 1970s? What methodological changes were instituted in the second Duke study? Compare the findings. What does this suggest about the importance of methodology and investigator bias in research?

3) Read the most recent Kinsey report on sexual expression in older adults. How do the methods and findings from this report differ from those of earlier work by Kinsey? What does the most recent report suggest about how attitudes and behaviors of older adults toward sexuality have changed over the years?

4) Discuss the impact of social, psychological, and economic barriers to marriage or remarriage in old age, e.g., availability of partners, attitudes of adult children, Social Security laws, and inheritance laws.

5) Review the research on confidants and companions in old age. What is known about friendships in old age? Are friendships more important to women than to men? What does research suggest about the link between social support and health status? Between social support and well-being?

6) Review the research on hormone-replacement therapy. For women, read the findings from the Women's Health Initiative. Are there any federally sponsored trials of hormone replacement in men? What additional research is needed to determine the risks and benefits of hormone replacement in women and men?

Future Trends

An introduction to this assignment is provided by Dr. Payne when she proposes that, given the gender imbalance in old age, we may see an increase in polygamy and homosexuality in the future.

Consider trends in the following areas: life expectancy for men and women; medical and technological advances; options for social roles; attitudes toward sexuality; prevalence of AIDS and disabilities; etc. Write a two- to three-page paper in which you describe current trends and speculate about the future of love, intimacy, and sexuality for older adults. For example, what opportunities for love, intimacy, and sexuality will older adults have in 2020? What types of behaviors will be acceptable? What new programs will have been developed? What medical and technological advances will have occurred? What social changes will have taken place? Explain.

PROGRAM LESSON 5

LEARNING, MEMORY, AND SPEED OF BEHAVIOR

Learning Objectives

1) Give three examples that illustrate the concept of person-environment fit in an older adult's ability to learn.

2) Describe strategies used by older adults for storage and retrieval of information in long-term memory.

3) Describe how age changes in speed of behavior can affect physical, perceptual, and cognitive skills of older adults.

Summary of the Video and Text

Video

The video has three segments; these are on learning, memory, and speed of behavior. In the first segment, we hear how aging affects learning and how older adults can compensate for aging effects to enhance lifelong learning skills. In the segment on memory, changes in the ability to store and retrieve information from memory are discussed, along with suggestions for strengthening and aiding one's ability to remember things. The final segment addresses speed of behavior. Again, while research suggests a true age-related change, many older adults compensate with strategies developed over years of experience and through environmental modification.

The video features experts in the area of psychology, including Drs. James Birren, Gene Cohen, William Hoyer, Douglas Kimmel, K. Warner Schaie, and Sherry Willis. A number of older adults share their experience, including Elizabeth Allen, Charles Clark, Catherine (Kitty) Conroy, Ilse Darling, Louise Di Virgilio, Ruth Dow, Oliver Francisco, Mary and John Franggos, Jean Jaworski, Pat Nickerson, Jane Potter, Josephine Rosen, Jim Tate, Henrietta Towsley, and Mary Sue and Roger Wonson.

Text

The introduction to Part Three, "The Psychological Context of Aging" introduces Chapters 5 through 7 in the text. Included are examples of the wide variation in psychological functioning among older adults.

Chapter 5, "Cognitive Changes with Aging," presents information on the relationship between age and intelligence, learning, memory, wisdom, and creativity. The text also discusses factors that affect learning in old age, age-related changes in memory, and five recommended criteria to assess if the individual is regarded as "wise." For each topic, the text outlines the major findings from research in the area and then suggests things older people can do to maintain and enhance their cognitive functioning.

Your instructor may assign additional readings for this lesson.

Key Points

Enhancing an Older Adult's Ability to Learn

The saying, "you can't teach an old dog new tricks," reflects a common misconception that learning is impossible in old age. In fact, research suggests that healthy adults can maintain the ability to acquire new knowledge and skills well into late life. For example, Dr. James Birren tells us about findings from studies of vocabulary. While a well-educated young adult knows about 22,000 words, the same person at 65 knows about 45,000 words.

Many older adults in the video spoke of positive experiences with late-life learning. For example, Mary Franggos and Kitty Conroy are proud of having obtained college degrees in later life. Members of the Institute for Learning in Retirement express enthusiasm for their program of peer education in which "nobody is in class unless they want to learn [and] nobody is teaching unless they're fascinated with the subject...a perfect learning environment."

46

Jane Potter advises older adults who want to return to school: start with a single class to gain study skills and confidence, and don't be afraid to ask for help.

Aside from the satisfaction it affords participants, lifelong learning keeps us mentally fit. For example, Dr. Gene Cohen tells us that in a mentally challenging environment, the brain continues to build synapses, or extensions, between brain cells, thereby improving the communication between the neurons of higher intellectual functioning. This research gives support to the adage, "use it or lose it."

Dr. Sherry Willis concurs with these findings and warns against becoming a "mental couch potato" in late life. Louise Di Virgilio illustrates this point; she keeps her mind active by reading, doing crossword puzzles, and playing Jeopardy, and says she feels she is much sharper now than when she was younger.

However, even in healthy adults, learning new information can be impeded by normal aging changes. For example, declines in vision and hearing may hinder an older adult's ability to get information into sensory memory. The slowing of psychomotor processes with age slows speed of response, making timed tests difficult. Older adults also tend to respond more cautiously when they are uncertain or when risks are high.

Several things can be done to help compensate for age-related changes that can impede learning. For example, declining vision can be compensated for by reducing or eliminating glare in the classroom and on the blackboard, by using big print, and by verbally reviewing information that is presented visually. Classrooms should be well marked and accessible to older students.

Declining hearing can be compensated for by improving the acoustics of the classroom, speaking clearly and slowly, and providing visual material that matches what is being said. Decline in physical response time and increased caution in responding are not barriers to learning if the learning conditions are self-paced.

Instructors must remember that older adults have a lifetime of experiences and respond better in learning environments in which the teacher provides meaningful information through a mix of lecture, audio-visual aids, practical examples, and discussion of how the older students perceive and interpret the material.

Finally, older adults themselves act to compensate for potential disadvantages by sitting close to the instructor and blackboard, by paying close attention to what is being said, and by taking detailed notes.

Other barriers to late-life learning are fear and anxiety. Many older people believe they are not as good at learning as young people. Yet, research indicates that learning skills can improve with age, particularly when the individual is studying an area of special interest. Mary Franggos says she was afraid of learning to use the computer, but once she sat down and started experimenting with it, she found it was not difficult to learn. Test anxiety can also be conquered. Kitty Conroy tells us that her nervousness kept her from passing her typing test; but she persevered and passed it on the tenth try.

Dr. Douglas Kimmel reminds us of the potential for ageism in the educational system. Ageism can be reflected in the physical facilities of a campus, for example, large distances between building or classes held in rooms up three flights of stairs. Age differences are apparent inside the class as well. Because older adults enjoy discussion-based learning, some may spend class time talking about the applications of the new knowledge in real life whereas some younger students may wish to focus conversation on information for the next exam. In the video, Charles Clark and Jean Jaworski express their preference for class discussion over lectures and tests.

Storage and Retrieval of Information in Long-Term Memory

Memory depends on the storage and retrieval of stored information in the brain. In general, new information is received by the senses. It is passed through our eyes and ears (sensory memory) to short-term (primary) memory. If the information in primary memory is important, it is stored in long-term (secondary) memory.

Once stored, we must be able to retrieve the information from memory when we need it. A schematic representation of how we process information is shown in Figure 5.3 of the text.

Dr. Birren uses the analogy of a computer. Like a computer, the brain has short-term storage and long-term storage. We must save information from short-term storage to long-term storage if we want to remember it.

Like a computer, our long-term memory can hold a tremendous amount of information. We also have a scanning mechanism to see what is in long-term storage and a way to retrieve information from long-term memory.

What happens to our memories as we age? Compared to young adults, research suggests that older adults may be less efficient at moving information through sensory and short-term memories to long-term memory.

They also may have more difficulty retrieving information from long-term memory. Two reasons for this change are discussed in Chapter 5 of the text.

The disuse theory suggests that information in long-term (secondary) memory fades away or decays unless it is exercised, as in the adage, "use it or lose it." Interference theory suggests that older people have problems retrieving information because new information interferes with the material already in storage.

General slowing of the central nervous system also accounts for slower memory function in aging. Whatever the reason, older adults tend to do better on tests of recognition (like multiple choice or matching tests) than on tests of recall (like fill-in-the blank tests).

In addition, most older people are afraid of Alzheimer's disease and tend to suspect the worst when they misplace or forget something. Studies of attention and memory, however, suggest that young people have more lapses than old people. But because young people don't worry as much about these lapses, they do not think poorly of themselves.

Old people, on the other hand, blame themselves for memory lapses; their fear of incompetence may become a self-fulfilling prophecy by leading to real cognitive declines. Two older women in the video, Elizabeth Allen and Ilse Darling, are very disappointed by their lapses in memory.

Both internal and external memory aids can help enhance memory. Dr. Willis tells us that one of the most important memory strategies is organizing information. She uses the analogy of a filing cabinet, saying that the better we file something in long-term memory, the easier it is to retrieve it.

Mary Sue Wonson tells how she files people's names in her memory by the name's first letter, and this helps her to retrieve the name when she meets the person again. Another internal memory aid (or mediator) is rehearsal or repeating something several times to yourself to help it into long-term memory.

Sometimes information can best be remembered in categories. For example, it is easier to remember to eat fruits and vegetables than it is to eat apples, squash, pears, spinach, beans, peas, oranges, broccoli, peaches, lettuce, celery, and tomatoes.

Associating new information with an image is also successful. For example, Dr. Birren tells people to remember his name by thinking of a mug with "beer in" it. Association was used to improve memory in the Berlin study described by Dr. William Hoyer; participants associated new words with specific monuments and were able to recall the words by taking a mental trip from monument to monument.

Context also supports memory. Dr. Hoyer gives us the example of the surgeon who is supported in his/her work by the operating room environment. Jim Tate notices that just seeing a certain Civil War monument will trigger his memory of certain details of the battle.

Another internal tool is called mnemonics. These are rhymes or phrases that contain hints about the subject to be remembered, for example, "I before E, except after C."

External memory aids are also useful. For example, most adults make lists and keep calendar books. Jane Potter uses a purse clip to keep from misplacing her keys.

People of all ages can learn these techniques to improve their memory. Dr. Willis assures us that using these strategies is not "cheating;" they constitute effective tools by which we can all improve our ability to store and retrieve information in long-term memory.

Oliver Francisco describes two other strategies he uses when his memory fails him. Sometimes he feels comfortable admitting that he has forgotten something. Other times, he will try to cover a memory lapse. For example, if he cannot remember people's names, he says, "Oh, you two know each other, don't you?" The two strangers will proceed to introduce themselves, saving Oliver the embarrassment of admitting he has forgotten their names.

Older adults are susceptible to a number of conditions that impair mental functioning, such as Alzheimer's disease, depression, and alcoholism. Information on these conditions and their effects on cognitive skills will be presented in Lesson 10, "Illness and Disability." Cognitive functioning can also be impaired by cardiovascular disease, sensory deficits, and poor nutrition, conditions reviewed in Lessons 2 and 3.

Effects of Age Changes in Speed of Behavior

Speed of behavior refers to the quickness with which one responds to a stimulus. An example is how quickly one steps on the brakes when the traffic light turns red.

An individual's speed of behavior depends on how fast one perceives the stimulus, encodes it, remembers what it means, makes a decision about it, programs the appropriate movements, and then executes the movement. It also depends on muscle strength, endurance, and coordination.

Research suggests that, in older adults, encoding and response selection are slower due to changes in the central nervous system, and that strength, endurance, and coordination are reduced.

However, research also suggests that older adults can compensate for these decreases in a number of ways. First, speed of behavior appears to be enhanced by continued mental activity and physical fitness. Pat Nickerson agrees; she attributes the maintenance of her quick reflexes to her active lifestyle, which includes gardening and walking.

Second, older adults compensate for declining reaction time by relying on experience with the task, skill, and mental strategies such as anticipation. For example, Dr. Warner Schaie describes research that found that older typists compensated for slowed response time by picking up larger chunks of information from typescript than younger typists.

Dr. Birren notes that older pilots purposely avoid conditions that might require split-second maneuvers, while younger pilots tend to take more risks.

Older workers in manufacturing tend to seek out self-paced jobs that do not require quick reaction times. Dr. Hoyer describes how older musicians maintain playing speed and quality. Through experience with the music, they have advance knowledge of the notes and can anticipate the upcoming passages of their music.

Third, older adults may compensate by depending on other adults for clues about the environment and protection. For example, Dr. Birren noticed that an older adult may surreptitiously follow a young person while crossing a busy intersection. The young person unknowingly provides the older person with information about the traffic by the speed at which he/she walks and tends to protect the older person from passing cars and pedestrians.

It appears that older adults who age successfully also have a good attitude about their own changes in learning, memory, and speed of behavior. Mary Sue Wonson admits that her speed of behavior and endurance has decreased and she has prioritized her activities; she decided she wanted more time to be creative, so has cut back on housework. John Franggos feels he has become more easygoing and isn't as concerned about working at the pace he worked at 20 years ago. Mary Franggos feels a lot more peaceful about life.

Key Terms and Concepts from the Text, Video, and *Study Guide*

Attentional Control
Classic Aging Pattern
Cognitive Retraining
Crystallized Intelligence
Cued Recall
Creativity
Disuse Theory
General Slowing Hypothesis
Echoic Memory
Elderhostel
Encoding
Errors of Commission
Errors of Omission
External Memory Aids
Fluid Intelligence
Free Recall
Iconic Memory
Information Processing Model
Interference Theory
Learning
Mediators

Memory
Mnemonics
Primary Memory
Recall
Recognition
Seattle Longitudinal Study
Secondary Memory
Selective Attention
Self-Fulfilling Prophecy
Self-Paced Tests
Senior Learning Programs
Sensory Memory
Spatial Memory
Terminal Decline Hypothesis
Test Anxiety
Tip-of-the-Tongue States
Visual Mediators
Weschler Adult Intelligence Scale (WAIS)
Wisdom
Working (Primary) Memory

Self-Study Questions

Instructions: Fill in the blank with the appropriate word or phrase from the list of Key Terms and Concepts.
Note: Only 25 of the 41 key terms and concepts can be used.

1) In the information processing model, _____ is the place where information received through the sense organs is stored for a tenth of a second. Information is then either forgotten or passed on to _____, where it is held a little longer but still only temporarily. If you want to remember the information, you must pass it to _____ memory.

2) To help remember, we might use _____ such as calendars, alarms, and lists. Or we might use internal memory aids, also called _____, to help us file new information in long-term memory.

3) An example of an internal memory aid is a _____, which refers to a verbal riddle, rhyme, and code associated with new information, for example, 'i' before 'e' except after 'c.'

4) _____ is another term for visual memory and refers to the words, faces, and landscapes that we experience through our eyes. _____ is another term for auditory memory and refers to remembering what you hear as opposed to what you see or read.

5) _____ is the ability to recall where objects are in relationship to each other in space.

6) The acquisition of a new skill or the encoding of new information into one's memory is called _____.

7) Performance that is influenced by pre-performance expectations may lead to a _____. For example, people who are told that their age may keep them from performing well often perform poorly.

8) _____ is the process of searching through and retrieving information from the vast store of information in secondary memory. If you are given cues or hints to help you, this is called _____. If you have to retrieve information without any help, this is called _____.

9) Exams in which the subject can control the amount of time spent on each item are called _____.

50

10) _____ refers to the process of matching information in secondary memory with stimulus information. In testing, this ability is tested by multiple-choice exams questions.

11) _____ refers to nervousness about taking an exam; this nervousness may result in poor performance.

12) _____ implies that the individual does not act on impulse and can reflect on all aspects of a given situation.

13) The _____ suggests that people 65 and older tend to perform significally worse on Performance Scales (i.e., fluid intelligence), but their scores on Verbal Scales (i.e., crystallized intelligence) remain stable

14) The most widely used measure of adult intelligence is the _____. It consists of subtests, some of which are described as Verbal Scales (which measure, to some extent, _____ intelligence) and Performance Scales (providing some measure of _____ intelligence).

15) _____ refers to a specific type of difficulty in retrieval of information, distinguished by the sense or feeling that one can "almost" remember it.

16) _____ refers to the ability to apply unique and feasible solutions to new situations to come up with original ideas or material products.

17) _____ refers to being able to focus on information relevant to a task while ignoring irrelevant information.

Use the Glossary at the end of the Study Guide to check your answers.

Topics for Discussion

1) To what extent do age-related changes in sensory processes and physiological functioning affect older people's memory at the stages of sensory, primary, and secondary memory?

2) How have older persons been found to compensate for declines in information processing and perceptual-motor speed?

Website Challenge

Visit the following websites that can provide more information on this lesson's topics. Bookmark them for easy access in the future.

1) Elderhostel at http://www.elderhostel.org

2) SPRY Foundation at http://www.spry.org

Written Assignments

Your instructor may ask you to complete one or more of the written assignments that follow.

Reaction Paper: New Knowledge and Feelings Stimulated by the Video

Write a two-page paper describing: 1) new information gained from watching the video; 2) how the experiences of the older adults in the video affected your personal view of aging.

3) Include other comments to the instructor regarding this lesson or the course.

Older-Adult Interview

Contact Elderhostel, an older-adult learning program at your college or university, or a senior center that offers educational classes. Ask the program leader to arrange for you to interview an older adult who is participating in a late-life learning program, asking the questions below. Write a three- to five-page paper on your findings.

Interview Questions

1) Which courses are you taking?

2) Why did you decide to take these courses? What are the benefits?

3) Have you gotten involved in an educational program after a long absence from formal schooling? If so, when were you last in school? Compared to when you were a young adult, is it easier or harder for you to learn and remember new material? Why?

4) Which learning conditions work best for you? For example:

a) Do you like to sit in the front of the room?

b) Are you more comfortable in large or small classes?

c) Which types of exams do you prefer (for example, true-false, multiple choice, essay, in-class, take-home)?

d) Which teaching style is most educational for you (for example, films, class discussion, guest speakers, lectures, individual research)?

5) What could the college, program, or center do to improve its learning environment for older adults?

6) What are your study habits? How well do they work?

Student Questions

1) How do the experiences of the older adult compare with the information provided by the text on adult learning and memory?

2) How has this interview affected your personal view of aging and older adults?

Community Interview

Listed below are examples of programs designed to help older people assess whether or not they are having changes in psychological function.

Professionals	Programs
- Geriatrician	- Geriatric assessment program
- Neurologist	- Veterans Administration clinic
- Psychiatrist	or hospital
- Psychologist	- Mental health center

Work with your instructor to identify a program or professional providing services to adults aged 60 or older. Arrange to interview a staff member who frequently works with older adults, asking the questions below. Write a three- to five-page paper on your findings.

Interview Questions

1) What is your name and job title? Who else works with you?

2) Which cognitive or psychological assessment services do you provide?

3) How are people referred to you for an assessment? How many clients are assessed in a year? About what proportion is 60 or older?

4) For the older-adult clients, which kinds of tests are done during the assessment, for example, lab tests, written tests, skills tests? How long does the assessment take?

5) How much does the assessment cost? Does Medicare cover it?

6) What are the qualifications of the people conducting the assessment?

7) Do you share the results with the older adult being assessed? If not, who do you share it with?

8) What recommendations are made to older adults after the assessment is complete? Give examples.

9) How would expanding the program help it better meet its goals?

Research Paper

Select one of the topics below for in-depth study. Read a book or five journal articles on the topic. A good place to start searching for reading material is in the reference section provided at the end of each text chapter. Write a five- to ten-page research paper that describes the historical and current thinking on the topic. Identify things about the topic that are not yet resolved or may benefit from further study.

1) What is the definition of mental competence in your state? According to the law, when is a person incompetent and how is that determined? What are the advantages and disadvantages of declaring someone incompetent?

2) Read about the work of Dr. Timothy Salthouse on the effects of age on skill performance. Who was studied? Which methods were used? What were the findings? Which other investigators are studying the effects of age on skill performance? How do their findings compare with those of Salthouse?

3) Read studies by Drs. K. Warner Schaie and Sherry Willis on cognitive retraining. Describe how their studies were conducted. What were the findings? Which other investigators are studying cognitive retraining? How do their findings compare with those of Schaie and Willis?

INTELLECT, PERSONALITY, AND MENTAL HEALTH

Learning Objectives

1) Discuss strengths and weaknesses of longitudinal and cross-sectional designs in the study of adult intellectual development.

2) Describe the major findings from research on personality development over the life span.

3) Identify three factors that promote or help maintain good mental health for older adults.

Summary of the Video and Text

Video

The video has four segments. The first segment focuses on intellectual skills over the life span. The second segment reviews the current thinking on personality and aging. In the third segment, experts and elders discuss factors that promote or maintain good mental health in later life. The final segment provides a brief look at future directions for research in the psychology of aging.

Experts who appear in the video include Drs. Herbert Benson, James Birren, Gene Cohen, Paul Costa, William Hoyer, K. Warner Schaie, Sherry Willis, and Steven Zarit. Older adults who help illustrate the lesson's main concepts include: Elizabeth Allen, Eric and Doris Birchander, Louise Di Virgilio, Ruth Dow, Oliver Francisco, Mary Franggos, Pat Nickerson, Mollie Pier, David Reese, Vi Smith, Ben Tamashiro, Jim Tate, Virginia Templeton, and Mary Sue and Roger Wonson.

Text

New Readings. Chapter 6, "Personality and Mental Health in Old Age," presents information on stability and change in personality over the life course, how personality affects how we cope with and adapt to age-related and environmental changes, and the concepts of successful and robust aging. Also presented is information on mental disorders among older people, Alzheimer's disease, and use of mental health services.

Review. "The Psychological Context of Aging" is a short overview of Chapters 5 through 7 in the text. Three vignettes in this section provide examples of the diversity in psychological functioning among older adults.

Chapter 5, "Cognitive Changes with Aging," presents information on intelligence and aging, problems in measuring cognitive function, longitudinal studies of intelligence, and factors that may influence intelligence in adulthood.

Your instructor may assign additional readings for this lesson.

Key Points

Studies of Adult Intelligence

Intelligence is difficult to measure, especially in later years, and it has not been proven whether or not older adults are more or less intelligent than young people. Research does suggest "a classic aging pattern" in which older adults experience a decline in fluid intelligence (spatial orientation, abstract reasoning, and speed of perception) but not crystallized intelligence (knowledge acquired through education and experience, e.g., verbal skills and social judgment). However, as we saw with learning, memory, and speed of behavior in the previous lesson, a number of factors may influence the measurement of intelligence. For example, older adults tend to be more cautious and thoughtful than younger adults and therefore may answer questions more slowly or give multiple, situation-based answers. Increased anxiety, especially in timed test situations, may reduce performance as well.

It is important to understand research design before being able to draw conclusions from research findings. Many studies, including those of intelligence, have cross-sectional designs, i.e., they compare two or more age groups at a single point in time. Findings from cross-sectional studies suggest that older adults are less intelligent than young adults. Because our world has changed so much in the past 50 years, however, it is hard to determine if group differences are related to age or related to historical and technological changes over time.

For example, a cross-sectional survey may suggest that 20-year-old adults do better on computerized tests than do 60-year-old adults. But does this represent a difference in intelligence, or just in the relative levels of exposure to computers in the two groups? In the last lesson, Mary Franggos said that many older people are afraid of computers, but found she had no trouble with her computer once she decided to learn to use it. Dr. Warner Schaie found in his research that older participants were more skilled at adding numbers than younger participants. Does this mean that we become better at addition as we age? Dr. Schaie suggests that this might be due to the widespread use of inexpensive, hand-held calculators among younger people who rarely have to add by hand or in their heads.

Researchers are more likely to get a more accurate measure of age-related changes by conducting longitudinal studies, i.e., interviewing the same people over a number of years. The text reviews longitudinal studies conducted in Seattle (by Dr. Schaie and Dr. Sherry Willis in the video), in Iowa, New York State, and North Carolina that examined intelligence. Longitudinal studies have limitations too, including attrition (participants dropping out over the course of the study) and terminal drop (a marked decline in cognitive function within five years of death). Ruth Dow, a participant in the Seattle Longitudinal Study since 1954, is referring to attrition when she notes that not many participants in her age group are still in the study.

Despite these limitations, research has found that people who have good health and good educational backgrounds experience relatively small changes in cognitive functioning over the life span, especially if they exercise their brains regularly. In other words, adults should "use it or lose it" as research shows that older adults who are less intellectually active tend to experience declines at younger ages than their more active counterparts. Even if losses occur, Dr. Willis's research on cognitive retraining suggests that intellectual declines can be reversed in some older adults when they engage in intellectually stimulating activities.

Several widows talk about how they improved their spatial abilities in reading maps after their husbands died. Dr. James Birren notes that if we control illness and offer older people more opportunities for learning, we find that intellectual function changes very little with age.

Will we see changes in the intellectual functioning of older adults in the future? Dr. Willis believes so. More women are working in intellectually stimulating jobs and more older adults are exposed to interactive technology. According to the "use it or lose it" theory, we can expect this exposure to help adults maintain their intellectual skills well into late life.

Dr. Birren is excited about research underway on the 20,000 brain-specific proteins. What functions do these proteins perform? Can we manipulate them? Another research question is "why don't neurons continue to divide?" As we discover more about the brain, we may find we can help older adults with brain damage or disease maintain or extend their intellectual functioning.

Personality Development over the Life Span

Chapter 6 of the text reviews a number of theories of personality. In contrast to Sigmund Freud's belief that personality achieves stability by adolescence, more recent psychological theorists emphasize developmental stages of personality. For example, Erik Erikson theorized that individuals pass through eight psychosocial stages (see Page 196 in the text). Older adults are likely to experience the last two stages.

"Generativity vs. stagnation" is the stage in which an adult establishes a sense of concern for the well-being of future generations, looks toward the future, and does not stagnate in the past. "Ego integrity vs. despair" is the stage in which an older adult integrates life experiences to establish a sense of meaning about one's life, rather than feeling despair or bitterness that life was wasted. Many of the older adults in the video display generativity and ego integrity. For example, Mollie Pier tells us how she continues to look forward to the future and finds satisfaction in being a role model to younger people.

Carl Jung's model of personality emphasizes that consciousness develops from the self-centered focus of the child to a more worldly and less selfish view as the older adult. He also proposed that people, as they age, adopt psychological traits commonly associated with the opposite sex, i.e., men become more passive and nurturing as they age while women become more assertive and achievement-oriented. We see evidence of this in Mary Sue Wonson, Ruth Dow, and Vi Smith who feel they have become more assertive and independent, and in David Reese who says he has become more tolerant over time. Bernice Neugarten and her associates found support for Jung's theory in their longitudinal research in Kansas City. They also found that, contrary to popular stereotypes at the time, older adults became more different from each other in old age rather than more alike.

Dr. Paul Costa and his colleagues propose that personality has five primary components or traits: neuroticism, extroversion, openness to experience, agreeableness, and conscientiousness. Following adults for more than 25 years through the Baltimore Longitudinal Study of Aging, they found that personality was fairly stable between the ages of 30 and 65. This doesn't mean that older people cannot change; older adults who want to modify their personalities can do so through individual therapy and group support, say Drs. Costa and Cohen.

Four personality factors are thought to help older adults maintain self-esteem in their later years. These are: accepting the aging process with its consequential limitations and opportunities; adapting goals and expectations as circumstances change; defining oneself in terms of internal qualities rather than in terms of the roles one plays (e.g., spouse, worker, volunteer); and being able to objectively review one's life and learn from experience. The relatively recent Nun Study by Snowdon and his associates indicate a significant link between positive emotions and mortality. They hypothesize that positive emotions may trigger a lifetime of positive behaviors.

Dr. Costa feels that research will eventually help us understand more about the relationship between personality and successful aging. He would "love to ... [know] what kinds of changes or interventions we need to do for what kinds of people, when, and under what conditions that will allow them to lead the lives that they want...to reach their own goals, to self-actualize."

Mental Health Promotion and Maintenance

Drs. Steven Zarit, Birren, and Cohen assure us that most older adults enjoy good mental health and that only a small minority experience psychological crisis in adulthood. The older adults in the video give tips for maintaining good mental health in later life. Several, like the Birchanders, say to keep busy. Mary Sue Wonson and Mollie Pier recommend a positive attitude and a sense of humor. Roger Wonson is creatively involved with photography and music. Elizabeth Allen relies on her "inner resources." Pat Nickerson and Oliver Francisco enjoy exploring their spiritual sides.

Do the older adults in the video represent the privileged few? On the contrary, many of them have experienced losses and changes over the life course. For example, Mollie Pier has lost her husband and, more recently, a son. Oliver Francisco's discovery of his homosexuality led to major changes in his family relationships and now he is coping with a terminal illness. Most older adults experience a variety of life events and losses, such as retirement, loss of a spouse or child, birth of a grandchild, becoming a caregiver to a parent, and becoming ill themselves.

When a life event is viewed as a positive challenge, people usually cope with the event in a productive way. When an event is viewed as a threat, coping is usually less successful. Researchers have identified a number of responses used by adults when faced with a crisis. Ego defense mechanisms (text page 208) are unconscious reactions that help protect the self; primitive defense mechanisms include denial or repression. Coping strategies include responses that aim to solve the problem or to deal with the emotional distress the problem might cause (see page 209 in the text).

How we cope with a loss or change also depends on our cognitive appraisal of the event, whether or not it is anticipated, if the event is normative (on-time) or non-normative (off-time), past experiences with similar events, personality style, perception of how much control we have over the event (i.e., if the locus of control is perceived as internal or external), and degree of social support. Sometimes, anticipation of an event can be more stressful than its actual occurrence.

The most successful efforts to alleviate stress will address both the problem and any associated distress. If coping mechanisms are not successful, stress can accumulate. Dr. Benson tells us that unchecked stress can cause hypertension, decrease tolerance of pain, and increase feelings of anxiety and depression.

Mary Sue and Roger Wonson describe their different coping styles. Mary Sue tends to discuss stressful events with her supportive husband, Roger. He helps her reappraise the situation in a positive light or see how she can act to solve the problem. Roger, on the other hand, admits to ignoring problems that he feels he cannot change. Doris Birchander talks about a time when she was particularly stressed by providing care to her parents and in-laws. She tried to cope with her feelings by scrubbing the floor until she found a more successful approach through talking with and accepting the support of her sister-in-law.

Dr. Herbert Benson describes the relaxation response, which can be learned by individuals as a tool to cope with stress. Relaxation response techniques reduce anxiety, slow heart rate, and reduce blood pressure. Once relaxed, people are better able to modify their lifestyles (e.g., improve nutrition and increase exercise) and their perceptions to control stress.

Psychotherapy also helps people cope with stress and has been found to be quite effective for older adults willing to try it.

Although the majority of older adults have developed successful coping strategies and are satisfied with life, Dr. Cohen states that as many as 15% of older people have symptoms of depression.

It is important to identify and treat depression in older adults and to help people develop effective coping skills, as depression is the leading risk factor for suicide. Late-life depression is costly not only in regards to the older adult's psychological and physical well-being, it also results in a large economic toll.

Depression is more likely to be undetected or misdiagnosed in minority elders partly because cultural factors can be barriers to diagnosis and treatment.

Recent epidemiological data have led to the general agreement that the incidence of dementias increases with age, especially between ages 75 and 90. While significant efforts are made to develop drugs for Alzheimer's disease, all of them thus far appear to slow the rate of decline in moderate to advanced stages of Alzheimer's disease. So far, none of these drugs reverse the destruction of brain tissue by plaques and tangles.

The text states that the majority of older adults experience normal psychological development with aging that includes some changes in cognitive processes. However, some older adults experience more severe psychological disorders that can impair interpersonal and self-care behaviors. While these conditions are not unique to older adults and are found across the life span, they may be more difficult to diagnose because of co-morbidities such as chronic systemic diseases and impaired sensory function.

More information on diseases that effect psychological functioning is provided in Program Lesson 10, "Illness and Disability."

Key Terms and Concepts from the Text, Video, and *Study Guide*

Adaptation
Archetype
Cognitive Appraisal
Cognitive Functioning
Convergent Validity

Coping Strategies
Defense Mechanisms
Dialectical Models of Adult Personality
Erikson's Psychosocial Development Model
Extraversion

Freud's Psychosexual Development Model
Hassles
Intelligence
Intelligence Quotient
Introversion
Jung's Model of Personality
Levinson's Model of Personality Development
Life Change Unit
Life Events
Life Structures
Locus of Control
Mastery, Active and Passive
Non-Events
Non-Normative Events
Normative Events
Off-Time Events

On-Time Events
Personality
Resilience
Robust Aging
Seattle Longitudinal Study
Self-Concept
Self-Efficacy
Self-Esteem
Stage Theories of Personality
Stress
Stress Responses
Stressors
Successful Aging
Terminal Decline or Terminal Drop
Trait Theories of Personality

Self-Study Questions

Instructions: Fill in the blank with the appropriate word or phrase from the list of Key Terms and Concepts.
Note: Only 29 of the 41 key terms and concepts can be used.

1) _____ refers to the combination of intelligence, learning, memory, perception, creativity, and wisdom.

2) _____ refers to one's cognitive image of oneself and one's identity. _____ is one's emotional assessment of self.

3) Intelligence has been conceptualized into two components. _____ relates to the brain's organization of neurons in areas responsible for memory and associations and to the speed of processing information, measure of which include spatial orientation, abstract reasoning, and perceptual speed. _____ refers to the knowledge and abilities that individuals acquire through education and lifelong experiences, e.g., verbal skills and social judgment.

4) The _____ is an instrument used to measure adult intelligence, which consists of eleven sub-tests: six Verbal Scales measuring mostly crystallized intelligence and five Performance Scales measuring mostly fluid intelligence. The _____ refers to a consistent pattern of scores on this test that suggest that, as we age, decline in fluid intelligence precedes decline in crystallized intelligence.

5) _____ refers to a rapid decline in cognitive function within five years of death.

6) The text describes several models of personality development. For example:

a) _____ suggests that one's personality achieves stability by adolescence and that little change in personality is seen subsequently in the life span.

b) _____ proposes eight stages of development; each stage presenting a major crisis, the outcome of which influences one's subsequent development.

c) _____ outlines four "seasons" of life: pre-adulthood, early adulthood, middle adulthood, and late adulthood.

d) _____ emphasizes life span development of consciousness ego moves from the narrow focus of the child to the other-worldliness of the adult. This theory also suggests that the ego moves from a focus on the external world (called _____) as an adult to a focus on one's inner world (also called _____) in old age.

7) Everyone experiences life events that cause change in an individual's daily life, e.g., marriage, childbirth, divorce, change in financial status, and caregiving. When events happen at the expected time in one's life, they are called _____ or _____. When they happen at an unexpected time in life given one's age, they are called _____ or _____.

When life events are expected but fail to materialize, they are called _____.

8) In contrast to life events, _____ are bothersome or negative day-to-day activities and feelings that are long-term.

9) One's _____, or individual perception, of a life event can minimize or magnify one's ability to cope with it.

10) _____ refers to the place from which an individual feels his/her life is being controlled, externally (by fate or powerful others) or internally (by themselves).

11) Sometimes, life events and hassles cause _____.

12) When faced with stress, there are two major _____. _____ are unconscious reactions to

stress and include denial and repression. _____ are conscious approaches to reducing or managing stress, and subsequent discomfort, from life events and chronic daily hassles.

13) _____ refers to a combination of good physical and functional health, high cognitive functioning, and active involvement with society in old age.

14) _____ refers to the ability to thrive under adversity or multiple challenges by taking life's ups and downs in stride.

15) _____, a broader perspective on successful aging, considers exceptional functioning on measures of physical health, cognitive abilities, and emotional wellbeing.

Use the Glossary at the end of the Study Guide to check your answers.

Topics for Discussion

1) Discuss the advantages and disadvantages of longitudinal research designs in the study of intelligence in old age.

2) Self-concept is generally established early in life, but is modified through social roles and life experiences. Discuss some experiences of the later years that may affect self-concept and those that may negatively influence self-esteem.

3) Discuss the qualities that result in "successful aging." How can health promotion help older people achieve a successful old age?

Website Challenge

Visit the following websites that can provide more information on this lesson's topics. Bookmark them for easy access in the future:

1) American Association on Geriatric Psychiatry at http://www.aagponline.org/

2) Geropsychology at http://www.premier.net/~gero/geropsyc.html

3) Older Jokes for Older Folks at http://seniors-site.com/funstuff/

Written Assignments

Your instructor may ask you to complete one or more of the written assignments that follow.

Reaction Paper: New Knowledge and Feelings Stimulated by the Video

Write a two-page paper describing: 1) new information gained from watching the video; 2) how the experiences of the older adults in the video affected your personal view of aging; and 3) other comments to the instructor regarding this lesson or the course.

Analyzing the Text Vignettes

Read about Mr. Wallace, Mrs. Johnson, and Mr. Adams in the introduction to Part Three "The Psychological Context of Social Aging" in your text. Write a two- to three-page paper in which you compare and contrast these adults, using the questions below as a guide:

1) What memory changes have they experienced, if any?

2) What personality changes have they experienced, if any?

3) What were the causes of these changes?

4) How did these changes disturb them and their family members and friends?

5) How did the older adults and/or their families cope with the changes?

6) What more could the adults in the vignettes do to enhance coping and mental health?

Older-Adult Interview

Prior to interviewing an older adult, review this list of life events and note which ones you have experienced in the past five years. Then arrange to interview a person who is 65 or older. Have the interviewee review the same list of life events and answer the questions below. Write a three- to five-page paper on your findings.

Life Events
New love relationship
Divorce or separation
Marriage
Change in living arrangements
Birth of a child or grandchild
Death of a family member or close friend
Major change in financial status
Personal illness or disability
Increase in job or volunteer responsibilities
Loss of or decrease in job or volunteer
 responsibilities.

Interview Questions

1) Please look at this list of life events. Please tell me which ones you are experiencing now or have experienced within the past two years. What kinds of things do you do to cope with stress at this time?

2) Is this the most stressful time of your life? Why or why not? If not, think back to a time when you were under a lot of stress. Look at the list of life events and tell me what was going on in your life at that time? What kinds of things helped you cope during that time?

3) Which life events on this list do you anticipate experiencing in the future? Will they be stressful? What can you do to reduce their impact when they happen?

4) Research suggests that the death of a spouse is the most stressful life event. Do you agree or disagree? Why? If you disagree, what do you think is the most stressful life event? (Student: if appropriate, you may want to share your perceptions of the most stressful life event.)

Student Questions

1) Compare your experience with stressful life events with that of your interviewee. Compare coping mechanisms.

2) How do your findings compare with the information on stressful life events and coping provided in the text?

3) How has this interview affected your personal view of aging and older adults?

Community Interview

Listed below are examples of support groups designed to help people adjust to common changes in aging that can lead to emotional stress:
 -Retirement support group
 -Alzheimer's support group
 -Cancer support group
 -Hospice
 -Senior center support group
 -Caregiver support group
 -Bereavement support group
 -Widow support group

Work with your instructor to identify the support groups in your community. Interview an employee or facilitator who is knowledgeable about the support group, asking the questions below. Write a three- to five-page paper on your findings.

1) What is your name and position within the support group? How long have you been affiliated with it?

2) What is the history of the support group or program? When was it started? Why was it started? What are its goals and objectives?

3) Who can participate in this group or program?

4) What kind of assistance is provided within the support group or program? How does this assistance help members adjust to change or reduce emotional stress?

5) How do individuals involved in the program benefit from it? Give examples of clients whom you have helped adjust to change or whose emotional stress has been reduced.

6) How many facilitators work with the program? What are their qualifications? Are they volunteer or paid? Do they attend a special training?

7) How is the support group or program funded?

8) What do you feel are the program's limitations, if any (for example, hours or location)?

9) In what ways, if any, would expanding the program help it better meet its goals?

Research Paper

Select one of the topics below for in-depth study. Read a book or five journal articles on the topic. A good place to start searching for reading material is in the reference section provided at the end of each text chapter. Write a five- to ten-page research paper that describes the historical and current thinking on the topic. Identify things about the topic that are not yet resolved or may benefit from further study.

1) Read source documents about one of the following studies of intelligence: the Seattle Longitudinal Study, the New York Study of Aging Twins, or the Duke Longitudinal Studies. Describe the sample and methodology of the study. How did the study measure intelligence? Describe the findings. What were the limitations of the study? What further research questions did the study stimulate?

2) Read source documents on the findings concerning personality from the Baltimore Longitudinal Study of Aging or the Kansas City studies by Neugarten and her associates. Discuss the study's methods and findings regarding personality. What are the study's limitations?

3) Read the section on "Emotional Expression and Regulation" in Chapter 6 and the article by Magai (2001) on "Emotions Over the Life Span" in the fifth edition of the "Handbook of the Psychology of Aging." Then interview two individuals, one in his or her 60s and another in his or her 80, and discuss whether your findings from these interviews parallel the notion of early familial and cultural expectations can influence emotional expression across the life span and remain powerful messages in old age.

4) Read and analyze a popular book on developmental psychology, for example, *Passages* by Gail Sheehy. Which theories of personality does it draw on? What makes the book popular?

5) Being a caregiver for a disabled spouse or parent can cause considerable stress. A number of organizations sponsor support groups to help adults cope with the stresses of caregiving. Review the literature on caregiver support groups. Have any been shown to help caregivers increase their coping skills? If so, in what ways? What methods were used to test the usefulness of the support groups? What further research questions did the studies stimulate?

6) Examine the latest research on Alzheimer's Disease. What theories have been developed to explain the probable causes of AD? What new developments have taken place in treatment? What is the outlook for further developments in this field?

PROGRAM LESSON 7

SOCIAL ROLES AND RELATIONSHIPS IN OLD AGE

Learning Objectives

1) Give an example of each of the following in old age: role continuity, role development, role loss, and role gain.

2) Discuss three social theories of aging: activity theory, disengagement theory, and continuity theory.

3) Explain why and how role options are expanding for today's older adults.

Summary of the Video and Text

Video

The video has four segments. The first segment explains that older adults have a variety of role options available to them today, as illustrated by several older adults. The second segment presents information on how researchers study social roles. Three methods of inquiry are described: observation, interview, and survey.

Role stability and role change over the life span are topics of the third segment. A number of older adults share examples of role continuity, role development, role loss, and role gain in their lives. The final segment of the video presents information on expanded roles for older adults in the future, for example, new roles in politics, diplomacy, community service, grandparenthood, and great-grandparenthood.

Experts appearing in the video include Msgr. Charles Fahey and Drs. Robert Atchley, Vern Bengtson, Herman Feifel, and Fernando Torres-Gil, and service providers Betty Crowder and Mary Alice Stevenson. Illustrations are provided by several older adults, including Florence Austin, Doris and Eric Birchander, Thac Do Bui, Frank Catanzaro, Marian Cowan, Faye Cruse, Sylvia Davis, Dean Gotham, Hayward King, Mollie Pier, Leo and Lillian Salazar, Mildred Tuttle, and Blanche Woodbury.

Text

"The Social Context of Aging" provides a short introduction to Chapters 8 through 14 in the text. It includes three vignettes that illustrate the diversity in social functioning among older adults.

Chapter 8, "Social Theories of Aging," first presents an outline of role theory and three of the early social theories of aging--activity theory, disengagement theory, and continuity theory--which focused primarily on individual adjustment to aging. The text gives more information about the second and third generation of social theories, which focus more on structural factors and interactive processes. These include: symbolic interactionism, subculture of aging, age stratification, social exchange theory, and the political economy of aging perspective, social phenomenologist and social constructionist perspectives, critical theory, and feminist perspectives.

In Chapter 12, "Productive Aging: Paid and Nonpaid Roles and Activities," read the sections on Leisure, Membership in Voluntary Associations, Volunteer Work, Educational Programs, Religious Participation, Religiousness and Spirituality, Value of Spiritual Well-Being, Political Participation, and Senior Power.

Your instructor may provide additional readings for this lesson.

Key Points

Role Continuity, Development, Loss, and Gain

The roles we play throughout our lives help define us and help form our self-concept. Some roles can be maintained throughout life. This is called role continuity. For example, Hayward King maintained his role as the artist throughout life and the Birchanders, like most parents, have maintained their roles as parents.

61

We see continuity between past and present leisure activities in Mildred Tuttle's pursuit of gardening and golf and in Marian Cowan's active involvement with her church.

Roles also develop and change as we age. Ever since becoming a grandparent, Thac Do Bui has had the role of repository of Vietnamese culture. But his recent migration to the United States has forced him to further develop this role as sole representative and teacher of Vietnamese culture for his grandchildren.

Msgr. Charles Fahey's parents provide us with another example of role development. They had experience as parents, but have further developed this role as surrogate caregivers for neighborhood children whose parents work. Faye Cruse points out that although her parents, siblings, and husband are deceased; she has successfully developed a new family within her community at Leisure World. Dr. Feifel notes that, in fact, older adults demonstrate a great deal of flexibility in developing new aspects of existing roles.

All older adults will experience role loss. For example, most of the older adults in the video are retired. Mollie Pier, Marian Cowan, and Florence Austin are widowed. Sylvia Davis has lost the role of sibling, having watched her nine brothers and sisters die before her.

As a Vietnamese refugee, Thac Do Bui experienced the loss of roles that would have been available to him in his homeland. Frank Catanzaro and Dean Gotham have lost their homes and Dean Gotham has lost touch with his family. Role loss can lead to a decline in identity and self-esteem.

Roles may also be gained in later life. For example, several of the elders in the video have become grandparents. Mollie Pier found a new role for herself as "senior ambassador."

Leo Salazar gained a new work role as counselor for his ophthalmologist's Hispanic patients. His wife, Lillian, who spent much of her life as caregiver to her children and parents, went back to school as an older adult and now teaches at a community college.

Organizations that help older adults gain and develop roles or cope with role loss are described in Chapter 12 of the text and in the video. Blanche Woodbury relates how her neighborhood senior center provided her with new roles and relationships after her vision declined.

Mary Alice Stevenson discusses how a senior center in San Francisco's Tenderloin helps some members connect with needed health care and social services, and gives other members the opportunity to fill roles as volunteers. Volunteering is also very important to Florence Austin, a volunteer Senior Companion. Marian Cowan finds satisfying roles within her church. Leo Salazar, as a graduate senator at his university, became involved politically.

It should be noted that only a small percentage of older adults spend their leisure time in public recreation programs designed specifically for them. For example, many like to engage in activities and hobbies that are solitary and sedentary, like reading, writing, and visiting family and friends. About 40% of older adults volunteer. About 60% belong to religious groups and attend services regularly. Over 35 million seniors belong to the American Association of Retired Persons (AARP). Voting rates among older adults are almost three times higher than voting rates for adults 18-20 years old. Research suggests that older people are not necessarily more religious or more political than younger people but that they may have more time to express their religious and political beliefs than younger people.

Engagement in activities is also influenced by gender, ethnicity, and health status. For example, Dr. Bengtson describes research that suggests that older women have more roles than older men. Older African Americans tend to be more active in voluntary and religious organizations than older adults of other ethnicities. In Chapter 12 of the text, Flippen and Tienda found that African Americans and Hispanics tend to have lengthy periods of non-work at an early age and lack access to pensions, in part because of diminished opportunities that "pushed" them into retirement. Not surprisingly, as health declines, leisure activities usually become more home-based.

Social Theories of Aging

A social theory of aging provides a framework within which to explain role changes in late adulthood and the optimal way for older people to adapt to these changes. A social theory known as role theory forms the basis for the three of the earliest and best-known social theories of aging: activity theory, disengagement theory, and continuity theory. These theories attempt to explain how older people successfully adapt to role changes with age.

Role theory is based on the belief that roles (student, parent, businessperson, homemaker) define our self-concept. People are socialized through a process of learning to perform new roles, adjusting to changing roles, and relinquishing old ones.

Age norms are culturally or even legally defined expectations about the roles we can fill at various ages. For example, we expect people to retire between 62 and 65; this expectation is reflected in our Social Security laws. People who retire in their 40s or in their 80s are exceptions and violate our age norms.

Activity theory suggests that high self-esteem in old age is associated with keeping busy and staying involved in a variety of roles and with a variety of people. Several of the older adults in the video relate stories that tend to support this theory. For example, the Salazars, Florence Austin, Marian Cowan, and Mollie Pier have all expanded their roles and activities in later life and they obviously enjoy and gain a sense of purpose from their busy lives. Mr. Catanzaro's statements also support activity theory; he experienced a loss of role and activity when he became homeless and links these losses to a sense of uselessness. Two more examples are provided in the text.

In contrast to activity theory, disengagement theory links well-being in old age with successful withdrawal from public life and increased introspection. Msgr. Fahey feels that people should take the opportunity in later life to develop their interiority, i.e., to take the time to contemplate, to make sense out of lives and losses, and thus gain an increased awareness of themselves.

Research shows that older people are more likely than younger people to engage in solitary and sedentary pursuits. Two vignettes in Chapter 8 illustrate disengagement in old age.

Unfortunately, neither activity nor disengagement theory takes into account individuals' personalities or the historical and cultural context within which they are aging. Continuity theory proposes that individuals age successfully if they maintain their preferred roles and adaptation techniques. To illustrate, Dr. Atchley tells about a woman who maintained her identity as a teacher in retirement. Hayward King (artist) and Marian Cowan (church activist) both demonstrate how avocations continue throughout life.

Two more examples are given in Chapter 8. Researchers have found support for continuity theory in their study of volunteerism. Specifically, volunteering appears to be a pattern established early in life and recruiters are not usually successful in recruiting retirees who have never volunteered before.

Looking back at these early social theories of aging, developed before 1961, they seem simplistic and individualistic. While it is important to understand activity, disengagement, and continuity theory, several other social theories have been developed. Chapter 8 of the text provides an introduction to these other theories, which tend to look beyond the individual to larger issues, like the structures of society and the way elders interact in their environments.

An example is the social exchange theory, which is based in the belief that an individual's status is defined by the balance between his/her contributions to society and the cost of supporting him/her. In other words, if an older person experiences declines in health and income and becomes more dependent on others, he/she may be less "valued" and have to withdraw from decision making roles. In many communities, elders who freely contribute nonmaterial resources, like time to volunteer or willingness to mentor young people, may not lose status despite declines in their material resources.

The principles of social exchange theory are relevant to discussions intergenerational exchange, which we will address in Program Lesson 8, "Family and Intergenerational Relationships," and in Program Lesson 13, "The Future of Aging."

Recent developments in social gerontological theory have provided important insights as to how old age is defined or portrayed. For example, the negative ways in which age is socially constructed has numerous consequences for social policy and employer practices.

How do researchers gather information upon which social theories are built? Dr. Bengtson gave an example of how multiple research methods can be used to answer social questions. He described starting to explore a social issue through observational analysis, then focusing inquiry by conducting structured interviews.

A survey questionnaire can be used to gather data from a large sample of older adults. Observational, interview, and survey methods can be used by themselves or in combination, depending on the research question to be answered.

Sometimes research findings disprove the hypotheses. This was true for Dr. Atchley in his first study of social roles. From his review of the literature, he thought that retirement had negative effects on older adults. His first interviewee, however, told him of the positive aspects of retirement, forcing him to revise his hypothesis and his research questionnaire.

Expanding Roles for Older Adults

This rapid evolution in social theories of aging is related to, in part, our great increase in life expectancy. More and more people are living longer, and some can expect to spend up to 40 years in retirement. Dr. Bengtson calls it a "demographic revolution" that has profound implications for individuals and society.

Because this extended time of post-retirement leisure is a relatively new phenomenon, many older adults lack clear-cut age norms and role models for late-life behavior. How can people so dedicated to the work ethic make a transition to 40 years of post-retirement leisure? This dilemma is sometimes referred to as the rolelessness of old age. Msgr. Fahey describes how Father X, a former professor of biology, did not find new roles for himself after retirement. Dr. Bengtson warns young people, especially young men, to "begin investing effort in a variety of roles" so that they have several role options for themselves in later life. Dr. Atchley agrees, and has suggested that "activity competence" needs to be learned by middle age.

Most of the older adults in the video have made a successful transition to retirement. Very few of them are involved in senior-specific activities, however. In fact, several of them are involved in roles that are not traditionally occupied by older adults. Some enjoy roles as older students. Leo Salazar developed a new work role for himself. Mollie Pier enjoys her new role as "ambassador" through a senior exchange program between the U.S. and Japan.

Dr. Torres-Gil hopes older adults' political activity will go beyond just voting. He recommends the role of political leader for retired adults, a role that older members of the tribe used to occupy. Msgr. Fahey gives us examples of this in former President Jimmy Carter, his wife Rosalyn Carter, and Maggie Kuhn, founder of the Gray Panthers. The text box in Chapter 12 on "Political Activism and Older Women" introduces Tish Sommers, founder of the Older Women's League.

Today's older adults will be pioneers in the development of brand-new social roles, most notably that of the great-grandparent. Dr. Bengtson notes that in the 21st century, people will spend as long in the great-grandparent role as their own grandparents spent in the grandparent role. He finds this opportunity to define new roles very exciting. What other new roles await us in later life?

Key Terms and Concepts from the Text, Video, and *Study Guide*

Activity Theory
Age Norm
Age Stratification Theory
American Association of Retired Persons
American Society on Aging
Busy Ethic
Continuity Theory
Critical Theory
Disengagement Theory
Elderhostel
Feminist Perspective
Foster Grandparent Program
Generations United
Gerontological Society of America
Gray Panthers
Hypothesis
Interactionist Perspective
Interiority
Labeling Theory
Leadership Council of Aging
Leisure
Life Course Capital
Life Course Perspective
National Asian Pacific Center on Aging
National Association of Retired Federal
    Employees
National Caucus for the Black Aged
National Council of Senior Citizens
National Council on Aging
National Retired Teachers Association
Observational Analysis
Older American Volunteer Program

Older Women's League
Opportunity Structures
Peace Corps
Political Economy of Aging
Positivism
Postmodern Theory
Retired Senior Volunteer Program
Role
Role Change
Role Continuity
Role Development
Role Dilemma
Role Discontinuity
Role Gain
Role Loss
Role Model
Role Theory
Rolelessness
Senior Companion Program
Senior Net
Senior Power
Service Corps of Retired Executives
Social Exchange Theory
Social Phenomenology and Constructionism
Social Theories
Socialization
Spiritual Well-Being
Structural Lag
Subculture Theory
Symbolic Interactionism
Work Ethic

Self Study Questions

*Instructions: Fill in the blank with the appropriate word or phrase from the list of Key Terms and Concepts.
Note: Only 27 of the 62 key terms and concepts can be used.*

---

1) In role theory, _____ refers to the addition of a new function or position; _____ happens when one loses a function or position; _____ refers to the idea that behaviors learned early in life remain useful and are continued at later stages of life; and _____ refers to the evolution or changes within existing roles over time.

2) _____ is a lifelong process by which individuals learn how to perform new roles, adjust to changing roles, relinquish old ones, and thereby become integrated into society.

3) If a behavior learned early in life becomes useless or conflicting at a later stage of life, an individual may experience a _____ or _____.

4) If someone is without a specified set of standards to guide behavior, they may feel a sense of _____.

5) _____ is a set of behaviors and roles normally associated with a specific age group.

6) In research, a _____ is an assumption or proposition that is then tested through observation or experimentation.

7) In research, _____ is a method whereby the researcher simply watches the subjects to describe and develop hypotheses about their interactions.

8) _____ are plausible, general principles that provide frameworks within which to understand human behavior and social structures.

9) The text reviews several social theories of aging. For example:

    a) _____ is based on the belief that roles (student, parent, business person, homemaker) define us and our self-concept.

    b) _____ is based on the belief that older people must remain active and that older people should therefore replace lost roles with new roles to maintain their integration with society.

    c) _____ is based on the belief that central personality characteristics become more pronounced with age or are retained as "life threads" with little change. People age successfully if they maintain their preferred roles and adaptation techniques throughout life.

    d) _____ is based on the belief that older people, due to their inevitable decline with age, become less active in the outer world and more preoccupied with their inner lives.

    e) _____ is based on the belief that an individual's status is defined by the balance between his/her contributions to society and the cost of supporting him/her.

10) _____ is a program in which older adults enjoy inexpensive, short-term academic programs at colleges and universities around the world.

11) _____ refers to well-being that manifests as self-determined wisdom, self-transcendence, achievement of meaning and purpose for one's continued existence, and acceptance of the wholeness of life. According to Msgr. Fahey in the video, an important way to achieve it may be to develop one's _____.

12) Someone who has a strong _____ or _____ feels that work is valuable and that nonproductive use of time is wasteful and suspect.

13) Senior citizens and gerontologists join together in a number of organizations whose primary function is to lobby for social change. For example:

    a) _____ is a national organization open to all adults 50 and above, offering a wide range of informational materials, discounted services and products, and a powerful lobby. It is the most influential senior group, with more than 35 million members.

    b) _____ is a national organization, founded by Maggie Kuhn, which encourages work on social issues through intergenerational, grassroots alliances.

    c) _____ is a national organization of professionals concerned with increasing the responsiveness of aging programs to African Americans.

    d) _____ is a national organization concerned about issues affecting older women, especially health care and finances.

14) The _____ refers to the expansion of the life course perspective that addresses impact of differential acquisition of resources among different members of a cohort.

Use the Glossary at the end of the Study Guide to check your answers.

Topics for Discussion

1) List several ways that an older person may act contrary to age norms. What happens when an older individual violates age norms?

2) If you were a director of a senior center dependent on volunteers, what would you do to recruit and retain volunteers?

Web Site Challenge

Visit the following websites that can provide more information on this lesson's topics. Bookmark them for easy access in the future.

1) AARP at http://www.aarp.org

2) SCORE Counselors to America's Small Business at http://www.score.org/volunteer.html

Written Assignments

Your instructor may ask you to complete one or more of the written assignments that follow.

Reaction Paper: New Knowledge and Feelings Stimulated by the Video

Write a two-page paper describing: 1) new information gained from watching the video; 2) how the experiences of the older adults in the video affected your personal view of aging; and 3) other comments to the instructor regarding this lesson or the course.

Analyzing the Text Vignettes

Read the text vignettes about Mr. Valdres, Mrs. Howard, and Mr. Mansfield in the introduction to Part Four, "The Social Context of Aging." Write a two- to three-page paper in which you compare and contrast the social roles and relationships of these three older adults, using the questions below as a guide:

1) What roles and relationships are these older adults involved in currently?

2) How have their roles and relationships changed over the years? Give examples of role stability, role loss, role gain, and role development for these adults.

3) How have their roles and relationships been influenced by their gender, finances, health status, living arrangements, support systems, and the expectations of others?

4) Do the role experiences of these adults fit into patterns suggested by any of the social theories discussed in Chapter 8? Explain.

Older-Adult Interview

Interview a retired, older person about the role changes he/she has experienced to date, asking the questions below. Does the pattern of his/her experiences fit any of the social theories discussed in the text? Write a three- to five-page paper on your findings.

Interview Questions

1) What were your major roles as a young and middle-aged adult? For example, were you a parent, spouse, worker, boss, volunteer?

2) How much time did you spend in each role?

3) Did your gender influence your choice of roles? What else do you think influenced your choice of roles (health status, money, social supports, other's expectations)?

4) What are your major roles now? For example, are you a grandparent, spouse, worker, boss, volunteer? How are these different from your roles in middle age? What roles were lost? gained? continued? further developed?

5) How much time do you spend in each role?

6) Does your gender influence your choice of roles now? What else may be influencing your options for roles (health status, money, social supports, others' expectations)?

7) Do you (or did you) have any role models for a successful old age?

8) Have you experienced discrimination because of age?

Student Questions

1) Do the role experiences of the interviewee fit into patterns suggested by activity theory, disengagement theory, or continuity theory? Explain.

2) How has this interview affected your personal view of aging and older adults?

Community Interview

Listed below are examples of programs that provide role options for older adults.

-Associations to which seniors belong, for example, AARP, Gray Panthers, Older Women's Network

-Advisory Boards to which seniors belong, for example, a State Unit on Aging

-Agencies for which seniors volunteer, for example, literacy programs, Meals-On-Wheels, Red Cross

-Places that employ seniors, for example, McDonald's, Senior Companions, Wal-Mart

Work with your instructor to identify a program in your community. Interview an employee who is knowledgeable about the organization, asking the questions below. Write a three- to five-page paper on your findings.

1) What is your name and position within the organization? How long have you worked here?

2) What is the history of the organization? When was it started? Why was it started? What are its goals and objectives?

3) Who are the clients? What are the eligibility requirements?

4) What programs/services are offered? How do they help older adults maintain or enhance social roles and relationships?

5) How do adults involved in the program benefit from it? Give examples of adults whose social roles and/or relationships have been maintained or strengthened through association with your program.

6) How many staff work here? What are their qualifications?

7) How many volunteers work here? What are their roles?

8) How is the program funded?

9) What do you feel are the program's limitations (e.g., the types of services provided, the hours of operation, the location of the services, the eligibility requirements)?

10) How would expanding the program help it better meet its goals?

Research Paper

Select one of the topics below for in-depth study. Read a book or five journal articles on the topic. A good place to start searching for reading material is in the reference section provided at the end of each text chapter. Write a five- to ten-page research paper that describes the current thinking in the area. Identify things about the topic that are not yet resolved or may benefit from further study.

1) The text presents information on social theories of aging. Choose one of them and read the source materials on the theory. How and why was the theory developed? What evidence justified it at the time of its development? What subsequent research has supported it or discredited it?

2) Estes and Minkler have written on the political economy of aging and the aging enterprise. What do these terms mean? How does current policy perpetuate the aging enterprise? A good book to start you off is *The Aging Enterprise* by Carol Estes.

3) The text mentions that early theories of aging were developed and tested using quantitative methods while several of the newer theories were developed out of studies that used qualitative methods. Read the book by John Creswell titled *Research Design: Quantitative & Qualitative Approaches* (published by Sage Publications in 1994). Write a paper comparing and contrasting the two approaches.

FAMILY AND INTERGENERATIONAL RELATIONSHIPS

Learning Objectives

1) Describe how family roles can evolve in old age.

2) Give five examples of intergenerational exchange.

3) Explain how community services can help build social supports for older adults.

4) Discuss similarities among ethnic and cultural groups in marital, parental, and caregiving roles.

Summary of the Video and Text

Video

The video has three segments; each features older adults who discuss changes they have experienced in family relationships and activities over time. In the first segment on marital relations, experts and older adults discuss marriage, widowhood, divorce, and being single. The second segment describes parent and grandparent roles in late life. In this segment, we begin to see examples of intergenerational exchange within families. In the final segment, caregiving roles are defined and illustrated. This segment also shows how community services can strengthen a family's ability to care for a loved one who is frail or disabled.

Experts appearing in the video include Drs. Colette Browne, Herman Feifel, Linda Martin, and E. Percil Stanford. We also hear from service provider Ruth Sifton. Older adults who share their experiences and insights include Pasquale Capone, Ethel Cooper, Celestine Eggleston, Tatsuno Ogawa, Mollie Pier, Leo and Lillian Salazar, and Ben and Gloria Tamashiro. Younger family members are also featured, including Buster and Raymond Capone, Marguerite Ogawa, and Mary Saladino.

Text

New Reading. Chapter 9, "The Importance of Social Supports: Family, Friends, and Neighbors," focuses primarily on informal supports (family and friends).

It includes sections on family relationships (partners, children, grandchildren, siblings, and other kin), intergenerational assistance, older adults caring for even older parents, friends and neighbors, and services that can strengthen these relationships.

Chapter 10, "Opportunities and stresses of informal caregiving," addresses the important role of informal family caregiving in the context of the long-term care system. Topics of discussion include the benefits and costs of caregiving, policies and programs that support family caregivers, and issues relating to elder mistreatment.

Chapter 11, "Living Arrangements and Social Interactions," provides information on neighborhoods and on programs that address the changing housing needs of older adults, including independent living, shared housing, planned housing, congregate housing, retirement communities, assisted living, and nursing homes.

Review. "The Social Context of Aging," especially the three vignettes illustrating the diversity in family resources and relationships among older adults.

In Chapter 15, "The Resiliency of Older Women," review the section on Older Women's Social Status.

Your instructor may provide additional readings for this lesson.

Key Points

Family Relationships for Older Adults

The average length of marriage at the time one spouse dies is now more than 45 years. Research suggests that most marriages become more intimate and satisfying in old age. This is most likely due to two factors:

1) couples have more time for each other after retirement and after children leave home; and 2) decreased attention on traditional sex roles can increase feelings of equality within the marriage.

In addition, studies of personality suggests that men become more affectionate and less career-oriented in old age. Women, freed from child-rearing duties, can pursue work and volunteer roles.

Partners who give one another the space to grow and change find their long-term marriages an important source of strength and happiness. The Salazars and the Tamashiros both illustrate this phenomenon.

Most older men have spouses (from original or serially monogamous marriages); however, because women usually marry older men and then outlive them for 10 to 20 years, they experience a high degree of widowhood. Divorce in old age is also becoming more common, and about 4% of adults never marry. Life satisfaction is not necessarily diminished, however, for single elders. Mollie Pier (widowed), Celestine Eggleston (divorced), and Ethel Cooper (never married) report that they are engaged in many satisfying roles and relationships and are not looking to add a spouse role. Another reasons why women tend not to remarry as much as men is because women tend to have more social support networks than men and therefore feel less of a need to seek companionship through marriage.

About 80% of older adults have children. Some older adults experience sadness when their adult children move out of the house; this is known as the empty nest syndrome. On the other hand, some older adults now find that their adult children don't want to move out, or may want to move back home, perhaps after a divorce or because they've lost their jobs. This is referred to as the cluttered nest. Whether living with them or not, most older adults are in regular contact with their adult children.

Of older adults with children, 94% of them have grandchildren. The grandparent role is especially fulfilling to many older adults. Celestine Eggleston feels she has more leisure time to devote to her grandchildren than she did to her own children. Ben Tamashiro (Japanese American) and Leo Salazar (Hispanic American) are making efforts to document and pass on information about their culture to their grandchildren.

Some grandparents feel so strongly about continued interaction with their grandchildren that they will petition the courts for grandparents' rights of visitation (and in some cases custody) when the grandchildren's parents divorce.

About 3.7 million grandparents in the U.S. have become "parents" to their grandchildren, often because the children's parents have problems with substance abuse. Such is the case for Mary, described in a text box in Chapter 9.

An increasing number of older adults are single, either because they never married, were divorced, or were widowed. About 20% of older adults are childless. Many of these older adults become involved in nontraditional families. For example, while most older adults strengthen relationships with siblings in old age, some may decide to live together. Others depend on nieces and nephews for social support. Others create families comprised of unrelated people brought together through friendship, cohabitation, homosexual partnerships, adoption, shared housing, foster care, and other arrangements. Others will develop a blended or reconstituted family composed of spouses, ex-spouses, children, ex-children-in-law, grandchildren, step-grandchildren, and so forth. In fact, very few older adults purposely avoid building social networks or engaging in reciprocal relationships. Even Mr. Valdres in the text vignette has developed a surrogate family of other single men who reside in the inner-city hotel where he has a room.

In some cases, older adults gain caregiving roles as their aged parents or spouses become frail and dependent. This is true for the Salazars and the Ogawas, families featured in the video.

Intergenerational Exchange

Families remain the primary institution for socializing individuals. This occurs through intergenerational transfer of knowledge and resources, a phenomenon that does not stop when children leave home. Instead, older adults stay involved in reciprocal relationships within their families throughout life. Celestine Eggleston, for example, loves to spend time with her granddaughters and take them on outings. The granddaughters plan to reciprocate in the future, promising that when they grow up they will take Celestine to lunch. She tells them she looks forward to their continued sharing for many, many years.

70

Even when family members move away from one another, as is common in our mobile society, they often remain "intimate at a distance." This means they have frequent and meaningful contact with children and grandchildren, but are vital members of their own communities and do not wish to relocate. Mollie Pier, for example, visits her children's families regularly. But she is not interested in moving in with any of them. She is very busy with activities in Los Angeles, which include going to school and volunteering. The text notes that about 30% of those over 65 years of age live alone.

When older people become frail, it is usual for them to receive intergenerational assistance from younger family members as is seen in the Salazar and Ogawa families. In fact, families provide about 70% of the in-home care needed by disabled older adults. And 70% of family caregivers are women. As people live longer and have fewer children, family caregiving pressures will continue to grow.

Older adults prefer to remain autonomous in old age. Thus relocation, for example, to a nursing home or even into a child's home can be traumatic. The Salazars and the Ogawas both make efforts to allow their aged parents to retain as much dignity and independence as possible although they live together in the same house.

Lillian Salazar and Marguerite Ogawa both demonstrate strong commitments to care for their aged parents. They also say that they are occasionally frustrated with the caregiving role, as they both perceive it as time consuming and demanding. Both can be referred to as "women in the middle" or members of the "sandwich generation" because they have responsibilities to their aged parents as well as to their spouses, children, and grandchildren.

They describe different strategies for coping with feelings of caregiver burden. Marguerite is helped by her husband's sisters and by several community programs. Lillian copes by keeping a sense of humor and by depending on her family for respite. Marguerite and Lillian act as role models to their children by showing how to care for aged parents. See text box on page 313 of Hooyman and Kiyak's for characteristics of women as caregivers.

Childless older adults are more likely to become socially isolated than adults with children. Without adequate support from non-family sources, an isolated older adult may face premature or unnecessary disability, nursing home admission, or death. While the number of childless elders is expected to increase, efforts made to develop reciprocal relationships with other family members, nontraditional family, and friends can reduce the chance of becoming isolated.

Dr. Colette Browne mentions "age wars," which refers to intergenerational conflict over resources. However, Dr. Browne does not feel that age wars are inevitable. Instead, we need to acknowledge our interdependence. "We're all on the same planet together," she says, and we need to continue sharing knowledge and resources among the generations.

Community Services That Build Social Supports

The vast majority of adults who cannot live independently depend on family caregivers for support and assistance. They may stay in their own homes and receive help from others. Alternatively, they may move in with a family member. The Ogawa's aged mother, for example, lives in a small apartment attached to their home. Elders who need extra human assistance that cannot be provided by the family may arrange formal support services. Tatsuno Ogawa uses two such services. She attends an adult day center three days a week where she socializes with other adults. She also is visited by a nurse and a personal care aide who monitors her medical problems and helps her bathe.

Some people are natural helpers and make good family caregivers. Others do not have the time, money, patience, skill, or social support to provide good care. Despite policy makers' concerns that formal care would substitute for informal support for older adults at public expense, two federal policy initiatives were approved to support families: the Family and medical Leave Act of 1993 (FMLA) and the National Caregiver Support Program of 2000 (NFCSP). With the NFCSP, for the first time in the history of the Older Americans Act, state units on aging and area agencies on aging are required to serve not only older adults, but also family caregivers.

71

We increasingly hear about elder abuse, including cases of financial exploitation, medical abuse, physical abuse, and psychological abuse. (A text box in Chapter 10, "Types and Symptoms of Elder Mistreatment," gives definitions of each type of abuse.) Other times, we hear of elders who are neglected by family members and elders whose level of self-care may be considered unsafe. Most states sponsor programs that intervene when elder abuse or neglect is suspected.

Several programs have been developed to assist older adults who do not wish to leave their neighborhoods and companions to move in with children. Some may benefit from a home equity conversion mortgage, in which the bank "buys back" the house, providing the elders with income while they continue to live in their own home. Home-bound elders may benefit from the attention of gatekeepers, service people (such as letter carriers) or neighbors who "keep an eye" on them and can intervene when they suspect a problem. As seen in the text vignette of Mr. Valdres, the hotel manager plays a gate keeping role by watching him and giving him extra money or food when needed.

When home or community care is unavailable or unsafe, older adults may relocate to planned housing, assisted living, congregate housing, lifecare communities, or nursing homes. These settings tend to be age-segregated and needed services are provided by professional caregivers. More information on community-based and institutional long-term care services is presented in Program Lesson 10, "Illness and Disability."

Similarities Among Ethnic and Cultural Groups

America is composed of dozens of ethnic and cultural groups. The extent to which ethnicity and culture influence family relations is unclear.

Some of the differences seen within and across ethnic groups are likely to be due to an underlying difference in socio-economic status. In the video, older adults of various ethnic groups shared many of the same concerns within their families.

For example, Leo Salazar and Ben Tamashiro share the desire to teach their progeny about their cultural heritages. Leo Salazar is very proud of his Hispanic upbringing and works to pass on this pride to his children. Ben Tamashiro rejected his Japanese heritage during his youth, but is learning more about it now and documenting it for his grandson. Celestine Eggleston and Mollie Pier come from different ethnic and religious backgrounds. Yet both are satisfied with the freedoms of being single, both are busy pursuing new activities, and both have maintained close relationships with their children.

Two couples are involved in cross-cultural marriages. Lillian Salazar (Armenian American) and Leo Salazar (Hispanic American) discuss the adjustments they have made over their marriage. Some of these adjustments were made because of their different cultural expectations of marriage and family; others, however, appeared to be based on differences in their ages (16 years) and on the great expansion over the past 40 years in roles available to women. Ben Tamashiro (Japanese American) and Gloria Tamashiro (Chinese American) also talk of adjustments they have made as their family and work roles have changed over time.

Lillian Salazar and Marguerite Ogawa (Japanese American) both demonstrate strong commitments to care for their aged parents. They also express occasional frustration with the caregiving role, as they both perceive it as time consuming and demanding. Celestine Eggleston and Marguerite Ogawa, although of different ethnic backgrounds, share the expectation that they will be cared for by their children when they themselves become frail.

Key Terms and Concepts from the Text, Video, and *Study Guide*

Adult Day Care
Adult Day Health
Age-Heterogeneous
Age-Homogeneous
Age-Segregated
Age Wars
Assisted Living
Autonomy
Blended Families
Caregiver, Formal
Caregiver, Informal
Caregiver Burden
Caregiving
Case Management
Cluttered Nest
Cohabiting
Congregate Housing
Continuous Care Retirement Community
Direct Care Workers
Elder Mistreatment
Elder Neglect
Eldercare
Empty Nest Syndrome
Familial Piety
Foster Care
Foster Grandparent Program
Gatekeepers
Grandparents' Rights
Home and Community-Based Services
Home Equity Conversion Mortgages
Home Health Care
Home Sharing Programs
Inelastic Ego

Institutionalization
Intergenerational Assistance
Intergenerational Exchange
Intergenerational Inequity
Intergenerational Living
Intergenerational Programming
Intergenerational Transfer of Knowledge
Intergenerational Transfer of Resources
Intimacy at a Distance
Lifecare Communities
Lifecare Contract
Mobile Society
Multigenerational Family
Multilevel Facilities
National Family Caregiver Support Program
Natural Helpers
Naturally Occurring Retirement Community
Nontraditional Families
Nursing Homes
Personal Care Aide
Planned Housing
Reciprocal Relationship
Relocation
Respite Care
Reverse Mortgages
Samurai
Sandwich Generation
Serial Monogamy
Shared Housing
Single Room Occupancy
Surrogate Family
Women in the Middle

Self-Study Questions

Instructions. Fill in the blank with the appropriate word or phrase from the list of Key Terms and Concepts. Note: Only 40 of the 65 key terms and concepts can be used.

1) If an unmarried couple is living together, we say they are _____.

2) _____ refers to legal rights of grandparents to interact with grandchildren following divorce of the grandchildren's parents.

3) Saying that we live in a _____ refers to the fact that most of us move from place to place rather than live in the same place forever.

4) A _____ has three or more generations living at the same time.

5) Even though family members do not live near each other, they may still have strong emotional ties. This is known as _____.

6) Families whose membership is comprised of blood and nonblood relations through adoption, divorce, and remarriage are called _____. A person with no blood relations may develop strong ties with friends to make a _____.

7) _____ refers to having several different partners over a lifetime, but being involved with only one person at a time.

73

8) A parent who experiences sadness after his/her children leave home is experiencing the _____. When an adult child delays leaving home, or moves back in later in life, the parents may experience a _____.

9) A program that includes people of different ages would be called _____ while a program that is comprised of people of similar age is called _____ or _____.

10) A person with a high level of _____ or _____ is devoted to his/her family.

11) Sometimes members of different generations fight over resources, resulting in _____.

12) The personal energy, time restrictions, financial commitments, and/or psychological frustrations associated with assisting disabled persons is called _____.

13) There are two types of caregivers. An _____ caregiver is a family member who assists an elderly loved one with personal care, household and financial chores, and transportation, usually without compensation. A _____ caregiver is a trained person who assists an unrelated elder with nursing, personal care, and household tasks, usually for compensation.

14) If you were a middle-aged woman who cared for parents, spouse, and children, and perhaps also worked outside the home, you would be called a _____. You would also be a member of the _____.

15) When a niece cooks and cleans for her aunt, while the aunt puts money aside for the niece's tuition, they are engaged in _____ or _____.

16) A _____ is a formal caregiver specially trained to assist disabled adults with bathing, dressing, and grooming.

17) There are two types of adult day programs. _____ programs are for elderly people who need stimulation and supervision, but little medical attention and rehabilitation. _____ programs are for elderly people who need medical attention and rehabilitation in addition to stimulation and supervision.

18) Older people often give things to younger people. The giving of property or resources is called _____. The giving of ideas and information is called _____.

19) If you yell at or hit an older adult, you may be accused of _____

20) With a _____, the bank provides a monthly annuity to the homeowner and, upon the homeowner's death and the home's sale, receives a refund on the loan as well as a portion of the home's appreciated value. These are also called _____.

21) _____ are people in service positions who, because of regular interactions with older adults, can watch for signs indicating a need for assistance or attention.

22) In a _____ program, older persons who own homes are provided live-in companions (of any age) who may pay rent, share household chores, and/or provide services (such as shopping or personal care) to the elderly home owner.

23) A _____ offers a variety of living arrangements, from independent living to congregate living arrangements and nursing home care. Such communities that guarantee to let you live there and care for you until you die may also be called _____.

24) _____ can be traumatic for older adults, especially if they are not prepared for or in agreement with the move.

25) A building, neighborhood, or region (such as Florida) largely occupied by older people, but not planned specifically for this population can be called a _____.

26) The _____ requires state and area agencies on aging to provide services to support family caregivers.

27) _____ refers to short term (rest) for caregivers and may be provided in the home or out of home (e.g., through adult day health).

28) _____ is the coordination and monitoring of services to meet older adults' assessed service needs.

Use the Glossary at the end of the Study Guide to check your answers.

Topics for Discussion

1) Discuss trends that will affect the aging family in the future.

2) Discuss some options available to an older woman who does not wish to move to retirement housing, but prefers to stay in the large mortgage-free home she has lived in for 40 years, which she can no longer maintain.

3) Assume that you are the director of a retirement home. What programs might you develop to foster intergenerational contacts?

Website Challenge

Visit the following websites that can provide more information on this lesson's topics. Bookmark them for easy access in the future.

1) Family Caregiver Alliance at http://www.caregiver.org/

2) Center on Elder Abuse at http://www.elderabusecenter.org

3) Foundation for Grandparenting at http://www.grandparenting.org

Written Assignments

Your instructor may ask you to complete one or more of the written assignments that follow.

Reaction Paper

Write a two-page paper describing: 1) new information gained from watching the video; 2) how the experiences of the older adults in the video affected your personal view of aging; and 3) other comments to the instructor regarding this lesson or the course.

Analyzing the Text Vignettes

Read about Mr. Valdres, Mrs. Howard, and Mr. Mansfield in the introduction to Part Four, "The Social Context of Aging," in the text. Write a two- to three-page paper in which you compare and contrast these adults, using the questions below as a guide:

1) Who is in their family? To what extent is their family traditional or nontraditional?

2) What roles do they play within their respective families?
3) How do they maintain their autonomy within their respective families?

4) What kinds of formal and informal supports do they receive?

5) What reciprocal relationships are they involved in? What intergenerational relationships are they involved in?

Older-Adult Interview

Interview a person who is 65 or older, asking the questions below. Write a three- to five-page paper about the social support structure of the interviewee and how it has changed over time. Pay close attention to the influence of gender, ethnicity, and other socio-cultural factors on social support.

Interview Questions

1) What was your family like when you were a child? How your ethnicity, income, family structure, and lifestyle affect the way you were raised?

2) What is your family like now? How is your current family structure affected by your ethnicity, income, and life events?

3) Think about your family and friends as a social support network. What kinds of things do you do for each other? Who can you count on when you need help? Who counts on you when they need help? Give examples.

4) Are any service providers part of your support network, for example, physicians, day care providers, delivery people, or housekeepers? What do they do for you and how are they compensated?

5) How has living in this neighborhood or community affected your support network?

6) How important is this support network to your well-being?

Student Questions

1) Reread the information on Social Exchange Theory in the text. How do the situations described by the interviewee illustrate this theory?

2) How has this interview affected your personal view of aging and older adults?

Community Interview

Listed below are examples of community programs designed to provide formal support to older adults, to assist families and friends who provide informal support to older adults, or to facilitate intergenerational sharing.

- Caregiver support groups
- Joint elder/child day care programs
- Foster Grandparents Program
- Friendly visitor programs
- Geriatric foster care programs
- Grandparents in the schools programs
- Neighbor-helping-neighbor programs
- Protective services programs

Work with your instructor to identify a program in your community. Interview an employee who is knowledgeable about the organization, asking the questions below. Write a three- to five-page paper on your findings.

1) What is your name and position within the organization? How long have you worked here?

2) What is the history of the organization? When was it started? Why was it started? What are its goals and objectives?

3) Who are the clients? What are the eligibility requirements?

4) What programs/services are offered? How do they help strengthen family and/or intergenerational relationships?

5) How do clients involved in the program benefit from it? Give examples of clients whose family and/or intergenerational relationships have been maintained or strengthened through association with your program.

6) How many staff work here? What are their qualifications?

7) How many volunteers work here? What are their roles?

8) How is the program funded?

9) What do you feel are the program's limitations (for example, types of services, eligibility requirements, location and hours of services)?

10) What could be done to help the program better meet its goals?

Research Paper

Select one of the topics below for in-depth study. Read a book or five journal articles on the topic. A good place to start searching for reading material is in the reference section provided at the end of each text chapter. Write a five- to ten-page research paper that describes the historical and current thinking on the topic. Identify things about the topic that are not yet resolved or may benefit from further study.

1) A number of studies have been conducted on grandparents who are caring for their grandchildren. Why were these studies undertaken? What kinds of research methods were used? What were their major findings? What questions have been left unanswered and would benefit from further research?

2) What does research tell us about the positive and negative aspects of providing care to a disabled family member? What programs, if any, have been able to help strengthen the positive aspects or reduce the negative aspects of caregiving?

3) What are elder abuse and elder neglect? What is known about why people abuse and/or neglect older adults? What are your state laws on reporting elder abuse? What programs are helpful in preventing and reducing elder abuse and neglect?

4) How does culture influence family relationships? How do other factors, such as socio-economic status, language, or recent immigration affect family relationships in old age?

Future Trends

Think about current trends in longevity and family structure that were discussed in the video and assigned text readings. Write a two- to three-page paper in which you speculate about what you think your family life will be like when you are 75.

For example, where will you live? What kind of family will you have? What kinds of relationships will you have with family members, friends, and neighbors?

How will you spend your day? What kind of assistance will you receive if you are disabled and who will provide it? What new programs or services might be available to you that are not available today?

If you are already 65 or older, describe the kind of family life you would wish for senior citizens living 50 years in the future. What differences would you see 50 years from now? What changes would need to be made to the present system to assure quality family lives for future seniors?

PROGRAM LESSON 9
WORK, RETIREMENT, AND ECONOMIC STATUS

Learning Objectives

1) Identify important aspects of successful employment and successful retirement in old age.

2) Explain the reasons for the poverty found among older minorities and women.

3) Describe three factors that may change the work patterns of elders in the future.

Summary of the Video and Text

Video

The video has three segments. In the first, older adults discuss their experiences with paid and voluntary work in old age. We learn that a lifetime of low income forces many African American and Hispanic elders to continue working well past the age that most Caucasian Americans retire. Senior employment programs that provide low-income elders with paying jobs are described. Ageist and sexist attitudes and recessionary times, however, can keep older adults out of the workforce.

The second segment discusses how the experience of retirement differs by gender and ethnicity. Regardless of race and sex, however, advance planning can help assure financial security and social support in retirement. The third segment presents information on economic status in old age, including a discussion of why older women and minorities are at risk of poverty. The experts advocate for changes in our Social Security, pension, and employment systems to close these gaps.

Experts appearing in the video include Representative Neil Abercrombie, Msgr. Fahey, Lou Glasse, Samuel Simmons, and Drs. Robert Atchley, Colette Browne, Herman Feifel, Douglas Kimmel, H. Asuman Kiyak, Barbara Payne, Marta Sotomayor, E. Percil Stanford, Robyn Stone, Richard Suzman, and Jeanette Takamura.

Older adults who share their experiences with us include Florence Austin, Charles Clark, Faye Cruse, Ilse Darling, Mary and John Franggos, Haruko Kiyabu, Robert Okura, Michael Orlando, Jane Potter, Eleanor Reese, Nancy Rice, Josephine Rosen, Leo Salazar, James Tate, Henrietta Towsley, Mildred Tuttle, and Mary Sue and Roger Wonson.

Text

New Reading. Chapter 12, "Productive Aging: Paid and Nonpaid Roles and Activities" defines and provides critiques of the concept of productive aging. Read the sections on Retirement, Employment Status, Economic Status, and Poverty Among Old and Young. These sections present information on the types of jobs older people have, the extent of unemployment among the elderly, barriers to employment in old age, timing of and satisfaction with retirement, sources of income in retirement, and the causes of and extensiveness of poverty in old age.

In Chapter 16, "Social Policies to Address Social Problems," read the sections on Income Security Programs and Private Pensions and Income Tax Provisions.

Review. Chapter 14, "Resiliency of Elders of Color," provides information about the special conditions of older African Americans, Hispanic Americans, Native Americans, and Pacific Asian Americans. In general, older Americans of these ethnicities are at higher risk of poverty and job discrimination than are older Caucasian Americans.

In Chapter 15, "Resiliency of Older Women," review the section on Older Women's Economic Status.

Key Points

Successful Employment and Retirement in Old Age

Some older adults never fully retire. About 18% of men and 10% of women who are 65 and older are still in the labor force. On the other hand, more older women than older men work part-time (Figure 12.2). In fact, part-time work among women 65 years and older has increased significantly between 1960 and 1998 while the opposite is true for older men—part-time work for men 65 years and older decreased in the same period of time. Interestingly, more older workers (23%) than younger workers (7%) are self-employed.

Dr. Robert Atchley says that older adults most often desire work that is part-time, self-paced, meaningful, and project-oriented. Dr. Atchley reminds us that most older people are at a stage of personality development in which they want to show concern for future generations and realize meaning in their lives. Thus, they are not interested in bureaucratic jobs, which tend to be impersonal and frustrating. Instead, they seek out jobs that provide them with opportunities to be creative, to teach, to personally touch other human beings, or to produce something of value to them.

A number of older adults illustrate these points. For example, Mary Franggos enjoys working part-time. She does not want to be tied down to a 9-to-5 job because she wants time to do other things she enjoys. John Franggos, who owns a store, and Nancy Rice, who runs a bed and breakfast, enjoy being self-employed. James Tate, a Gettysburg guide, likes the flexibility of setting his own hours. Dr. Barbara Payne opened a consulting business after retiring from the university.

Faye Cruse has maintained her identity as a nurse and continues to enjoy work in which she can help others. Leo Salazar tells us he is busier than ever in retirement. One of his volunteer jobs includes tutoring fourth-grade students as a member of a group called Dedicated Older Volunteers in Educational Service (DOVES).

Haruko Kiyabu works at her son's nursery. Jane Potter found that continuing to work helped her adjust to being widowed. Her work colleagues were supportive of her situation and the work helped focus her attention away from her loss.

Dr. Atchley talks about age discrimination in the workforce, which results from a presumption that older adults are less productive, less creative, and less motivated than younger workers, and that they are too old to learn new skills. The Age Discrimination in Employment Act, enacted in 1967, and the elimination of mandatory retirement in 1986 have helped reduce ageism in the workplace. But Robert Okura has experienced difficulty getting work in later life and Dr. Payne resented being forced to retire at age 70. In 2002, the U.S. Census Bureau reported that about 13.2% of older adults sought employment, and the rate was higher for older persons of color.

People who attempt career changes late in life may still face a number of obstacles, including employers' reluctance to retrain older workers and subtle forms of age discrimination. This is illustrated in the stories about Jane Feld and Sarah Nelson presented in a text box in Chapter 12. Several other barriers to employment for older adults are also discussed in this chapter.

Contrary to these stereotypes, there is evidence that older people make excellent employees, especially in information and service industries. When the hotel chain, Days Inn, installed its computerized reservation system, it found that older workers learned the system just as quickly as younger workers. In addition, older workers booked more reservations because they spent more time talking to customers and trying to meet their needs. Finally, the older workers stayed with Days Inn longer than the younger workers, providing a better return on the training investment.

Traveler's Insurance hired its retired employees, instead of agency workers, to fill temporary work needs and found that they saved nearly a million dollars. Samuel Simmons tells of an 87-year-old man who was retrained as a successful housing manager. In 2004, Home Depot, the national chain of home improvement stores, publicly announced and encouraged older adults to apply for jobs in their stores.

Among older adults who can afford to retire, attitudes toward retirement vary. Charles Clark says he was glad to retire and enjoys being able to travel and paint. Leo Salazar became involved in his community. Ilse Darling found retirement a bit of a shock, but now fills her time relaxing, reading, and spending time with her grandchildren. Faye Cruse writes poetry. On the other hand, Mildred Tuttle and Dr. Payne feel that people are forced to retire too early.

Dr. Jeanette Takamura urges men and women to plan for their retirement, financially and socially. For example, how much money do you need to save to live comfortably in retirement? What leisure activities will you pursue? Will you explore another line of work? Will you volunteer? How can you develop and maintain relationships with your children, grandchildren, and others younger than yourself? Where will you live?

Michael Orlando had several plans for retirement: to spend more time exploring his religion, keeping his body in shape, and participating with the Institute for Learning in Retirement. Henrietta Towsley and Dr. Payne admit that they could have been better prepared to fill the leisure time that retirement provides.

Dr. Colette Browne tells us that, in later life, gender role expectations tend to loosen up. With retirement, couples may need to renegotiate their roles and their boundaries. For example, Mary Sue Wonson found that she lost some privacy when her husband retired. It took a little time to adjust so that they each had their own space. Mary Sue spends time by herself in the early morning before Roger wakes up; Roger has his hobbies set up in the basement.

Retirement may be difficult for older adults who have been workaholics and have few interests outside of work. Inadequate retirement income, poor health, and poor family relations can also decrease satisfaction with retirement.

Poverty Among Older Minorities and Women

The "poverty level" is a fixed dollar amount of income; if a household makes less than this dollar amount, it is deemed poor. The number of older people living in poverty has decreased over the years, but 10.4% of older adults still had incomes below the poverty line in 2002.

The percentage of minority elders living in poverty is greater than Caucasian elders. Figure 14.1 shows that 29.4% of American Indian elders, 26.4% of African American elders, 21% of Hispanic American elders, compared to only 8-9% of Caucasian elders live in poverty. Being both old and a minority may put someone in "double jeopardy." As noted in Chapter 12, women of color remain at the lowest income levels across decades, and in the video, Dr. Percil Stanford tells us, retirement is not an option for everyone.

As noted by Lou Glasse, the official poverty level is too low for comfort and tends to be "ageist." For example, the official poverty level for older adults is lower than for younger adults because it was assumed that older people eat less and need less to live on. But, in fact, older people may need more money to meet needs related to declining health. Many advocacy groups define low-income individuals as those whose income falls below 125% of the official poverty level. According to Samuel Simmons, the overwhelming majority of older African Americans in the United States live on incomes less than 125% of the official poverty level. The text introduces the term "tweeners," meaning people who are too well off for public assistance but too poor to make ends meet.

The video and text describe why minority elders are economically disadvantaged. A number of factors keep minorities out of the workforce, including racial discrimination, lack of educational and training opportunities, and lack of employment opportunities. When they do work, these same factors often force minority individuals to work in low-paying jobs, jobs without pensions, jobs that do not contribute to the Social Security system (for example, domestic helper jobs), and jobs with no or inadequate health insurance. They may also work in jobs involving heavy labor or hazardous conditions. If such a worker is hurt or sick, the entire family income can be threatened. Young family members may have to stop attending school to support the family while the primary wage earner recovers.

Dr. Marta Sotomayor notes that Hispanics face additional problems obtaining jobs with good pay and benefits because many are not fluent in English and many are illiterate. Hispanics who have entered the country illegally are not supposed to work, so are unlikely to get jobs that contribute to the Social Security system or provide other benefits.

Older women are economically disadvantaged as well. Dr. Robyn Stone explains that, for many centuries, women were considered chattel, or slaves, of men. Women have not had the same access to the job market and are not paid for their work as housekeepers and family caregivers.

Social policies help perpetuate a system where women are dependent on their husbands (see the text boxes in Chapter 12, "Gender Inequities and Social Security," and "Pensions and Gender Inequities"). Today, more and more women are joining the workforce, but traditional female jobs (e.g., teaching, nursing, food service) tend to pay less than traditional male jobs (e.g., medicine, law, business, construction).

Even in comparable jobs, women tend to make less than men. Women are more likely to leave the workforce at various times to care for children or parents. Lower earnings throughout life and fewer years contributing to the Social Security system translate to lower earnings upon retirement. Finally, older women have to stretch their retirement income further than men because women are more likely to live longer and to face widowhood and disability.

Chapter 15 explores the economic status of women. For example, women over 65 account for nearly 75% of the poor older population, and Social Security is the primary source of income for older women. As shown in Figure 12.4 of the text, Social Security is the largest source of income for older adults. About 95% of older Americans receive Social Security, and without Social Security income, the poverty rate for older adults would increase from 10% to nearly 55%.

Social Security was enacted in 1935 to provide a minimum floor of protection in old age or disability. To participate, a worker must have contributed a portion of income to the system for at least ten years. Upon retirement, the individual receives a monthly check based on a percentage of average monthly earnings subject to Social Security tax. Other sources of income include assets (e.g., savings, property, home equity), pensions (job-specific retirement pay), and earnings from current employment.

Although it is the largest source of income, older adults find it difficult to live on Social Security alone. In the video, Jim Tate tells us that he does not receive a pension for any of the companies he worked for so that the income he receives as a tour guide at Gettysburg is an important supplement to his Social Security check. Haruko Kiyabu says that Social Security is important, but feels sorry for seniors who have to live on Social Security alone.

Florence Austin is happy that she at least qualifies to receive Social Security. She worked as a caregiver in people's homes; neither she nor her employers knew to contribute a portion to the Social Security system. When she learned about the system at age 65, she began to contribute. Over the next 15 years, she kept working and made the required contributions from her paycheck. Today she receives a monthly check from Social Security.

Samuel Simmons describes several federally sponsored employment programs for low-income seniors: one program pays seniors to work at nonprofit agencies, one pays seniors to educate communities about toxic wastes and the Environmental Protection Agency's Superfund project, and one trains seniors to be managers and maintenance people in housing projects. These programs are important in helping older adults earn an adequate income while contributing to society.

What about older adults who do not have income from Social Security, pensions, assets, or earnings? About 14% of older adults (more women than men) fall into this category and they may be eligible for financial assistance from the Supplemental Security Income (SSI) or Medicaid programs. SSI, enacted in 1972, is designed to bring the incomes of very poor elderly to a minimal level (about $400 a month, which is still below the official poverty level).

As the text outlines, SSI has a number of restrictions. Applicants may have only a small amount of assets or savings and applicants who accept money, food, clothing, or housing from other sources may see their SSI benefits cut.

In the video, Lou Glasse is critical of SSI. She says it does not pay enough to save older adults from poverty and the difficult application process discourages eligible seniors from applying. She feels that our income maintenance system needs a complete overhaul. Samuel Simmons describes a coalition (involving the National Caucus for the Black Aged, the Gray Panthers, and other groups) dedicated to increasing the "income floor" to a livable level. The coalition would like society to assure that no American's income falls below a level that is adequate to meet his/her basic needs.

Work Patterns of Elders in the Future

Several factors will shape work patterns of older adults in the future. Older people are living longer and may choose to stay in the workforce longer rather than risk boredom in retirement. As the Baby Boomers age, more old people and fewer young people will be available to the workforce. We may be increasingly dependent on older people to work. The text reminds us, for example, that older people are already filling jobs in fast-food restaurants.

Economic trends are important too. When the Baby Boomers retire, the country will need to expend more for Social Security at a time when fewer workers are contributing. Baby boomers worry, however, that Social Security will be bankrupt by the time they are ready to retire. In fact, the text notes that more Americans under age 35 believe in UFOs than believe in the future of Social Security. While short-term

danger of bankruptcy was averted through 1983 legislation, Representative Neil Abercrombie warns that if we do not prepare financially for the aging of America, it could spell economic ruin for the United States.

The text also notes that, by 2040, Social Security will be able to pay only 75% of its obligation to retirees. Proposed solutions include raising the age at which older adults become eligible for benefits, raising payroll taxes, or establishing a means test (see section on the Future of Social Security in Chapter 16).

Dr. Takamura and Dr. Asuman Kiyak note that, in a recession, government and business may be less able and willing to provide income subsidies or job opportunities to low-income elders.

To save money, government and businesses may consider reducing pension and health benefits that have helped maintain the retirement income of the middle class. In retirement, income tends to be fixed while the cost of living continuously increases. How many years can anyone live on a fixed income?

As Dr. Atchley reminds us, the nation's elite will probably weather the changing times. But he feels that the middle class will be squeezed and that the economically disadvantaged could be forced further into poverty. Dr. Kiyak wonders if future generations of older adults will be able to afford to retire.

82

Key Terms and Concepts from the Text, Video, and *Study Guide*

Age Discrimination in Employment Act
Apocalyptic Demography
Assets
Baby Boomers
Cost-of-Living Adjustment
Discrimination
Displaced Homemakers
Double Decker System
Double Jeopardy Hypothesis
Earnings
Economically Marginal
Employment Retirement Income Security Act
Graying of the Welfare State

Mandatory Retirement
Pensions
Poverty Level
Retirement
Safety Net
Senior Employment Programs
Serial Retirement
Social Security
Supplemental Security Income
Tweeners
Unemployment Rate
Universal Eligibility
Workaholic

Self-Study Questions

Instructions. Fill in the blank with the appropriate word or phrase from the list of Key Terms and Concepts. Note: Only 15 of the 26 Key Terms and Concepts can be used.

1) The number of people without jobs compared to the total population within a specific age group is called the _____.

2) An individual who works compulsively and has few interests outside of work is sometimes called a _____.

3) _____ refers to judging someone a certain way based on age, gender, ethnicity, or sexual orientation, rather than on individual characteristics.

4) The _____ is a federal law that protects workers age 45 and over from denial of employment strictly because of age.

5) _____ are women who do not have a paid work history (usually because they depended on a husband's income while raising a family) and do not qualify for credit or personal retirement benefits.

6) The _____ refers to the supposition that older women are discriminated against both for being old and for being female.

7) An individual's savings, home equity, and personal property are called _____ while money received in payment for a job is called _____.

8) _____ are retirement plans sponsored by employers.

9) The _____ is a fixed dollar amount of income determined by the federal government below which a household is deemed "poor."

10) _____ describes the work pattern of individuals who move in and out of the workforce, perhaps retiring at age 50 from a first career and retiring again at age 65 from a second career.

11) A company that requires workers to retire at a certain age has a _____ policy.

12) Programs sponsored by government or business that encourage the employment of older workers are called _____.

13) _____ is a federal program into which a worker contributes a portion of his/her income during adulthood and then, in retirement, receives a monthly check based on the amount earned.

14) _____ is a federal program that provides a minimal income for elderly living on the margin of poverty.

Use the Glossary at the end of the Study Guide to check your answers.

Topics for Discussion

1) If you were the director of personnel in a corporation and wanted to hire more older workers, what steps would you take?

2) If you were advocating for reforms in the Social Security and Supplemental Security Income programs, what changes would you suggest?

Website Challenge

Visit the following websites that can provide more information on this lesson's topics. Bookmark them for easy access in the future.

1) Commission on Law and the Aging at http://www.abanet.org/aging/

2) AARP's Senior Employment Program at http://www.aarp.org/scsep/

3) National Senior Service Corps at http://www.seniorcorps.org/

Written Assignments

Your instructor may ask you to complete one or more of the written assignments that follow.

Reaction Paper: New Knowledge and Feelings Stimulated by the Video

Write a two-page paper describing: 1) new information gained from watching the video; 2) how the experiences of the older adults in the video affected your personal view of aging; and 3) other comments to the instructor regarding this lesson or the course.

Older-Adult Interview #1

Work with your instructor to contact a senior employment program in your community. Ask them to help arrange an interview with a person 60 or older whom they have helped place in a job. Write a three- to five-page paper on your findings, answering the questions below.

Interview Questions

1) Tell me about your job? What do you do? How often do you work?

2) When you were looking for this job, what type of work and work environment were you seeking? Did you experience any barriers in your job search?

3) How did you find out about the senior employment program? How did they help you obtain your job?

4) What qualifications are needed for this job? What prior experience and personal characteristics are useful in this job? Is it a good job for you at this time?

5) Please tell me two accomplishments in this job that have given you the most satisfaction.

6) How long do you expect to work? Why?

7) What messages do you have for mature adults who are seeking work?

8) What messages do you have for employers regarding the hiring of mature adults?

9) What changes would you like the government or private sector to put in place to help older adults gain employment?

Student Questions

1) How do the interviewee's reasons for continued work compare with those mentioned in the text?

2) How did the barriers experienced by the interviewee compare with those described in the text? Explain.

3) How has this interview affected your personal view of aging and older adults?

Older-Adult Interview #2

Interview a person 60 or older who has retired from full-time work. Write a three- to five-page paper on your findings, answering the questions below.

Interview Questions

1) Before you retired from full-time work, what jobs did you hold (starting from when you were 20)? If your occupation changed over your life, why did it change? If it stayed the same, why didn't it change?

2) When did you retire from full-time work? Why did you retire at that particular time? Who, if anyone, helped you make the decision to retire when you did?

3) Did you plan for your retirement from full-time work? Did you attend any programs about retirement?

4) What are your sources of income? Do you worry about your financial future? Explain.

5) When you retired from full-time work, how did your life change? Did you have any trouble adjusting to retirement? If so, how long did it take to adjust? What helped you make the adjustment?

6) What do you do with your free time? Do you relax? Do you have a part-time job? Do you volunteer? Do you care for someone who is dependent on you? Do you have hobbies?

7) What things about your retirement give you the most satisfaction? the least satisfaction? What would you change about your retirement, if anything?

8) Would you consider returning to full-time work? If so, under what conditions?

9) What messages do you have for older adults who are thinking about retiring from full-time employment?

Student Questions

1) How do the interviewee's experiences with retirement compare with those mentioned in the text?

2) How has this interview affected your personal view of aging and older adults?

Community Interview

Listed below are examples of programs that help older people obtain jobs or that hire older adults.

-Senior employment programs
-State employment services
-Senior Companions
-Companies at which senior employment programs have placed older workers

Work with your instructor to identify either: 1) a company that hires adults who are 60 years or older, or 2) a program that helps adults who are 60 or older obtain employment. Interview someone who is knowledgeable about the organization, asking the questions below. Write a three- to five-page paper on your findings.

1) What is your name and position within the organization? How long have you worked here?

2) What are the goals and objectives of the organization regarding the employment of older adult workers?

3) How many older adults are employed at this time? What percentage of your total workforce does this represent?

4) What kinds of jobs are older workers most often employed in? Give examples.

5) Do older adults usually work full-time or part-time?

6) How do older adult workers involved in the organization benefit from it?

7) How do companies benefit from hiring older adult workers?

8) Name some of the organizational limitations regarding job opportunities for older adults (e.g., the types of jobs available, the hours of the job, the location of the job, the requirements of the job). Explain.

9) How could your organization better meet the needs of older adult workers?

Research Paper

Select one of the topics below for in-depth study. Read a book or five journal articles on the topic. A good place to start searching for reading material is in the reference section provided at the end of each text chapter. Write a five- to ten-page research paper that provides historical and current thinking on the topic. Identify things about the topic that are not yet resolved or may benefit from further study.

1) Research the history of the Social Security program (Title XVIII of the Social Security Act). Why was it established? What benefits does it provide to older adults? How much money has the government accrued in Social Security trust accounts? Will the program go broke when the baby boomers retire? What are the program's limitations, especially in regards to older women and minorities? How much can older people earn and still obtain their Social Security benefits?

2) What is the poverty level in your state? How does it compare with the federal poverty level? What proportion of the older adults in your state fall below the state and federal poverty levels? How does this compare with the proportion of people under 65 years of age who fall below the state and federal poverty levels?

Are certain groups of people more likely to be living in poverty than others, e.g., groups defined by age, gender, ethnicity, type of occupation, county, etc.? What programs in your state are available to older adults living below the poverty level? How many people participate in these programs?

3) Read the source documents about the Normative Aging Study of the Veterans Administration Hospital in Boston. What is the study's sample and methodology? What did the study find out about the phases of retirement? What else did the study's findings suggest about retirement?

Future Trends

Consider the demographic trends and concerns about the future discussed in the video and in Chapter 12 of the text, "Productive Aging: Paid and Nonpaid Roles and Activities." Write a two- to three-page paper in which you speculate about what you think will happen 50 years from now.

For example, will more people seek early retirement? How will the future economy affect employment opportunities for older adults? How will the cost and structure of health care influence an older adult's willingness to stay on the job?

What new types of employment or leisure activities will be popular? How will older adults be assured an adequate income as life expectancy increases? Will advances in social policy reduce the disparity in income we currently see between genders and among ethnic groups? Explain.

PROGRAM LESSON 10
ILLNESS AND DISABILITY

Learning Objectives

1) Identify the major physical and mental health problems of older people in the United States today.

2) Discuss the theory and reality of the "continuum of care" for chronically ill or disabled older adults.

3) Discuss how gender and ethnicity affect use of health services.

Summary of the Video and Text

Video

The video has four segments. The first segment discusses the impact of chronic, physical health problems on an elder's ability to function independently. Described in the second segment are three common mental health problems in old age: depression, dementia, and alcoholism. The third segment provides examples of how older people cope with physical and mental illness. The important roles of family support and health providers are highlighted. The fourth segment introduces some of the services available to compensate for losses caused by chronic disease.

Experts featured in the video include Drs. Vern Bengtson, Kenneth Brummel-Smith, Theodore Koff, Meredith Minkler, Steven Zarit, and Rabbi Earl Grollman. Dr. Thomas Lapine, Pat Nickerson, Jane Potter, and Robert Shaw share their perspectives as service providers. A number of older adults illustrate how they cope with physical and mental health conditions. They include Marian Cowan, Louise Di Virgilio, Ruth Dow, Oliver Francisco, Tatsuno Ogawa, Leo and Lillian Salazar, and Lindsey and Betty Tuff. Family members, Helen Sunahara and Allen Tateishi, are also featured.

Text

New Reading. In Chapter 4: "Managing Chronic Diseases and Promoting Well-Being in Old Age," read the sections on Chronic and Acute Diseases, Causes of Death in Later Years, Common Chronic Conditions, Falls and Their Prevention, and Use of Physician Services by Older People.

In Chapter 6, "Personality and Mental Health in Old Age," read the sections on Psychological Disorders Among Older Persons, Depression, Suicide Among Older People, Dementia, Alzheimer's Disease, Alcoholism, Drug Abuse, Paranoid Disorders and Schizophrenia, Anxiety, and Older Adults Who Are Chronically Mentally Ill.

Review. "The Biological and Physiological Context of Social Aging" provides a short overview of Chapters 3 and 4 in the text, including two vignettes that illustrate the variation in health status in older adults.

In Chapter 11, "Living Arrangements and Social Interactions," review the section on the theories of person-environment interaction that apply when trying to develop or provide services to compensate for individual losses. Also review the sections on Nursing Homes, Newer Options for Long-Term Care, and Services to Aid Older People in the Community.

Chapter 14, "The Resiliency of Elders of Color," which provides information about the special conditions of older African Americans, Hispanic Americans, Native Americans, and Pacific Asian Americans. In general, older Americans of these ethnicities live fewer years and are at higher risk of poor health than are older Caucasian Americans.

In Chapter 15, "The Resiliency of Older Women," review the section on Older Women's Health Status.

Your instructor may provide additional readings for this lesson.

87

Physical and Mental Health Problems of Older People

The physical health problems experienced by older people are more likely to be chronic (long-term) than acute (short-term). The incidence of acute illnesses, such as influenza, infections, and colds, decreases with age, and the discovery of antibiotics has greatly reduced the number of people who die from acute illnesses. But the incidence of chronic conditions increases with age and more than 80% of people over age 65 have at least one chronic disease.

The most frequently reported chronic conditions causing limitation of activity in persons age 70 and over are shown in Figure 4.2 in the text. For both genders, conditions include arthritis, hypertension (high blood pressure), heart disease, diabetes, respiratory diseases, stroke and cancer.

Older adults may have multiple conditions and these may interact with one another. In the video, we learn that Louise Di Virgilio had bowel cancer, which was surgically removed, and has degenerative joint disease, Addison's disease, diabetes, and chronic obstructive pulmonary disease (COPD). Her physician, Dr. Thomas Lapine, explains that the medication she takes for Addison's disease exacerbates her diabetes and mobility problems. The COPD, which restricts her ability to breathe, further complicates her health and reduces her ability to get around.

Chronic diseases are also responsible for the majority of deaths among the elderly. The top causes of mortality include heart disease, cancer, cerebrovascular disease (stroke), and COPD. How do physical changes associated with these diseases differ from the changes that accompany normal aging are discussed in Program Lesson 2, "How the Body Ages."

In normal aging, the heart muscle loses elasticity, lipids (fats) accumulate in the vessels leading to the heart, and the heart muscle is replaced with fat. Heart disease is a condition in which the blood supply to the heart is severely restricted.

This leads to angina pectoris (characterized by chest pain and shortness of breath), myocardial infarction (heart attack), or congestive heart failure (decreased pumping efficiency). In the video, Lindsey Tuff has heart disease; his coronary circulation has been improved through open-heart surgery in which vessels from his leg were grafted onto his heart to increase coronary blood flow. Heart disease is the leading cause of death in older adults.

In normal aging, blood vessels throughout the body lose elasticity and accumulate lipids. If the flow of blood and oxygen to the brain is severely restricted, malfunction or death of brain cells can result.

In strokes, whole portions of the brain are denied blood through the narrowing of vessels in the brain, the presence of a blood clot that restricts blood flow (cerebral thrombosis), or the rupturing of a weak spot in a blood vessel in the brain (cerebral hemorrhage). The extent of impairment from a stroke depends on the area of the brain affected and the length of time the area is denied blood.

In cancer, cell reproduction goes "out of control." Caught at an early stage, many cancers can be treated. However, cancerous cells can migrate from the organ they originate in and may eventually interfere with vital body functions, causing death. Common cancers among older adults are cancer of the bowel, lung cancer, colon cancer, and breast cancer. Louise Di Virgilio had cancer of the bowel, but the cancer was surgically removed.

With normal aging, breathing capacity decreases as lung muscles loss elasticity and strength. With Chronic Obstructive Pulmonary Disease (COPD), however, lung tissue is actually damaged. COPD is a broad term for lung-damaging respiratory diseases, including chronic bronchitis, asthma, and emphysema. As these diseases progress, it becomes harder and harder to breathe. The least amount of physical exertion can cause shortness of breath.

Even though they don't usually cause death, other chronic illnesses can disable older adults. The World Health Organization defines disability as impairment in the ability to complete multiple daily tasks. About 20% of older adults have a mild disability, but only about 4% are severely disabled.

Diabetes, one of the most prevalent of chronic diseases, for example, results when the pancreas produces insufficient insulin for the proper metabolism of carbohydrates. Most of the time, diabetes can be managed through changes in diet and intake (either orally or by injection) of insulin. However, when diabetes is not under control, high blood glucose (sugar) levels can contribute to nerve damage, blindness, kidney problems, stroke, and poor circulation in the extremities (sometimes leading to gangrene and amputation). In the video, Louise Di Virgilio's diabetes appears to be under control.

Normal aging is also associated with loss of bone density, which results in loss of stature. In osteoporosis, however, the loss of bone mass is extreme and bones become brittle and more prone to collapse or fracture. It occurs mostly in women after menopause. Arthritis is a term that encompasses more than 100 conditions that result in the degeneration or inflammation of bones and joints. Surprisingly, of all the health problems experienced by Louise Di Virgilio, she feels most restricted by her arthritis. Arthritis is the most common chronic condition in old age.

Sensory impairments can be very frustrating to the aged. With normal aging, the ability to see and hear diminishes. Interventions such as glasses, cataract surgery, and hearing aids can help compensate for mild and moderate losses. Information on sensory impairment was covered is Program Lesson 3, "Maximizing Physical Potential in Old Age."

The video describes three major disorders that affect cognitive functioning: depression, dementia, and alcoholism. These are discussed in Chapter 6 of the text, "Personality and Mental Health in Old Age."

Depression is the most common psychiatric illness among older adults. Some depressions in old age are called reactive depressions, which results from losses (for example, the loss of a spouse or of a family home). Symptoms may include sadness, weight loss, inability to concentrate, sleeplessness, and suicidal thoughts. Premature death, by suicide or accident, can also result.

In the video, Lindsey Tuff, Betty Tuff, Oliver Francisco, and Allen Tateishi talk about their experiences with depression. Some practitioners erroneously believe that depression is a not worth treating in older adults. Research suggests, however, that treatment is usually effective in older people and can improve their quality of life. Types of treatment include individual therapy, antidepressant drugs, talking to a friend or spouse, or participating in a support group.

Dementia is a broad term for disorders that cause a progressive deterioration of intellectual functioning, learning, and memory. In most cases, dementias have physical causes and are not "mental illnesses." However, because they affect cognitive functioning, many books, including the text, discuss them under mental disorders. Some dementias may be reversible, like those caused by brain tumors, substance abuse, nutritional deficiencies, or depression. People with hearing loss may also appear to have mental or cognitive impairments. If these conditions are treated successfully, however, the associated dementia should disappear. Nonreversible dementias include those caused by Alzheimer's disease, mini-strokes (multi-infarct dementia), and Huntington's Chorea. Mrs. Tateishi, in the video, has Alzheimer's disease, for which there is yet no cure. Her son, Allen, tells of Mrs. Tateishi's progressive loss of cognitive skills.

Substance abuse can also impair mental functioning. Alcoholism is the most common form of substance abuse among the aged. However, it is important to consider the effects of polypharmacy (the interaction of multiple medications) when assessing mental status in older adults. Some medications compound or cancel out the effects of other medications. In addition, with normal aging the kidneys become less efficient at purifying toxins and drugs from the blood. Medication levels can build up and actually begin to poison an older person and may cause changes in mental function.

Multiple diseases, medication and sensory impairment can cause older adults to fall. A seemingly simple fall incident for an older adult may trigger a series of events that can lead to disability. This may then dramatically alter the quality of life of the older adult and his or her family members.

Falls are the leading cause of injuries for people 65 and older in the U.S. and account for 90% of all hip fractures. See table 4.1 and the text box on page 139 for risk factors for falls in older adults.

Especially important to older people is the effect that health problems have on their ability to function independently. As Dr. Theodore Koff explains in the video, we measure the impact of illness by how it limits Activities of Daily Living (ADLs), which include bathing, dressing, grooming, eating, toileting, and walking.

Another measure of independent functioning is known as Instrumental Activities of Daily Living (IADLs). IADLs include cooking, cleaning, doing laundry, running errands, using the telephone, and managing money. It is true that having an acute illness can limit one's activities temporarily. But chronic conditions can limit one's ability to function independently altogether. For example, a stroke can limit mobility and make it difficult to shop, cook, and clean the house.

Severe arthritis makes it difficult to dress and feed oneself. A person with Alzheimer's disease will eventually need help with all IADLs and ADLs, even toileting.

Even the potential loss of ADL and IADL functioning can motivate older adults to make changes in their lifestyles and living arrangements. For example, Marian Cowan is planning to move into a more sheltered living environment before she becomes dependent. Ruth Dow knows that the stairs in her home will eventually become a barrier that will either force her to move or will make her homebound.

It is important for older adults and their health professionals to learn to distinguish the effects of illness from the effects of normal aging. The video and text warn that many people tend to regard physical and mental complaints in later life as the inevitable result of "just getting old."

According to Dr. Steven Zarit, some health professionals feel that older people won't benefit from examination or treatment; he refers to this as an example of age prejudice or ageism. Concerns about cost may also keep older adults from seeking medical care.

As we have learned, the normal aging process is accompanied by physical and sensory decline. Even older people who watch what they eat and continue to exercise find that they move less quickly and have less strength than they did in their younger years. Even older people with strong social networks and positive attitudes can become depressed as they face the multiple losses that accompany aging. However, acute and chronic illness will compound the declines of normal aging. An older person should review his/her health status regularly with a health professional who understands the aging process and can prescribe treatment for any reversible loss of function.

Despite the fact that physical functioning declines with age, Dr. Meredith Minkler tells us that more than 80% of older adults rate their health as good or excellent. Reasons for this may be that people measure health by how well they can function and people tend to compare themselves with their peers.

For example, Louise Di Virgilio says she is not depressed about her health because she can still "get around" and she sees people who are "worse off" than she.

Coping is improved by social support. For example, Betty Tuff reduces her anxiety by talking things over with her husband Lindsey. Allen Tateishi improves his coping abilities by sharing his concerns and feelings with a support group for adults caring for loved ones with dementia. Dr. Minkler reminds us that people who have high levels of social support have lower rates of death and illness than people with low levels of social support.

What will happen to the Baby Boomers as they age? Will we see growing numbers of disabled elders in the future? Will the current focus on healthy lifestyles and advances in medical science reduce the incidence of chronic disease and disability in the next century?

Dr. Minkler feels that both will happen. Today's older adults are varied, and there's a good chance that we will see even more diversity in the years ahead. As Dr. Minkler says, "we need to plan for both."

The "Continuum of Care"

The table and flow chart on the following pages list the variety of services that can help to meet the needs of older adults and their families. Certain services are appropriate for certain older adults, depending on how much assistance an older adult requires with ADLs and IADLs and whether the service is provided in the home, in the community, or in an institution.

In theory, the "continuum of care" refers to a seamless system of services that can be used by older adults as they move from being totally independent in functioning to being totally dependent on others for care. In reality, few communities have all these services. Even when services exist, they may be difficult to access because of their varying funding mechanisms, eligibility requirements, and waiting lists.

The primary service provider encountered by older adults is the physician. Geriatrics is a relatively new field, and few physicians are certified in this specialty. But many physicians have learned to understand and treat the multiple, interactive problems experienced in later life. Louise Di Virgilio and Oliver Francisco say they appreciate physicians who take a good history, who listen to them, who are responsive to their concerns, and who show their human side. Physicians and hospital staff can benefit from continuing education about aging. Pat Nickerson describes a training program in her hospital that explained the aging process to staff. She found that this increased the staff's understanding of aging and their empathy for older patients.

Older adults who do not see private physicians can visit health professionals through outpatient and mental health clinics, often funded by state and local governments.

Treatment for mental health concerns can include counseling and/or medications. Support groups play an important role in mental health promotion as they provide adults with opportunities to share their feelings with people in similar situations. Oliver Francisco belongs to two men's support groups and tells us he enjoys the sharing that goes on within the groups.

Older adults who are socially isolated can benefit from outreach services. Jane Potter describes an outreach service in which volunteers go to the homes of older people for a friendly visit; while there, the volunteer can assess the living situation and help the older person obtain additional services if needed.

Independent older residents at Leisure World, a retirement community near Los Angeles, benefit from the presence of building captains who watch out for residents and intervene if something looks amiss. Some residents of Leisure World also have emergency alarms that they can activate when they need emergency assistance in their homes. Older adults who are relatively independent in functioning can attend senior centers and meal sites, which offer opportunities for activity, exercise, nutrition, and companionship.

The majority of older adults depend on family members to help them compensate for the losses that accompany aging and illness. For example, Betty Tuff depends on her husband Lindsey to vacuum; she can't do it because of her bad back.

Louise Di Virgilio relies on her daughter to take her shopping. Lillian Salazar's father receives most of his care from Lillian and her family. In fact, Dr. Minkler notes that "Americans go to great lengths to keep our elderly family members at home." It may be necessary to modify the home to maintain disabled adults at home. Common modifications include raising toilet seats, installing grab bars in the bath, and building wheel-chair ramps.

Sometimes, family members cannot meet all the needs of a disabled older person living at home and may benefit from home- and community-based services. For example, Louise Di Virgilio has a chore worker help clean her house and do her grocery shopping. Lillian Salazar hired a home care worker to help her father groom, dress, eat, and walk. Allen Tateishi's mother participates in a group respite program, where she engages in exercise, crafts, and outings supervised by staff and volunteers who understand the needs of dementia patients.

At the same time, Allen gets a needed break and uses the time to go shopping or be with his children. According to Allen, the respite and support group services provided by the Alzheimer's Association helped save his marriage.

Continuum of Care: Location and Target Group of Services

Target Group	Location of Services		
	In the Home	In the Community	In Institutions
Older Adults of All Functional Levels		Support Groups Advocacy Services Outpatient Clinics Mental Health Clinics Private Physicians	
Older Adults Who Function Independently		Senior Centers Meal Sites	Retirement Facilities
Older Adults who Need Some Help with IADLs	Chore Services Housekeeping Escort Transportation Emergency Alarms Home Modifications Home-Delivered Meals Friendly Visitors	Senior Centers Meal Sites Adult Day Care Case Management Group Respite Care	Retirement Facilities Assisted Living Boarding Homes
Older Adults Who Need Some Help with IADLs and ADLs	All of the Above, plus Personal Care Home Health Aides Public Health Nurse Home Respite Care	Adult Day Care Adult Day Health Adult Foster Care Case Management Group Respite Care	Assisted Living Care Homes
Older Adults Who Need Help with Most IADLs and ADLs	All of the Above	Adult Day Health Adult Foster Care Case Management	Nursing Homes Institutional Respite
Older Adults Who Are Acutely Ill, Need Rehabilitation, or Are Dying	All of the Above, plus Visiting Nurse Visiting Therapist Home Hospice Care	Adult Day Health Adult Foster Care Case Management	Hospitals Rehabilitation Facilities Nursing Homes Institutional Respite Institutional Hospice
Family Caregivers		Caregiver Support Caregiver Training	

Steps to Avoid Institutionalization
Goal: Elder to stay in the home with help of family and caregiver(s), or to have in-home services for as long as possible
Source: Jill Tamashiro and Valerie Yontz, 2004

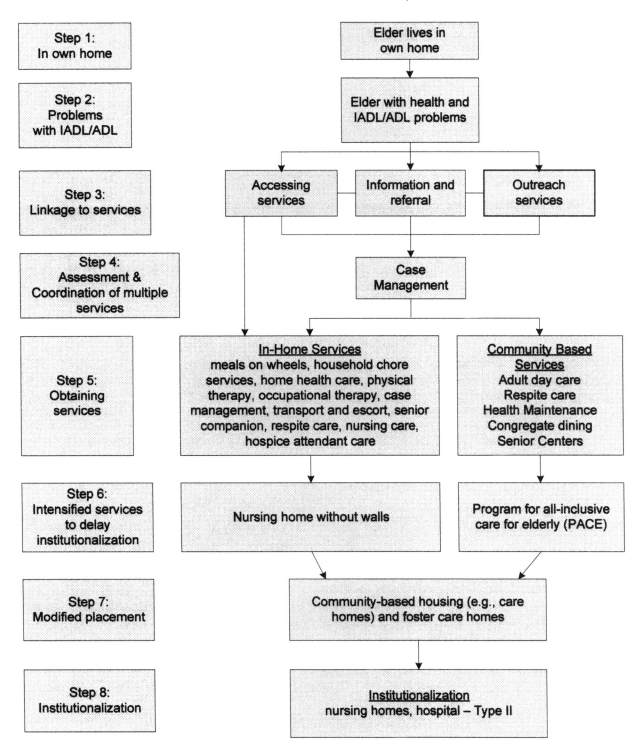

Step 1:
In own home

Step 2:
Problems
with IADL/ADL

Step 3:
Linkage to services

Step 4:
Assessment &
Coordination of multiple
services

Step 5:
Obtaining
services

Step 6:
Intensified services
to delay
institutionalization

Step 7:
Modified placement

Step 8:
Institutionalization

Elder lives in
own home

Elder with health and
IADL/ADL problems

Accessing
services

Information and
referral

Outreach
services

Case
Management

In-Home Services
meals on wheels, household chore
services, home health care, physical
therapy, occupational therapy, case
management, transport and escort, senior
companion, respite care, nursing care,
hospice attendant care

Community Based
Services
Adult day care
Respite care
Health Maintenance
Congregate dining
Senior Centers

Nursing home without walls

Program for all-inclusive
care for elderly (PACE)

Community-based housing (e.g., care
homes) and foster care homes

Institutionalization
nursing homes, hospital – Type II

In some cases, home- and community-based services may not be appropriate, for example, when an older adult is socially isolated and homebound, has no family support, or needs more help than can be provided in the current living environment. For them, a range of institutional services are available.

Relatively independent adults may consider a retirement community like Leisure World or congregate housing. Care homes, boarding homes, and adult foster homes provide 24-hour supervision, but less intensive levels of nursing care than do nursing homes. Nursing homes provide 24-hour nursing care and supervision to extremely disabled adults.

There is a myth that all older adults end up in nursing homes. In actuality, only 4.5% of older adults reside in nursing homes at any given time. However, Chapter 11 of the text notes that an older person's risk of staying in a nursing home increases with age. At age 65, the lifetime risk of admission is 39% while at age 85, the risk is 49%.

Mrs. Ogawa provides us an example of an older person whose disabilities and care needs have changed over time. For many years after being widowed, she lived alone. We met her in a previous video when, after an injury, she had moved in with one of her children. Home care workers visited regularly to help with bathing, grooming, and exercise, and to check her health status. She also attended an adult day care program in the neighborhood. In this video we learn that, after breaking her hip, she needed 24-hour care and her physician recommended nursing home care.

Her daughter, Helen Sunahara, says the family felt guilty about placing her in a nursing home, but the 24-hour care was too much for them to handle. Mrs. Ogawa says she does not like being dependent on others and is looking forward to her death. She hopes her children are lucky enough to live long, healthy lives and die suddenly before they become dependent.

When selecting services, it is important to remember the concepts of "person-environment fit" and "least restrictive environment." Consider the older person and his/her environment.

What does the older person want and need? What can be done to meet these needs while keeping the older adult in an environment that provides as much independence as possible? What modifications can enhance the current environment? What services will help strengthen current supports?

Because of the vast array of services, each with its own rules for eligibility and payment, families often benefit from the services of a case manager, someone who can arrange the most appropriate services at the least cost and the least amount of confinement for a disabled older adult.

Chapters 16 and 17 in the text provide information on the common social and health services and their funding mechanisms. The video and text admit that services for disabled older adults are not comprehensive or universally available in the United States. We will discuss the reasons for and the implications of this fact in Lesson 12, "Societal and Political Aspects of Aging."

Effects of Gender and Ethnicity on Use of Health Services

Older people are more likely to visit their physicians and to be hospitalized than young people. However, we see differences in the use of health services among older adults depending on their gender, ethnicity, income, and country of residence.

Dr. Minkler tells us that women outlive men by eight years but as Dr. Kenneth Brummel-Smith notes, women have a higher level of disability than men. Although women are more likely than men to seek medical care, more women than men lack health insurance. Thus, more older women are more likely to need long-term care services than men and more are dependent on Medicaid.

Ethnic differences in use of health services are seen as well. In research in Los Angeles, Dr. Brummel-Smith found that Hispanic Americans had two to three times more disability than did Caucasian Americans, but that their use of health services, especially mental health services, was much lower.

The text notes that African Americans have lower survival rates than do Caucasian Americans for several types of cancer, in part because they access health services less often and their cancers are diagnosed at a later, more dangerous, stage.

Ethnic differences may really reflect differences in socio-economic status, a concept that describes how "well off" someone is as determined by their income and occupation. Dr. Minkler points out that poor health among older African Americans may reflect an earlier life lived under serious segregation and discrimination. These conditions limited their opportunities for education and jobs, which limited their earnings, which limited the amount of money they could spend on housing, food, children, recreational activities, personal health, and so forth.

Similarities exist among ethnic groups, as well. In his research in Los Angeles, Dr. Vern Bengtson found that African Americans, Hispanic Americans, and Caucasian Americans, all identified their top concerns as personal health, income, and not being a burden to their children.

It may surprise many Americans that access to health services is affected most by one's country of residence. Drs. Minkler and Brummel-Smith both refer to the institutional and surgical biases in the U.S. health care system. Dr. Brummel-Smith notes that it is much easier and cheaper for an older person to get cataract surgery than to get a new pair of glasses.

Both experts suggest that most other developed countries have some form of national health service and that this helps them address the service needs of older adults. As Dr. Minkler says, in "Sweden or Canada or Great Britain, if you're an older person and you need home-delivered meals, there's no question about whether you qualify...it's just understood that older people may need these services and that the government provides them."

Key Terms and Concepts from the Text, Video, and *Study Guide*

Accessibility
Activities of Daily Living
Acute Illness
Adult Day Care
Adult Foster Care
Alcoholics Anonymous
Alzheimer's Disease
Angina Pectoris
Anxiety Disorder
Aphasia
Arteriosclerosis
Arthritis
Assisted Living
Atherosclerosis
Boarding and Care Homes
Cancer
Cardiovascular Diseases
Cerebral Hemorrhage
Cerebral Trombosis
Cerebrovascular Accident
Cerebrovascular Disease
Chronic Illness

Chronic Obstructive Pulmonary Disease
Congestive Heart Failure
Congregate Living Facilities
Congregate Meals
Continuum of Care
Contractures
DSM-4
Dementia
Depression
Diabetes Mellitus
Disability
Dowager's Hump
Electroconvulsive Therapy
Edentulous
Emphysema
Group Therapy
Health Status
Hemiplegia
Home Health Care
Homebound
Home-Delivered Meals
Hypertension

Hypotension
Incontinent
Infarct
Instrumental Activities of Daily Living (IADL)
Kyphosis
Least Restrictive Environment
Lifeline System
Life Review Therapy
Long-Term Care
Meal Sites
Mental Health Centers
Morbidity
Mortality
Myocardial Infarction
Nursing Homes
Older Americans Act
Osteoarthritis

Osteopenia
Osteoporosis
Person-Environment Fit or Congruence
Pharmacotherapy
Polypharmacy
Pseudodementia
Psychopathology
Psychotherapy
Range-of-Motion Exercises
Reactive Depression
Reality Orientation
Rehabilitation
Remotivation Therapy
Retirement Community
Rheumatoid Arthritis
Schizophrenia
Stroke

Self-Study Questions

Instructions. Fill in the blank with the appropriate word or phrase from the list of Key Terms and Concepts. Note: Only 40 of the 78 key terms and concepts can be used.

1) An individual's _____ refers to a summary of his/her vital signs, diseases, disabilities, and self-perceptions regarding health.

2) The concept of _____ refers to the match between an individual's needs and the environment.

3) Personal care tasks such as bathing, dressing, grooming, using the toilet, eating, and getting in and out of bed are called _____ .

4) Tasks such as shopping, meal preparation, money management, and housekeeping are called _____ .

5) A _____ refers to an impairment that affects one's ability to function within normal ranges.

6) An illness that is short-term and usually allows a full recovery is called _____ .

7) A _____ illness lasts more than three months, is often permanent, and leaves a residual disability that may require long-term management rather than cure. Examples include arthritis, emphysema, hypertension, some cancers, and diabetes.

8) _____ is another word for illness or disability. _____ is another word for death.

9) Someone who is _____ is unable to leave the house because of illness, disability, or social isolation.

10) _____ is the formal name for a stroke. It occurs when a portion of the brain is completely denied blood and oxygen.

11) If someone has severe memory loss, we say that he/she has a _____ . Sometimes, it is caused by underlying conditions that can be cured. When it is caused by _____, however, it is not reversible.

12) _____ is a general term for diseases that damage lung tissue, such as chronic bronchitis, asthma, and emphysema.

13) _____ is another word for a heart attack.

14) Someone who is _____ has no teeth.

15) There are two common causes of stroke. A _____ can cause a stroke when a weak spot in a blood vessel of the brain bursts. _____ can cause a stroke when a blood clot either diminishes or closes off the blood flow in an artery of the brain or neck.

16) _____ is a disease in which cells grow at an abnormal and excessive rate. It usually starts in one part of the body but may spread to distant organs and eventually cause death.

17) _____ is a disease that results in an above-normal amount of sugar (glucose) in the blood and urine, caused by insufficient insulin that is necessary to process carbohydrates.

18) _____ is another word for high blood pressure. _____ is another word for low blood pressure.

19) A person with _____ experiences a loss of bone that results in decreased bone strength, diminished height, and increased bone brittleness.

20) Someone who is _____ cannot control his/her urine and/or feces.

21) _____ is the name for a psychiatric disorder marked by sadness, diminished interest in activities, poor concentration, weight loss, and sleep disturbances. This condition may also cause a person to become disoriented and confused, and this is called a _____.

22) Feeling sad in response to specific distress such as illness or the death of a spouse is known as _____.

23) The _____ refers to the array of health services that should be available to meet the needs of older adults, including services provided in the home, community settings, and institutions to adults with all levels of health, illness, and disability.

24) Therapy that involves drugs is called _____.

25) The concept of _____ refers to arranging services and environments that allow a disabled person to be as independent, and least confined, as possible.

26) An emergency alarm system used by vulnerable older adults during periods of isolation is called _____.

27) A _____, after making an assessment of need, helps obtain and orchestrate services for disabled older adults.

28) _____ is different from individual therapy in that it provides participants the opportunity for peer support, social interaction, and role modeling as well as psychotherapy.

29) _____ are usually prepared by a church or voluntary agency and distributed to homes of people who have trouble cooking for themselves.

30) _____ provide ambulatory treatment for psychological and psychiatric disorders.

31) In a _____ program, family caregivers are temporarily relieved of their duties so that they can rest or run errands.

32) _____ is a housing model aimed at elders who want to live in a small apartment of their own and receive some assistance with IADLs and ADLs personal care, but who are not so physically or cognitively impaired as to need 24-hour attention.

33) Usually considered the most restrictive care environment, _____ are residential facilities in which nursing staff provide 24-hour care to people with chronic illnesses who need assistance with ADL and IADL. Slightly less restrictive environments into which elders can move to receive care from unrelated providers are _____ and _____.

Use the Glossary at the end of the Study Guide to check your answers.

Topics for Discussion

1) You are the case manager for an 80-year-old woman who has recently broken her hip. You need to help her make plans about how she will be cared for after she leaves the hospital. She will need help for about a month. What options are available to her if she has a big family in town? What options are available if she has no family in town?

2) A 75-year-old man seeks advice from his family doctor about his increasing memory problems. What could be causing this? What should the doctor do to help the older man and his family?

Website Challenge

Visit these websites that can provide more information on this lesson's topics. Bookmark them for easy access in the future.

1) Alzheimer's Association at http://www.alz.org

2) Leisure World at http://www.leisureworld.ca/

3) Caregiving Online at http://www.caregiving.com

Written Assignments

Your instructor may ask you to complete one or more of the written assignments that follow.

Reaction Paper: New Knowledge and Feelings Stimulated by the Video

Write a two-page paper describing: 1) new information gained from watching the video; 2) how the experiences of the older adults in the video affected your personal view of aging; and 3) other comments to the instructor regarding this lesson or the course.

Analyzing the Text Vignettes

Read the text vignettes about Mrs. Hill and Mr. Jones in the introduction to Part Two, "The Physiological Context of Social Aging," and the vignette about Mr. Adams in the introduction to Part Three, "The Psychological Context of Social Aging."

Write a two- to three-page paper in which you compare and contrast the illnesses, disabilities, and care needs of these three adults, using the questions below as a guide:

1) What illnesses and disabilities are they experiencing? Which ones are due to normal aging? Which ones are due to disease?

2) How do these illnesses and disabilities affect their ability to function independently? What help do they need with Activities of Daily Living? with Instrumental Activities of Daily Living?

3) How do they compensate for their physical and mental losses? Is the family able to meet all the needs of the older adult? If not, who provides the other needed services? What services are needed but not provided?

4) If you were asked to help these adults, what recommendations would you make? Base your decisions on the concepts of person-environment fit and least restrictive environment.

Older-Adult Interview

Interview an older person with a physical disability or chronic condition (e.g., heart disease, cancer, stroke, diabetes, arthritis, a chronic lung disease, paralysis, amputation, or blindness), asking the questions below. Write a three- to five-page paper about the older person's experiences and how he or she has adapted to living with the physical disability or chronic condition.

Interview Questions

1) How would you rate your health... excellent, good, fair, poor? How does it compare to the health of other people your age?

2) How does it compare to the health of your grandparents and parents when they were your age?

3) How often do you get a cold or the flu? Compared to when you were younger, how quickly do you recover from these acute illnesses?

4) Please tell me about a physical disability or chronic condition you have. How old were you when you first noticed or developed it? How has it progressed over the years? What is your chance of recovery, stability, or further decline?

5) How does your physical disability or chronic condition limit your ability to get around or take care of yourself?

6) What has helped you adapt to your physical disability or chronic conditions? Which roles did the following play? Family members and friends? Physicians and health care facilities? Service providers? Support groups? Home modifications or assistive devices?

7) Has your health insurance coverage been adequate?

Student Questions

1) Does your interviewee have any of the major disabling diseases common among older adults in the United States?

2) How does your interviewee's experiences with disabilities and assistance illustrate the concept of person-environment interaction?

3) How has this interview affected your personal view of aging and older adults?

Community Interview

Listed below are examples of health and social services designed to assist disabled or chronically ill adults and their families.

-Alcoholics Anonymous
-Alzheimer's Association
-Arthritis support groups
-Case management
-Home care services
-Make Today Count
-Meal services
-Personal care services
-Nursing homes
-Retirement community
-Stroke support groups
-Transportation services

Work with your instructor to identify a program in your community. Interview an employee who is knowledgeable about the organization, asking the questions below. Write a three- to five-page paper on your findings.

1) What is your name and position within the organization? How long have you worked here?
2) What is the history of the organization? When was it started? Why was it started? What are its goals and objectives?

3) Who are the clients? What are the eligibility requirements?

4) What programs/services are offered? How do they assist disabled or chronically ill older adults?

5) How do clients involved in the program benefit from it? Give examples of ways in which specific disabled or chronically ill clients have been helped.

6) How many staff work here? What are their qualifications?

7) How many volunteers work here? What are their roles?

8) How is the program funded?

9) What do you feel are the program's limitations (for example, types of services provided, location, hours, eligibility requirements for clients)?

10) What could be done to help the program better meet its goals?

Research Paper

Select one of the topics below for in-depth study.

Read a book or five journal articles on the topic. A good place to start searching for reading material is in the reference section provided at the end of each text chapter. Write a five- to ten-page research paper that describes the historical and current thinking on the topic. Identify things about the topic that are not yet resolved or may benefit from further study.

1) Choose a psychotherapeutic approach used with depressed older adults, e.g., life review, support groups, milieu therapy, reality orientation, remotivation therapy. Describe how this approach has been evaluated by researchers. Has it been shown to be effective? What further research is needed?

2) In the video, Dr. Minkler says the United States does not do a good job of providing health and social services to older adults. Compare how health care is provided to older adults in the United States with that provided in a developed country with socialized medicine, e.g., Canada, Sweden, England, Germany, or Australia. What are the advantages and disadvantages of the two health care systems?

3) What are boarding homes and care homes? How do they compare to nursing homes in services provided, populations served, costs, and payment mechanisms?

4) Discuss in depth the problems of diagnosing dementia in older adults. Which tests differentiate dementia from delirium, depression, substance abuse, schizophrenia, and other conditions that affect memory and behavior?

5) How can nursing homes and other living environments be designed to maximize functioning of older adults with dementia?

DYING, DEATH, AND BEREAVEMENT

Learning Objectives

1) Discuss reactions and coping mechanisms in older adults experiencing bereavement.

2) Describe two services designed to help older adults cope with dying, death, and bereavement.

3) Describe two tools people can use to plan for their own deaths.

4) Discuss two ethical dilemmas posed by our technological ability to keep alive increasing numbers of older people.

Summary of the Video and Text

Video

The video has four segments. In the first, experts and medical students discuss societal and personal views of death. We learn how early experiences with death shape our perceptions of it. Grief and bereavement reactions are further discussed in the second segment, as older adults tell how they have faced the death of loved ones in their lives.

The third segment introduces services designed to help older adults cope with dying, death, and bereavement. These include support groups, rituals (like funerals and memorial services), and hospice. The fourth segment presents information on tools people can use to plan for their own deaths, such as the living will and the durable power of attorney for health care decisions. Also discussed are moral and ethical concerns posed by society's ability to prolong life, including euthanasia, rationing medical care to older adults, and suicide.

Featured experts include Drs. Herman Feifel, Theodore Koff, Meredith Minkler, Edwin Shneidman, and Msgr. Charles Fahey. Additional perspectives are provided by students Kevin Mack, Ivy Nip, and Darith Seng from the University of Hawai`i Medical School and physicians Dr. Jack Kevorkian and Dr. Susan Tolle.

We also hear from Melinda Grooms, coordinator of a hospice program, and Bev Ickes and Tanya Blume, who discuss their feelings about the deaths of their respective fathers.

Older adults in the video include Ron and Janet Adkins, Florence Austin, Robert Brown, Lawrence Collins, Marian Cowan, Faye Cruse, Sylvia Davis, Oliver Francisco, Bert and Suzanne Higert, Hayward King, Mollie Pier, Jane Potter, Leo and Lillian Salazar, June Troxell, and Mildred Tuttle.

Text

Chapter 13, "Death, Dying, Bereavement, and Widowhood," discusses the dying process, attitudes toward death, palliative care, the right to die, the increasing ethical, medical and legal issues of using life sustaining technologies, legal options of advance directives, services that assist terminally ill adults, bereavement, and widowhood.

Your instructor may provide additional readings for this lesson.

Key Points

Reactions and Coping Mechanisms in Bereavement

The longer we live, the more likely we are to lose a loved one and experience bereavement. Individuals show wide variations in their reactions to the death of a loved one. In general, research suggests that grieving involves three stages: initial shock and sorrow, a searching or questioning stage, and recovery or reorganization. The grieving process may last up to four years, and some remember the loss with pain throughout the rest of their lives.

Among women, about two-thirds of those 70 and older are widowed. Loss of a spouse is often accompanied by prolonged feelings of loss. For example, although Florence Austin's husband died in the attack on Pearl Harbor in 1941, her love for him is still strong. She moved to Hawai`i after his death and wants her ashes scattered at Pearl Harbor when she dies.

Marian Cowan still dreams of her deceased husband two years after his death. She feels his presence in the house that they shared and is reluctant to leave it although her children want her to move closer to them. Jane Potter says she talks to her husband's ghost.

The loss of a child may be especially traumatic because it is "off-time." While losing a loved one is always difficult, it is easier to rationalize the death of a grandparent or parent who has lived a long, productive life than it is to accept the death of a child. In the video, the Salazars and Mollie Pier describe the difficult emotions they encountered with the death of their respective sons.

Research suggests that individuals are more vulnerable during the year following the death of a loved one. In some cases this is due to a lowered resistance during the grieving process. In other cases, this is due to loss of social support once provided by the person who has died. For example, Dr. Meredith Minkler tells us that widowers have higher death rates within the first two years of widowhood than do non-widowed men. These men are sad to lose their wife and friend, but may also be unable to cook for themselves, forget to take medications, and lose touch with friends and family.

Women tend to have more social support than men in widowhood. Jane Potter describes how she was befriended by other widows and how this has helped her through her grieving process. Research shows that men are much more likely to remarry after being widowed than are women.

Speed of recovery after the death of a loved one also may be assisted by a feeling of completeness of the relationship. Having years to anticipate the death, for example when a loved one has a prolonged illness, may help prepare one for the actual death. However, this may not reduce the grief felt after the actual death, as we learn from the older adults in the video. For example, although Lillian Salazar feels that she did a lot of anticipatory grieving for her chronically ill son during his lifetime; tears fill her eyes when she reviews his death with us. After two years, Marian Cowan wishes she were recovering more quickly from the loss of her husband.

Lillian Salazar and Sylvia Davis were with their loved ones when they died. They both gave the person "permission" to die, i.e., they told them they could let go of life if they desired and not worry about the people left behind. This practice may have helped the survivors face death, but we can see that they still grieve deeply for their losses. Sylvia Davis reports that watching her brother die was the hardest thing she ever had to do.

Dr. Herman Feifel assures us that grieving represents a deep human psychological need and that we should not be afraid to feel and express our sorrow. Dr. Edwin Shneidman tells us not to expect a quick recovery for he feels that individuals never entirely "get over" the death of a loved one.

Dr. Elisabeth Kubler-Ross is well known as an early advocate for dying people. Dr. Ted Koff describes how Dr. Kubler-Ross would help dying mothers see their children even though children were not allowed in the hospital. Through her interviews with dying people, she identified five stages experienced by people facing their own death: denial, anger, bargaining, depression, and acceptance. There seems to be agreement now that there is no typical, unidirectional way to die through progressive stages, and subsequent research suggests that reactions to one's impending death are also very individual, influenced by personality and the specifics of the timing, type, and place of death.

In the video, we see Hayward King, who recently learned he has inoperable cancer, simultaneously express denial and depression about his imminent death. Oliver Francisco, now in the acceptance stage, is using his remaining time to resolve past conflicts. He tells us about reconciliation with one of his sons, in which they discussed their fears and regrets, forgave each other for past behaviors, and expressed their love for each other.

Dr. Feifel believes that we have distanced ourselves from the experience of death. In his youth, he remembers being involved in the death of his uncle and remembers when more people believed in life after death. These experiences led to a greater acceptance of death. Today, he says, we have "professionalized" death and view it as a finality, rather than as a door to another level of being.

Dr. Feifel sees some disadvantages with being a death-avoiding society. Melinda Grooms agrees. In her work as a hospice coordinator, she sees that "death is happening in everybody's neighborhood [but] not everybody is dealing with it real well."

On the other hand, Mildred Tuttle reports that the residents of her retirement community have become very philosophical about death. She says they talk about death all the time and feels that this helps to reduce the intensity and duration of the grieving period following the death of a fellow resident.

Services for Dying and Bereaved People

Culture helps individuals and society cope with death by providing guidelines about the entire death process, for example, our expectations about age and place of death, style of burial, behavior and dress of survivors, length of time spent in mourning, and so forth. In many cultures, religious groups and churches provide a broad spectrum of services to assist individuals with death and bereavement. Therefore, it's very important that service providers be sensitive to the cultural values, beliefs, and rituals of the dying person and his/her family.

The text refers to the "six-R process of mourning" as integrating much of what has been written about grief stages, phases, and tasks. The "six-Rs" include the ability to recognize and accept the reality of the loss, to react or experience and express pain of the separation, to reminisce, tell and re-tell the memories, to relinquish old attachments, to readjust to the environment in which the dead person is missing, and to reinvest in new personal relationships and actions of meaning instead of remaining tied to the past while recognizing that the pain of the loss may continue in life.

The classical paradigm of grief assumed grieving individuals needed to let go of their relationships with their loved ones who have passed away in order to complete their "grief work." However, later theoretical perspectives make no assumptions about the universality of how individuals respond to death. On the contrary, more recent views on grieving acknowledge the tremendous diversity of healthy grieving.

Support groups can play an important role. Although she did not discuss it in the video, Marian Cowan participated in a bereavement group following the death of her husband. Materials on death and dying illustrated for her the feelings she might experience, such as numbness. Although she expresses concern that she "continued to just float" for longer than expected, her behavior and language suggests that the group helped her better understand and cope with bereavement. Widowhood support groups also provide information on bereavement, give widows an avenue for expressing grief, and can provide a new social network. Individual psychotherapy can also be helpful.

For people who have terminal illnesses, hospice care is an important service. As described by Dr. Koff, its goals are to ease pain, to assist the terminally ill patient gain an understanding of death and a sense of completing an important lifetime journey, and to support the family of the dying person.

Melinda Grooms coordinates hospice care to Bert Higert and his wife Suzanne, and, as a nurse, monitors his health status and medications. She talks to Bert and Suzanne about their feelings and does her best to see that they are coping well with Bert's impending death. Other professionals on the hospice team include a social worker who helps Suzanne plan for future contingencies, a home health aid who helps with personal care, and other workers who can help with housework or run errands for the Higerts. A text box in Chapter 13 provides a case example of the services that hospice provided to a gentleman with rapidly advancing and painful lymphoma.

Planning for Death

People are becoming increasingly concerned with planning their own deaths. People see that it is easy to artificially prolong life and want to prevent being kept alive in a permanent, vegetative state. Many older adults, like Mollie Pier, do not want to become a burden to their children or to society. Planning for death can help adults gain some control over their final years.

Advance directives are legal documents that can provide individuals some control (a sample is included in Chapter 13 in the text and other samples can be obtained from organizations like Partnership in Caring and the Hemlock Society).

The most commonly used advance directives are the living will and the durable power of attorney for health care decisions. In contrast to a will, a living will outlines instructions to withhold life-prolonging treatment in the event of an irreversible terminal illness. A durable power of attorney for health care decisions empowers a trusted friend or family member (also called a surrogate decision maker) to make decisions about health care when you are incapacitated for any reason.

The specific definitions and authority of these documents vary from state to state, however, a federal law, called the Patient Self-Determination Act, requires that hospitals inform patients of their rights in deciding how they want to live or die.

Although all 50 states now have laws authorizing the use of some type of advance directives, the Agency for Healthcare Research and Quality (AHRQ) found in their study that less than 50% of the severely or terminally ill had an advance directive in their medical records. See text boxes on advance directives in Chapter 13.

Several of the older adults in the video have thought about their own deaths. Mollie Pier has an advance directive that states she would like to enter a nursing home if she becomes incapacitated. Florence Austin wants her ashes scattered over Pearl Harbor. Leo Salazar is planning his memorial service, including the particular songs he wants played. Lawrence Collins wants his ashes mixed with his wife's ashes and scattered on a favorite hilltop.

Hayward King is just beginning to think about how he will divide the things he's collected and how he can visit Paris one last time before his death.

Ethical Issues Concerning Dying

Average life expectancy has greatly increased since the turn of the last century. In 1900, the average life expectancy was 47 years. However, females born in 2000 can expect to live to 79.5 years while males born in the same year can expect to live to 74 years. This change is due to several factors: decreased infant mortality; improvements to diet, sanitation and public health; and the control of many infectious diseases through antibiotics.

As Dr. Feifel tells us, "in the old days, when you got old and sick, you usually didn't last very long. You died of T.B., gastritis... Today, however, because of this ability to keep people alive for longer periods of time, we die of chronic degenerative diseases like heart [disease], stroke, and cancer. And so what it's done is really elongated the time in which it takes us to die."

Advances in medical care allow us to prolong life artificially, often without increasing its quality and often at great cost. However, traditional medicine's emphasis on cure can make medical care inappropriate or unwanted at end-of-life. A study funded by the Robert Wood Johnson Foundation— SUPPORT (Study to Understand Prognoses and Preferences for Outcomes and Risks of Treatment)—found that patients and their physicians did not routinely make plans for end-of-life care. The study also found that patients most often died in pain and in intensive care for long periods of time, with their families financially devastated by their efforts to keep their loved one alive.

There are encouraging signs that end-of-life care may be improving. A trend towards being more responsive to the needs of dying patients and their families is the expansion of the hospice model of caring for the terminally ill, and professional associations of medicine, nursing, social work are instituting guidelines for better standards and training in end-of-life care.

A textbox in Chapter 13 defines pain management, hospice, and palliative care. See another textbox in the text pages which follow where the Institute of Medicine provides recommendations for improving en-of-life care.

Questions about the sanctity of life, an individual's right to die, and society's responsibility to both protect life and utilize resources for the common good are very much in the forefront of moral, ethical and legal arenas. "Right to Life" proponents argue that all life should be protected, regardless of individual wishes or societal costs. They warn that having the power to end life may lead to systematic killing of people deemed useless by society.

On the other hand, "Right to Die" proponents remind us that the United States was founded on individual rights, and that people should be able to take their own lives if they want to.

They would like to be able to have "death with dignity" meaning that they would like to die while they still have some control over their bodies and their decisions. Under the principles of informed consent and right-to-know, patients must be told of their diagnosis, prognosis, and treatment options and allowed to accept or refuse treatment based on their understanding of its risks and benefits.

Some individuals with degenerative and disabling diseases may consider a form of active euthanasia, for example, suicide or assisted death/suicide. Tanya Blume's father, for example, felt that the quality of his life was so low that suicide was an appropriate option for him. In his suicide note, he hopes his children will have access to legal euthanasia.

Bob Brown, who has Parkinson's disease, has told his family that he will want help with dying when the time comes. His daughter, Bev Ickes, respects his wishes although the thought of his death clearly distresses her. Janet Adkins, who had Alzheimer's disease, wanted to die before becoming mentally incapacitated. She was able to find assistance from Dr. Jack Kevorkian who loaned her a device that allowed her to inject herself with a lethal drug.

A text box in Chapter 13, "Oregon: The Only State to Legalize Physician-Assisted Suicide" briefly discusses "The Death with Dignity Act," while another text box documents the history of major events to the right to die movement in the U.S.

Passive euthanasia, on the other hand, refers to allowing a person to die by not using all available interventions. Examples of passive euthanasia include withholding medications, food, and water.

Euthanasia is most openly practiced in The Netherlands when certain criteria are met: repeated, enduring requests for euthanasia by the patient; unbearable physical or psychological suffering; opinions from at least two physicians that the patient is terminally ill; and the exhaustion of all acceptable medical treatments. See the text box in Chapter 13 on the "History of Major events Related to the Rght-to-Die Movement in the United States."

Rationing of health care to the frail elderly is another issue of public concern, as noted by Msgr. Fahey. On the one hand, we shouldn't deprive people access to health care simply because they are old. On the other hand, we shouldn't prolong life in very old people because this takes resources away from care and services for younger generations.

Msgr. Fahey feels we should avoid the extremes. He suggests that we respect individual rights, but not take away a person's life just because he/she is not productive. The young medical students discuss their experiences with death, and try to reconcile a patient's right to die with a professional mandate to heal and keep people alive. Dr. Susan Tolle, however, seems to have resolved this dichotomy in her mind as she treats June Troxell, a patient with ALS. June has said she wants nothing done to prolong her life. Dr. Tolle has agreed to respect June's wishes by helping prevent suffering but not artificially prolonging life.

Dr. Feifel provides the following insight. On both the personal level and societal level, we need to find a balance between our fight to survive and an acceptance, or appreciation, of death. For, he says, it is important to remember that "death enhances the meaning and the value of life," making life all the more precious.

Key Terms and Concepts from the Text, Video, and *Study Guide*

Advance Directives
Anticipatory Grief
Appropriate Death
Assisted Death, Assisted Suicide
Autonomy
Autopsy
Bereavement
Bereavement Overload
Bioethics
Compassion in Dying Federation
Conservatorship
Death System
Death with Dignity
Do Not Resuscitate (DNR) Order
Dying Person's Bill of Rights
Dying Process
Dying Trajectory
Durable Power of Attorney for Health Care
    Decisions
Ethics Committee

Euthanasia, Active
Euthanasis, Passive
Geronticide
Grief Process
Guardianship
Hemlock Society
Hospice
Informed Consent
Last Acts
Living Will
Mercy Killing
Mourning
Palliative Care
Partnership in Caring
Patient Self-Determination Act
Right-to-Die
Right-to-Know
Suicide
Surrogate Decision Maker
Terminal Illness

Self-Study Questions

Instructions. Fill in the blank with the appropriate word or phrase from the list of Key Terms and Concepts. Note: Only 22 of the 39 key terms and concepts can be used.

1) A _____ is a disease that will lead to death within a short period of time, usually less than a year.

2) The principles of _____ and _____ refer to a patient's right to understand his/her diagnosis, prognosis, and treatment options to make decisions about further care.

3) National organizations that want to improve care to dying people and provide information on advance directives include _____ and _____. An organization that advocates for the right-to-die is the _____.

4) The _____ is a federal law requiring that health care facilities inform their patients about their rights to decide how they want to live or die, for example, by providing them information on refusing treatment and on filing advance directives.

5) An examination of the body after death, usually done to identify or validate the cause of death, is called an _____.

6) In a _____ program, terminally ill people receive palliative care in concert with spiritual and/or psychosocial therapies to help them accept death.

7) A legal document that empowers a trusted friend or family member to make decisions about the kind of health care you receive in the event of your incapacitation is called a _____. This person is also known as a _____.

8) If you deliberately cause your own death, you are committing _____. If you help a friend or doctor to kill his/herself, you are engaging in

_____.

9) As defined by Elisabeth Kubler-Ross, dying persons experience five stages in reaction to their death: 1) denial and isolation, 2) anger and resentment, 3) bargaining, 4) depression, and 5) acceptance. This is called the _____.

10) The _____ refers to the experience of bereavement in three stages: shock and sorrow, questioning or searching, and recovery/reorganization.

11) A _____ is a legal document outlining one's desire that medical treatment be withheld or withdrawn if it will not provide cure and merely prolongs the dying process.

12) Treatment designed to relieve pain provided to a person with a terminal illness for whom death is imminent is called _____.

13) If you permit the death of a hopelessly sick or injured person by withholding medication, food, or water, you are engaging in _____.

If you help them overdose on sedatives, you are engaging in _____ or _____.

14) _____ are documents that outline actions to be taken for you by others when you cannot give directions yourself, for example in the event of death, incapacitation, or irreversible, terminal illness. The three most common of these are the will, the living will, and the durable power of attorney for health care decisions.

15) _____ is a national not-for profit organization that has provided national leadership on living wills, guided the enactment of advance directives in all states, and lobbied for the passage of the Patient Self-Determination Act.

Use the Glossary at the end of the Study Guide to check your answers.

Topics for Discussion

1) How does our society seek to deny or avoid death?

2) What are some issues for people to consider when preparing for death? What can you do in your own life to prepare for your own death?

Website Challenge

Visit the following websites that can provide more information on this lesson's topics. Bookmark them for easy access in the future:

1) Download state-specific advance directives from Partnership for Caring at http://www.partnershipforcaring.org/

2) Compassion in Dying at http://www.compassionindying.org

3) DeathNet at http://www.rights.org/lowband.shtml

4) GriefNet at http://rivendell.org

Written Assignments

Your instructor may ask you to complete one or more of the written assignments that follow.

Reaction Paper: New Knowledge and Feelings Stimulated by the Video

Write a two-page paper describing: 1) new information gained from watching the video; 2) how the experiences of the older adults in the video affected your personal view of aging; and 3) other comments to the instructor regarding this lesson or the course.

Older-Adult Interview

Interview a person who is 65 years or older, asking the questions below. Write a three-to-five page paper about the interviewee's experiences with death and bereavement. **Note**: This topic might be sensitive. If you encounter resistance to discussing these ideas, choose another person to interview. As Dr. Feifel says, "we are a death-avoiding society."

Interview Questions

1) Have you experienced the death of a loved one? If so, may I ask you some questions about this experience?

- Who died? Under what circumstances? How long ago was that?

- Do you remember the emotions that your loved one experienced during the process of dying? Explain.

- How did you feel about the death at that time? Why?

- Did you go through a grieving process? Did your feelings or thoughts change as time passed? How long did it take to go through this process? How do you feel about the death now?

2) Have you thought about your own death? If so, would you mind sharing your thoughts about it with me?

- When did you start thinking about death?

- How do you view death? Has your view of death changed over time? If so, in what ways, and what caused it to change?

- Are you familiar with advanced directives, such as the will, living will, and durable power of attorney for health care decisions? If so, have you filed, or would you file, advanced directives for yourself?

- Have you thought about other death preparations, such as buying a cemetery plot, or planning the type of funeral or memorial ceremony you would like? If so, please share your thoughts or plans with me.

Student Questions

1) Did the interviewee's grieving process follow the stages described in the text? Explain.

2) What additional preparations for death would you recommend for your interviewee?

3) How has this interview affected your personal view of aging and older adults?

Community Interview

Listed below are examples of health and social services designed to assist terminally ill or bereaved older adults. **Note**: The term "spiritual advisors" refers to priests, ministers, rabbis, monks, kahunas, gurus, imams, and shamans, i.e., spiritual leaders of various religious groups.

-Make Today Count
-Compassionate Friends
-AIDS support groups
-Bereavement support groups
-Widows groups
-Hospice
-Hemlock Society
-Funeral homes
-Choice in Dying
-Memorial societies
-Crematoriums
-Religious and spiritual advisors

Work with your instructor to identify a program or professional in your community. Interview someone who works with adults facing death, asking the questions below. Write a three- to five-page paper on your findings.

1) What is your name and position? How long have you been involved in this line of work?

2) What is the history of the organization, group, or service you are involved with? Why was it started? What are its goals and objectives?

3) Who are the clients? What are the eligibility requirements, if any?

4) What programs/services are offered? How do they help older adults and their families with the dying or bereavement process?

5) How do clients involved in your program/service benefit from it? Give examples of clients whom you have helped through the dying or bereavement process.

6) How many paid staff and volunteers work with you? What are their roles? What training is required?

7) How is the program/service funded?

8) What do you feel are the program's limitations (for example, types of services, location and hours of services, eligibility requirements of clients)?

9) What could be done to help the program/service better meet its goals?

Research Paper

Select one of the topics below for in-depth study. Read a book or five journal articles on the topic. A good place to start searching for reading material is in the reference section provided at the end of each text chapter. Write a five- to ten-page research paper that describes the historical and current thinking on the topic. Identify things about the topic that are not yet resolved or may benefit from further study.

1) What is hospice? What is the history of its development and funding? Compare its philosophical basis to that of acute hospital or nursing home. Which types of hospice programs work best?

2) Compare and contrast the "right to life" movement and the "right to die" movement. How did each develop? What are their philosophical platforms? Which policy decisions of concern to these two groups are being discussed at the current time?

3) Compare and contrast suicide rates and reasons for men and women by age groups.

4) Compare and contrast one of the Western religions (Christianity, Judaism) with one of the other major world religions (Islam, Hinduism, Buddhism, Taoism) on their views of death and their death practices.

5) Read publications by Elisabeth Kubler-Ross. How did she determine the stages of the dying process? Which research methods did she use to test her theories?

Thinking About the Future: Giving It All Away
(This assignment was adapted with permission from a similar assignment by Mitsuo Aoki, Ph.D., Professor Emeritus, University of Hawai`i at Manoa.)

In our culture, few of us take the time to write our wills until we have reason to believe that our death is imminent. We commonly assume that a will is not necessary until we are elderly. Even then, wills are often written in a language that does not adequately convey the personal feelings and meaning involved.

This exercise helps explore the feelings that might be associated with the process of giving up our prized possessions and leaving them to the persons of our own choosing.

1) Think about ten prized possessions you currently own.

- Write the name of each possession and what you value most about the possession.

- Then, for each possession, choose a person you would most like to give it to when you die.
- Choose a different person for each possession.

2) Write a paper about your ten prized possessions and who you gave them to and why. Include in the paper the answers to the following questions:

- What kinds of feelings did you become aware of during this experience?

- What was it like for you to describe your valued possessions?

- What was it like to choose people to whom to give your possessions?

- What kinds of feelings do you now have about your possessions? Your loved ones?

- What feelings do you now have about writing wills?

SOCIETAL AND POLITICAL ASPECTS OF AGING

Learning Objectives

1) Discuss factors that affect elders' participation and success in the political process.

2) Describe four major social programs developed to meet the needs of older adults in the United States.

3) Explain why long-term care presents a major policy issue for the United States.

Summary of the Video and Text

Video

The video has three segments. The first explains how the status of older adults corresponds to the resources they control. It also explores the roles older adults currently play in the political arena. The second segment presents information on a number of social programs developed to meet the needs of older adults in the U.S., including: Social Security, Supplemental Security Income, Medicare, Medicaid, the Older Americans Act, and various housing programs. The third segment focuses on long-term care. Because long-term care is so expensive and because the demand for long-term care is growing, its financing is a major policy issue facing the U.S.

Experts appearing in the video include Representative Neil Abercrombie, former Representative Thomas Downey, Msgr. Charles Fahey, Robert Harootyan, Samuel Simmons, and Drs. Robert Atchley, Colette Browne, Kenneth Brummel-Smith, Robert Clark, Linda Martin, Marta Sotomayor, Robyn Stone, Jeanette Takamura, and Fernando Torres-Gil. Two service providers, William Narang and Mary Alice Stevenson, also present their views. Older adults who share their experiences with us include Arthur Boudreault, Ilse Darling, Jean Jaworski, Mabel McConnell, Jack Rice, Leo Salazar, and Lois Swift.

Text

New Reading. "The Societal Context of Aging" provides an introduction to Chapters 16 and 17. Included are two vignettes that illustrate how the economic times and the presence or absence of social programs affect older adults.

Chapter 16, "Social Policies to Address Social Problems," presents information on how and why social policies are developed, traces the historical development of aging policy in the U.S., and describes several income and service programs that benefit older Americans.

Chapter 17, "Health and Long-Term Care Policy and Programs," discusses health programs that benefit older Americans, including Medicare, Medicaid, Title XX, and the Older Americans Act. Presented also are problems with the current method of financing acute and long-term care for the elderly and various strategies being piloted or being considered that may contain health care costs.

Review. In Chapter 12, "Productive Aging: Paid and Non-paid Roles and Activities," review the section on Political Participation.

Your instructor may provide additional readings for this lesson.

Key Points

Factors Affecting Political Participation

Political participation includes voting, participating in political parties and advocacy groups, and holding public office. As described in Chapter 12 of the text, research suggests that older adults are more politically active than young people. For example, a greater proportion of older adults vote. Older members of political parties tend to have more influence within the party. A number of elected officials are older adults. However, age is not a predictor of whether a person is liberal or conservative, as pointed out by Dr. Fernando Torres-Gil.

Political beliefs are usually related to personal experience and exposure, rather than age, and rarely change over the life course. To illustrate, Leo Salazar tells us he has always been a Democrat.

Political activity varies by gender, health status, educational status, and ethnicity. For example, women traditionally have been less politically active than men, people in poor health are less active than people in good health, and less educated people are less active than better educated people. Samuel Simmons thinks more elderly African Americans should be involved, but notes that older African Americans are much more active than younger people.

Many experts in the video see older adults as a powerful constituency. What factors affect power? Dr. Linda Martin reminds us that the status (or power) of older adults corresponds to their control of resources. (Illustrations of this concept are provided in Chapter 2 of the text.) The resources of today's older adults include the large number of programs (about 50) that are directed specifically toward older persons. In terms of government spending, about 23% of the federal budget is spent on Social Security and another 12% is spent on Medicare; that means that slightly more than a third of the federal budget is spent on two programs that primarily benefit older adults. In addition, seniors have power because of their vast numbers and their relatively high levels of political participation, wealth, health, and leisure time.

Former Representative Thomas Downey reminds us that many older adults belong to advocacy groups like the American Association of Retired Persons (AARP). Senior advocacy groups have been successful at involving older adults in organized lobbying campaigns. Samuel Simmons relates how older adults got their City Council to vote a certain way on an issue by bringing ten busloads of seniors to City Hall. Representative Neil Abercrombie sees the older voter as the "single most potent force in the political spectrum today."

How do older adults learn to lobby? Silver-Haired Legislatures teach older adults how to create and lobby for legislation. The National Council of Senior Citizens and AARP involve older adults in political activities.

Ilse Darling thinks that many older adults join AARP for its drug and travel discounts, rather than its advocacy. Still, with more than 35 million members, AARP represents a powerful force in Washington, DC.

A policy is a principle that governs societal action about a specific concern. The U.S. has been developing its aging policy for more than half a century (see Table 16.2 in the text). But many European nations already had developed programs for the elderly by the time the U.S. Social Security Act of 1935 was established. In addition, the level of federal commitment and the reasons behind this commitment have varied over the years.

In the 1960s and 1970s, Dr. Torres-Gil tells us, Congress automatically assumed that older people were deserving and worthy of special programs. It was during that time that major programs for older adults were developed, including Medicare, Medicaid, the Older Americans Act, Supplemental Security Income, Section 202 Housing, and Title XX social services legislation.

In the 1980s, societal attitudes toward older adults changed. In these times of fiscal constraints, older adults began to be viewed as "greedy geezers" who benefitted from their special federal programs at the expense of other age groups. This stereotype was reinforced in the Medicare Catastrophic debacle, as Dr. Robyn Stone calls it. The Medicare Catastrophic Health Care Act, passed in 1988, imposed an additional tax on upper-income elders so that the Medicare program could limit out-of-pocket expenses, provide protection against spousal impoverishment, and increase coverage for skilled nursing home and home care for older adults who experienced a severe illness.

Although it did not provide protection against the costs of extended long-term care, a number of professional groups and members of Congress thought it would reduce health care worries and acute care costs for older adults. Congress was surprised by the large numbers of older adults who protested the tax. These protests led to the legislation's repeal in 1989. Former Representative Downey remembers this experience as "one of the more unhappy moments in Congress."

Since then, politicians have been leery of funding new programs for the elderly. Some groups are lobbying to reduce government spending for the elderly in favor of other age groups; they think older adults are selfish. Representative Abercrombie believes that most older people are not selfish, but are acting out of fear. They are worried that increases in life span and spiraling costs of health care will put them into poverty. For more recent points of discussion on this issue, see text boxes on "Current Context Framing the Social Security Debates" and "Values Reflected in Current Social Security System" in Chapter 16.

As we move through the 1990s, the experts feel that greater emphasis will be placed on developing programs that are need-based (or means-based), rather than age-based, to fairly distribute resources to those of all ages who are in greatest need. But these efforts to resolve "age wars" must not be allowed to turn into "ethnic wars." Dr. Torres-Gil notes that in 2020, when 20% of the population will be elderly and the majority of them Caucasian, more people from minority populations will be in the labor force. Today's seniors must support today's minority youth so that they will become good contributors to the tax base that pays for many eldercare programs.

One way to do this is to agree to pay increased taxes to support public schools. At the same time, young minority Americans must support programs like Social Security and Medicare so that they will be available to minority Americans when they reach old age. As many of our experts suggest, we need to recognize and strengthen interdependence among generations and ethnic groups.

Major U.S. Programs Benefiting Older Adults

The Older Americans Act (OAA), enacted in 1965, funds the "aging services network." Within this network, funds flow from Washington, DC to State Units on Aging (one in each state), which plan and advocate for services for older adults in the state. Area Agencies on Aging (about 700 have been established) work under their states' guidelines to plan and coordinate services within their jurisdictions.

The types of services that receive full or partial funding through the OAA include senior centers, nutrition services, access services, transportation, in-home services, and legal assistance (see text box "Services Provided Under the Older Americans Act" in Chapter 16).

Some senior centers provide a range of services. For example, Mary Alice Stevenson, director of a senior center in downtown San Francisco, says they offer lunch, socialization, classes, legal assistance, financial counseling, access to the library, and other activities. She laments cuts in funding for such a worthwhile program. In fact, nationwide limitations in funding require OAA providers to try to target their services to older adults who are low-income, frail, minority, or rural. As Samuel Simmons tells us, African American elders and older adults living in rural areas often do not have access to needed services.

Title XX of the Social Security Act is another federal program that provides funds for eldercare services, including homemaker, chore services, home-delivered meals, adult day care, foster care, residential care, and adult protective services. The text explains that Title XX money is now part of the Social Services Block Grant program, in which states receive a large block of money for low-income people of all ages and can decide how to spend it. Under this new arrangement, many states have shifted money away from eldercare services and toward programs for children.

Housing policy also affects older adults. Compared to many European countries, the U.S. does not provide much public housing. Strong construction and real estate lobbies and the desire for private home ownership both work against the enactment of federal programs that would provide public housing on a large scale. A few small programs exist, even though support for them was slashed 80% during the Reagan-Bush administrations. Through Section 8 of the Department of Housing and Urban Development (HUD), for example, older adults can get rent subsidies. Lois Swift tells us she receives $215 a month to help pay her rent.

Through Section 202 of HUD, low-interest loans are available to nonprofit groups that agree to build housing for lower-income and disabled persons. Leisure World, which provides housing and support services to older adults, was built using HUD money and expects to pay off its mortgage by the year 2000. Once the payments are finished, William Narang says that Leisure World will no longer have to comply with HUD's rules to rent to lower-income and disabled people. Because the land Leisure World sits on is so valuable, he fears that a new manager may then change or even sell Leisure World.

The two major income programs, Social Security and Supplemental Security Income, were introduced in Program Lesson 9, "Work, Retirement, and Economic Status." To review, the 1935 Social Security Act and its amendments established a system by which workers contribute a portion of their pay throughout life in exchange for monthly Social Security checks after retirement.

Dr. Robert Atchley likens Social Security to car insurance; you pay premiums regularly and then receive payments when you are eligible. He also reminds us that Social Security benefits the entire society. Without it, fewer older adults could retire, increasing competition between older people and younger people for jobs. In addition, more older adults would be dependent on their children for support. On average, Social Security pays older recipients about 41% of their pre-retirement income and, for many older adults, it is their primary source of income in retirement.

Several factors are converging that threaten the Social Security Trust Fund, including increased numbers of long-living older people, increased numbers of older adults taking early retirement, and decreased numbers of employed young people in the workforce. In the video, Dr. Robert Clark tells us that the 1983 amendments to the program, which reduced benefits and increased revenues, will keep the Social Security system solvent for at least 75 more years.

The 2004 Old-Age and Survivors' Insurance and Disability (OASDI) Trust Funds Trustees' Report says that a funding shortfall will not occur until at least the year 2042. At that time, Congress will be able to pay only 75% of its obligations promised to future retirees. See the textbox in Chapter 16 on "Should a 25-year-old Worry About Future Social Security Benefits?"

Very poor elderly people can receive a small monthly income from the Supplemental Security Income (SSI) program. Samuel Simmons reminds us that SSI does **not** pay enough to bring recipients above the official poverty level. Many experts believe that, with minor reforms, the SSI programs could go a lot farther in keeping older adults from poverty.

Robert Harootyan tells us that the original proposal that led to Medicare was for a national health insurance program for all ages. Following protests by interest groups against national health insurance, the program was redesigned to target older adults who contribute to the Social Security system.

Still, it took two decades to pass Title XVIII of the Social Security Act, which established the current Medicare program. A textbox in Chapter 17 lists the components of Medicare's two parts: Part A, providing partial coverage of hospitalization and a very limited amount of skilled nursing and home care, and Part B, which provides partial coverage of physician services, outpatient services, diagnostic x-ray and laboratory services. For today's seniors, the bulk of their hospital stays and doctors' visits are covered, at least partially, by Medicare.

What is meant by partial coverage? Medicare pays only 80% of "allowable charges" and many physicians charge more than the amount established by Medicare. Who pays the rest? Some physicians "take assignment," which means they agree to charge what Medicare pays. Some older adults pay the difference out of their own pockets.

About 90% of the older population have additional insurance, known as "medigap" insurance, to cover the 20% Medicare does not pay. "Medigap" insurance also covers some of Medicare's required deductibles. Jack Rice and Lois Swift both tell us that they are happy with the coverage provided by Medicare and their "medigap" insurance (Blue Cross/Blue Shield). Ilse Darling, who belongs to three health insurance programs, tells us that she must apply to each program separately for coverage, making the process very time-consuming and frustrating. She feels this contributes to the high cost of medical care.

Adults 65 years and older consistently spend more on prescription drugs than younger adults. Older adults not only account for over 40% of total spending on medication, about 40% of Medicare beneficiaries also lack drug coverage at some point each year, most for the entire year. The text also states that the burden of drug costs falls the hardest on older women, those ove age 80, those without high school education, and those in poor health or with three or more ADL limitations.

While Medicare is an age-entitlement program financed by individual contributions over a lifetime, Medicaid is a need-entitlement program funded jointly by federal and state governments. This means that Medicaid is available only to low-income people, but of any age. States have some flexibility in how Medicaid funds are spent, but most states cover hospital care, physician services, outpatient services, skilled nursing home care, and intermediate (custodial) nursing home care.

To qualify for Medicaid, an individual must "spend down" income and assets very close to the poverty threshold. Sometimes, becoming eligible for Medicaid is the only way an individual can afford extended nursing home care, which may cost between $40,000 and $80,000 a year.

In fact, most nursing home care in the U.S. is paid for by Medicaid. A recent amendment to the Medicaid program, the Spousal Impoverishment Plan, now allows the spouse of an institutionalized person supported by Medicaid to retain a relatively generous amount of income and assets, rather than be subjected to impoverishment as previously required.

The video points out a number of problems with the Medicare and Medicaid programs. Dr. Kenneth Brummel-Smith tells us that Medicare has an "institutional bias" in that the majority of funds are used to pay for hospital and nursing home care, rather than community-based or home-based care. Dr. Stone says that Medicaid has an "institutional bias" as well. The exception is the Medicaid Waiver program, through which states can use Medicaid dollars to pay for home-based services. But these programs serve a limited number of people who need care.

These points are also reflected in the text— a key limitation of Medicare is its focus on acute care versus coverage for care of chronic illnesses which are common among older adults. Hence, the majority of Medicare dollars goes to hospital care, typically for catastrophic illness and increasingly for home care while nursing home care is restricted to the first 100 days. Recent research findings cited in the text also indicate that some people underestimate nursing home care costs while others, believing that Medicare pays for long-term care, become aware of the first 100 days limit for nursing homes only upon their first hospitalization or admission to a nursing home.

Another problem is that Medicare and Medicaid help perpetuate a two-tier system of health care, one for low-income people and one for middle-income and high-income people. For example, some health care providers refuse to treat Medicaid and poorer Medicare patients because the assigned reimbursement is too low. Thus, poor people have fewer options for care or may not have access to care at all. If a person has Medigap insurance or can pay high out-of-pocket expenses, he/she can go to any health care provider for care. Robert Harootyan tells us that 40 million U.S. citizens are uninsured or underinsured and that this is a form of health care rationing.

Representative Abercrombie advocates for a nationally sponsored system of providing adequate health care to all citizens regardless of their ability to pay. The U.S. and South Africa are the only developed countries in the world that do not provide their citizens with a form of national health care.

Long-Term Care as a Major U.S. Policy Issue

Many people in the U.S. are talking about national health care. But Dr. Stone tells us that the issues surrounding long-term care have, as yet, been left out of the health care debate.

Long-term care refers to medical, nursing, and social services provided to people with chronic illness who need daily assistance with self-care activities at home, in the community, or in an institution. In earlier programs, we met several older adults who needed long-term care, including Lillian Salazar's father (who was assisted by a home health worker); Tatsuno Ogawa (who eventually entered a nursing home); Allen Tateishi's mother (who had Alzheimer's disease); and Bert Higert (who was receiving help from a hospice program).

As we learned in Program Lesson 10, "Illness and Disability," a continuum of services may be needed to help older people with disabilities to live at home. However, the U.S. health care system is more oriented toward funding acute care. Private long-term care insurance is very expensive and may not cover every service in the continuum of care. Consequently, only between 10% and 20% of older adults can afford long-term care insurance, and older women are less likely than older men to be able to afford to do so.

The text also points out that most long-term care policies are written to exclude people with certain illnesses and conditions, and contain benefit restrictions that limit access to covered care. Ideally, a national long-term care policy would assure that all of the services in the continuum were available and affordable to all persons needing them.

While many communities currently have a variety of the long-term care services, they are usually difficult to access because of their varying funding mechanisms, eligibility requirements, and waiting lists. For example, Medicare pays for skilled nursing home care but not intermediate (custodial) nursing home care. OAA and Title XX funds cannot be spent on nursing homes at all and funding for home and community services is limited.

Except under a waiver, Medicaid does not pay for home-delivered meals or respite and individuals must "spend down" before qualifying for it. Only very low-income adults are eligible for SSI and rent subsidies. Older adults who never paid into the Social Security system do not receive Social Security checks after retirement and do not qualify for Medicare Part A. Because of these complexities, older adults often seek the services of a case manager who can link them with appropriate programs and sources of funds. When no services or no funding are available, older adults and their families must do without long-term care assistance. For such examples, see textbox, "The Impact of State Budget Cuts on Long-Term Care Services for Low Income Elders" in Chapter 17.

Why doesn't the U.S. have a comprehensive program of long-term care delivery and funding? Part of the problem, according to Dr. Stone, is our philosophy. Many Americans believe that citizens should take responsibility for their current and future survival and that the government should have a residual role. In other words, they feel strongly that the government should **not** be allowed to expand its control over goods, services, and individual behaviors or to promise citizens a lot of services. Dr. Stone tells us that Canada has a very different philosophy. Canadians feel that everyone is entitled to certain services, including acute and long-term care.

For them, "it is unfathomable...that a person cannot get access to a nursing home bed, or that there are no alternative services available in the home or community setting."

Dr. Jeanette Takamura reminds us that long-term care is a family issue. The majority of long-term care is provided by families and this is true for all ethnicities. Caregivers make tremendous sacrifices in time and money and Dr. Takamura warns that they risk burning out. Despite the failure of the federal government to develop a comprehensive long-term care policy, at least 35 states are proceeding to develop their own. Dr. Takamura led Hawai`i's efforts, never enacted, to establish a statewide program for financing long-term care, called the Family Hope program.

An important new program, the National Family Caregiver Support Program (NFCSP) was established in 2000 to help family caregivers. The program calls for all states, working in partnership with local area agencies on aging and faith- and community-service providers and tribes to offer five direct services that best meet the range of caregivers' needs.

These services include information to caregivers about available services, assistance to caregivers in gaining access to supportive services, and individual counseling, organization of support groups, and caregiver training to assist caregivers in making decisions and solving problems relating to their roles.

Other services include respite care to enable caregivers to be temporarily relieved from their caregiving responsibilities, and supplemental services, on a limited basis, to complement the care provided by caregivers.

The NFCSP received a congressional appropriation of $125 million in fiscal year 2001 and $141.5 million in fiscal year 2002. In fiscal year 2003, the program received $155.2 million. Most funds are allocated to states through a congressionally mandated formula that is based on a proportionate share of the 70+ population. For more information about this program in your county, contact the area agency on aging.

Key Terms and Concepts from the Text, Video, and *Study Guide*

Access Services
Age-Based Programs
Aging Network
Americans for Generational Equity
Area Agencies on Aging
Blaming the Victim
Block Grants
Cash Substitute
Cash Transfer
Categorical
Contributory Programs
Cost Containment
Cost Effectiveness
Cost Efficiency
Diagnostic Related Groupings
Direct Benefit
Discharge Planning
Eligibility Criteria
Entitlement Programs
Gap Group
Generation X
Generational Investment
Health Care Financing Administration (HCFA)
Health Maintenance Organizations (HMOs)
Income Redistribution
Incremental
Index
Indirect Benefit
In-Home Services
Long-Term Care Insurance
Means-Based Programs
Means-Tested Programs
Medicaid
Medicaid Waiver
Medicare

Medicare Catastrophic Health Care Act
Medigap Insurance
National Health Care
Need-Based Programs
Non-Contributory Programs
Nutrition Programs
Older Americans Act
Outreach
Payroll Taxes
Policy
Politics of Diversity
Politics of Entitlement
Politics of Productivity
Rationing of Health Care
Residual Role of Government
Safety Net
Selective Benefits
Senior Center Programs
Silver-Haired Legislatures
Social Adequacy
Social Health Maintenance Organizations (SHMOs)
Social Insurance
Social Program
Social Security
Social Services Block Grant
Spending Down
Spousal Impoverishment Plan
State Units on Aging
Supplemental Security Income
Title XX of the Social Security Act
Two-Tier System of Health Care
Universal Benefits
Veterans Administration

Self-Study Questions

Instructions. Fill in the blank with the appropriate word or phrase from the list of Key Terms and Concepts. Note: Only 23 of the 68 key terms and concepts can be used.

1) A _____ is a principle that governs societal action about a specific concern.

2) _____ are the rules that govern who can participate in a program.

3) _____ are state offices that engage in statewide planning and advocacy on behalf of older adults in the state. _____ operate at the regional and local level to develop and administer service plans to meet the needs of older adults within that locale.

4) The _____ is the federal law that established and funds state and local offices to plan, coordinate, provide, and contract services for older adults.

5) The system of social services for older adults funded by the Older Americans Act and other sources is also referred to as the _____.

6) _____ is a federal health insurance program that provides partial coverage for medical care costs of older adults who contributed to the Social Security system.

7) The U.S. and South Africa are the only developed countries in the world that do not provide their citizens with a form of _____.

8) Programs available to individuals based on need, like Supplemental Security Income, are sometimes called _____, _____, or _____.

9) The _____ was an amendment to the Medicaid program that allows the spouse of an institutionalized person supported by Medicaid to retain a relatively generous amount of income and assets, rather than spend down to poverty as previously required.

10) Programs, for example Social Security, that are available to all people of a certain age are sometimes called _____.

11) The _____ refers to attempts to restrict access to health care to save money.

12) The _____ is a government program that provides health care for war veterans through hospitals, nursing homes, and contracts with community facilities.

13) _____ is a program jointly financed by federal and state government that provides coverage for health care costs of low-income people regardless of age. It is the primary payment source for nursing homes.

14) _____ is insurance that can be purchased from private companies to cover some of the long-term care services that you might need in the future. Only a small number of adults have this kind of insurance.

15) Insurance that can be purchased to cover a large portion of health care expenses not covered by Medicare is called _____.

16) Spending one's savings until they are low enough to meet the income criteria for a program like Medicaid is called _____.

17) The _____ was federal law passed in 1988 that imposed an additional tax on upper-income elders so that the Medicare program could provide better protection to people with severe illness. A huge grassroots protest by older adults led to its repeal in 1989.

18) People in the _____ are neither rich enough to pay privately for services they need nor poor enough to qualify for government assistance.

19) Exceptions to the Medicaid rules that allow states to use Medicaid dollars (usually restricted to pay for nursing home care) to pay for selected home-based long-term care services are called

_____.

20) Under the _____ system, states decide which social programs to fund and which citizens are eligible for them.

21) _____ is a national program to help family caregivers.

Use the Glossary at the end of the Study Guide to check your answers.

Topics for Discussion

1) Discuss the pros and cons of age-based versus need-based services.

2) Discuss the pros and cons for the elderly and their families of a national, comprehensive long-term care financing program.

3) Discuss the pros and cons for privatizing the Social Security system.

Website Challenge

Visit the following websites that can provide more information on this lesson's topics. Bookmark them for easy access in the future.

1) Administration on Aging at http://www.aoa.gov

2) Medicare and Medicaid Consumer Information at http://www.cms.hhs.gov/

3) Long-Term Care Quiz at http://gltc.jhancock.com/ltcbasics/quiz.cfm#quiz

Written Assignments

Your instructor may ask you to complete one or more of the written assignments that follow.

Reaction Paper: New Knowledge and Feelings Stimulated by the Video

Write a two-page paper describing: 1) new information gained from watching the video; 2) how the experiences of the older adults in the video affected your personal view of aging; and 3) other comments to the instructor regarding this lesson or the course.

Older-Adult Interview

Work with your instructor to identify an older adult (60 or older) who is active with an organization concerned with laws and programs affecting older adults. Interview that person, asking the questions below. Write a three- to five-page paper about the interviewee's political activity.

Interview Questions
1) Do you vote? Has your voting behavior changed over the years? Why or why not?

2) Most people in the U.S. are Democrats or Republicans. What is your political affiliation? Has your party affiliation changed over the years? Why or why not?

3) Tell me about your current political activity. What issues are you most concerned about?

4) If you work with a particular lobbying organization, tell me about the organization.

   a) When was it founded?

   b) Who belongs? What are the benefits of belonging? What is your role in the organization?

   c) What lobbying successes has the organization had in the past? Please describe one of your successes.

   d) What issues is the group working on now? Explain the group's lobbying methods. Are they working?

   e) Would you recommend that other people join this organization? Why or why not?

Student Questions

1) How do the activities of your interviewee compare with the information on political participation provided in the text?

2) Is the interviewee concerned with improving one of the programs discussed in the text? Explain.

3) Has this interview affected in any way your personal view of aging and older adults? Explain.

Community Interview

Listed below are the generic names of agencies that study your community's population of older adults and coordinate services to meet their needs.

   -Area Agency on Aging
   -State Unit on Aging

Work with your instructor to identify a contact at one of these agencies.

Interview an employee who knows about your community's population of older adults, asking the questions below. Write a three- to five-page paper on your findings.

If you are interviewing someone at your State Unit on Aging, ask questions about the state. If you are interviewing someone at an Area Agency on Aging, apply these questions to the census areas covered by the agency.

1) What is your name and position within the agency? How long have you worked here?

2) What is the history of the agency? When was it started? How is it funded? What are its goals and objectives?

3) What services does the agency provide?

4) What policy issues is your agency concerned with at this time? How does your agency go about recommending and encouraging policy changes?

5) Tell me about your advisory committee. How many older adults belong to it? What are the ethnic and gender compositions of the committee? What role does the advisory committee play?

6) Do young adults support the work you do? How do you know?

7) How many staff work here? What do they do? What are their qualifications?

8) How many volunteers work here? What are their roles?

Elected Official Interview

Work with your instructor to identify an elected official who knows about past and current legislation concerning older adults. Interview the official, asking the questions below.

If the elected official is not available, interview a member of the staff. Ask the staff person to answer for the elected official as best as possible. Write a three- to five-page paper on your findings.

1) What is your name and title? When were you elected to this position? Did you hold any other political offices before you were elected to this office?

2) What is your background? When did you become interested in politics? Why?

3) On what committees do you serve? Tell me about the kinds of policy issues that come before your committees.

4) Can you tell me about any past or current policy issues concerning older adults that this body addressed? What are they? Please describe your stand on these issues.

5) Do older adults lobby you? How do they do it (e.g., do they write letters? do they give testimony?) Does their lobbying have an effect? Why or why not?

6) Overall, what do you see as the pressing social issues facing our community? How would you prioritize the needs of the elderly population in relationship to other community needs? Why?

Research Paper

Instructions to Students. Select one of the topics below for in-depth study. Each topic requires that you obtain current information, most likely available through the web.

1) Visit the websites of one of the following national organizations. Write a five- to ten-page paper on their programs, their past successes at lobbying Congress, and their current campaigns. Call or e-mail them if you need additional information.

-American Association of Retired Persons
-National Asian Pacific Center on Aging
-National Caucus and Center for the Black Aged
-National Council for Senior Citizens
-National Indian Council on Aging
-National Hispanic Council on Aging
-Older Women's League

2) Read about the National Family Caregiver Support Program at the Administration on Aging's website at http://www.aoa.gov. Write a five- to ten-page paper on explain why this program is significant and the extent to which can help family caregivers.

THE FUTURE OF AGING

Learning Objectives

1) Describe how demographic, health, sociological, and technological changes will impact families and society in the future.

2) Describe how older people and younger people can join together to create the best possible future.

Summary of the Video and Text

Video

The video tells us to expect three revolutions in the future--a demographic revolution, a health revolution, and a social revolution. Changes in these areas will present many challenges for families and society. Will these changes lead to generational competition for resources? Experts and elders outline ways in which people can work together to create a better world for all, regardless of age, gender, or ethnicity.

Experts appearing in the video include former Representative Thomas Downey, Msgr. Charles Fahey, Lou Glasse, Robert Harootyan, Samuel Simmons, and Drs. Robert Atchley, James Birren, Colette Browne, Gene Cohen, James Dator, Leonard Hayflick, Nancy Hooyman, H. Asuman Kiyak, Linda Martin, Richard Sprott, E. Percil Stanford, Robyn Stone, Richard Suzman, Jeanette Takamura, Fernando Torres-Gil and Sherry Willis. Service provider Ruth Sifton discusses her views. Older adults who share their experiences with us include Thac Do Bui, Faye Cruse, Ilse Darling, Sylvia Davis, Mollie Pier, David Reese, Leo Salazar, Robert Shaw, Betty Tuff, and Mildred Tuttle.

Text

Review. Read the "Implications for the Future" sections for Chapters 16 and 17. These sections point out that public perception of older people as well-to-do competing for limited government resources may affect the types of future policies and programs for older adults in the future.

The sections also suggest the need for new ways to address the complex needs of older adults as they live longer in larger numbers and proportions in such great diversity. If no major changes in the way long-term care is structured and financed, costs will continue to escalate for the individual, families and society as a whole.

Your instructor may provide additional readings for this lesson.

Key Points

The Impact of Demographic, Health, and Social Changes

As we have seen throughout the course, the dramatic growth in the number and proportion of older adults will continue to impact families and society. We are reminded that it may be as soon as 2020 when about 20% of the U.S. population will be over age 65. The population over age 85, currently almost four million, is projected to double by 2020. The U.S. Census estimates that, by 2050, 1 in 26 Baby Boomers will be living as centenarians.

What will the future look like as we experience the "graying of society?" Dr. James Dator and Robert Harootyan remind us that no one can predict the future. At best, we can project alternative futures based on demographic trends and policy decisions. The questions to ask are: "What will the future look like if today's trends continue?" and "What could it look like if trends change or different policy decisions are made?"

A first question for those who predict the future is: What are today's trends and will they continue? Dr. Richard Suzman illustrates the difficulty in projecting exactly how many people will be alive in the future and how long they will be living. For example, if we follow today's trends, we may have 18 million citizens over age 85 by the year 2040. If we assume that tomorrow's adults will be more health conscious than today's adults, and therefore live longer, we may have 40 million citizens over age 85 by the year 2040!

A large percentage of the 85-plus age group now experiences physical and mental disabilities and requires long-term care. For example, the current prevalence rate of Alzheimer's disease is one in every 12 adults 65 years and older, and one in every two for those 85 years and older. What will happen in 2040 if we need 12 times the amount of long-term care services we need now? Will we ration health care to the very old? Will we allow people with terminal illness to voluntarily end their lives? These issues pose ethnical dilemmas for society.

Robert Harootyan is optimistic about the future. He believes that three health trends may result in more people living long, healthy lives. The first area is health promotion. Already we see mass media campaigns about healthy lifestyles along with legislation aimed at discouraging smoking and mandating seat belt use. The second area is medical technology, which is increasing our ability to diagnose and treat disorders at very early stages and prevent or reverse disability. Third, genetic engineering efforts such as the Human Genome Project and stem cell research may allow us to correct defects at the genetic level so that individuals are better able to avoid the diseases to which they are genetically susceptible. We may be able to use growth hormones to promote health as well.

The most optimistic projection of these trends would suggest two things: 1) a dramatic decline in disease and disability for all age groups and 2) continued extension of life expectancy. Dr. James Birren feels that we will soon view any death before age 80 as premature. Dr. Dator even wonders if someday we will look at death as a curable disease, meaning that we will not have to die at all.

Several experts take a middle ground. Dr. Leonard Hayflick, for example, thinks it will take several generations before we are able to manipulate human aging. This delay will give us time, he says, to work out the ethical, social, and economic dilemmas that would be created if the most optimistic projection comes true. Dr. Asuman Kiyak believes that older adults will become more diverse in every way, including their health status. She suggests we plan for both healthy and frail adults in this age group.

Will frail older adults have to move in with family or relocate to nursing homes? Or will technology be developed to help them remain in their own homes and "age in place?" For hands-on care for frail elders, will we continue to depend on families, especially women? Will men take more responsibility for caregiving? Dr. Nancy Hooyman believes so, but that families will need more services to help them maintain elders at home, especially day care and respite services. Will government programs be expanded to help families provide care? If so, will we have enough young people in the workforce to pay taxes to support programs for older adults? Will we see a rise in the incidence of elder abuse and neglect if families are not supported in their caregiving efforts?

Women continue to outlive men and the number of ethnic elderly is also growing rapidly. Lou Glasse notes that women of today have more opportunities and independence than their mothers and grandmothers. Unfortunately, current-day inequities in education, employment, and economic status suggest that we will still see pockets of poverty in future cohorts of elderly women and minorities. In fact, some gerontologists believe we will see a "feminization of poverty," meaning that most poor people will be women. Will we allow these inequities to continue? Will we develop programs that will keep low-income elders from poverty? How can we correct inequities so that increasing portions of old people can support themselves?

Aging is a worldwide phenomenon. Msgr. Charles Fahey tells us that some European countries already are feeling that they don't have enough young people to produce the goods and services needed by their society. In Japan, Dr. Linda Martin tells us, the aging of the labor force is forcing the country to rely more and more on women workers. If women are working outside of the home, who cares for their growing number of older people? Dr. Suzman reminds us that China's one-child policy helped China get control over its burgeoning population of young people. But when single children marry, the couple becomes responsible for four parents and eight grandparents. Can they provide that care? Dr. Martin also notes that the elderly population is growing in countries around the world, even in the least developed. How will these countries care for their growing number of elders?

What about sociological changes? Will we continue to see a trend toward early retirement? Will we raise the retirement age? Samuel Simmons believes older adults should have more options for work and retirement. While it is important to be flexible, Robert Harootyan wonders if we can afford to have adults out of the workforce for half of their lives. Can the U.S. survive if 25% of the population is on Social Security? Dr. Robert Atchley feels that we will need to think of creative ways to retain older workers and postpone the age of retirement. Dr. Jeanette Takamura suggests more support of "cyclical life plans" that allow people to pursue several careers throughout life, taking breaks for school, caregiving, and leisure as needed.

Dr. Dator believes that advances in robotization and artificial intelligence will provide us more options in the future. Assistive technology can help us hurry through our chores or allow us to work at home rather than in an office. If people have more leisure time in the future, what new roles will they take on? Technology can also help individuals compensate for disabilities and age-related changes, increasing the "fit" between people and their environments so they can remain productive and independent.

Dr. Takamura reminds us that most of the infrastructure of today was designed at a time when fewer older people participated in the economy. How can we design future buildings and transportation systems so that they are age-sensitive? The passage of the Americans with Disabilities Act is helping, as it mandates that environments be made more "enabling" for all. The World Wide Web is growing daily and already, thousands of websites exist that provide health information or support (for example for people coping with health problems, caregiving, or bereavement).

How do today's older adults view the future? Leo Salazar says he has lots of plans for his future, between his art, his counseling work, his political activity, and his family commitments; he tells us quite adamantly that he's "not ready to go yet." Mildred Tuttle expects to live to be at least 90 years old. Robert Shaw wants to continue helping other people as long as he can. Thac Do Bui wants to live a long life so he has time to teach his grandchildren about their Vietnamese heritage. They all seem quite optimistic about the future.

Intergenerational Alliances for a Better Future

In the United States, the proportion of the population over 65 will make a dramatic jump starting in 2011 when the first Baby Boomers become senior citizens. Some experts, including Dr. Kiyak, feel that the Baby Boomers, who have always been a vocal bunch, will continue to win freedoms for the cohort as older adults.

But, as vocal as the Baby Boomers may be, the video and Chapters 16 and 17 of the text remind us that no single generation can make it on its own. Most gerontologists believe in an "interdependence of generations framework," which means they think that the needs and contributions of different generations are so intertwined that programs benefitting one age group directly or indirectly benefit other age groups. In contrast, the "intergenerational inequity framework" is based on the belief that age-entitlement programs for older adults benefit the elderly at the expense of younger age groups. With this type of thinking, we may soon be engaging in "age wars" as we compete for scarce resources!

Instead, the video and text call for the development of intergenerational alliances to address issues of concern to all citizens. A few intergenerational alliances already exist. Dr. Torres-Gil talks about Generations United, a coalition sponsored by the National Council on Aging and the Children's Defense Fund. They joined together to support legislation that would benefit both groups. In another example, Lou Glasse tells us that the Older Women's League has been working to unite old and young women around women's health issues, for example, pregnancy, menopause, and aging. By presenting a united front to policy makers, they are more likely to get the funding for research and programs needed to address these concerns.

What other kinds of issues can be addressed by intergenerational coalitions? Dr. Dator reminds us of environmental crises that may face us in the future. What if the greenhouse effect increases global temperatures and the sea level rises? What if crowded conditions lead to the spread of new diseases?

Dr. Hooyman believes that intergenerational groups working on environmental issues could have a very powerful effect on policy. He also reminds us that eldercare and child care programs shouldn't have to compete with each other for funds. They are just two ends of a continuum of services that help families care for their dependents. Intergenerational coalitions may be successful in establishing better support for family care.

Dr. Torres-Gil notes that seniors and minorities share a desperate need for better health care coverage and, if they came together, could develop a political alliance that would be very difficult to defeat. Long-term care is another good issue for intergenerational work, says Dr. Stone. As the text notes, about 60% of Americans who report using long-term care services are age 65 or older.

Former Representative Thomas Downey wants us to think of programs like Medicare and Social Security as family programs; without them, children would find themselves increasingly responsible for their parents' housing, food, and medical needs. In this context, all generations benefit when family care, health, and income issues are addressed.

Not all intergenerational work has to be political. Programs open to multiple generations have benefits as well. We saw several examples in the video. Mollie Pier talks about a project in Los Angeles in which older volunteers worked with city schools on courses that increased awareness of the negative effects of ageism and racism.

Ruth Sifton talks about intergenerational programming at her adult day care center, located next to a preschool. The two groups have become well acquainted and share holiday programs with each other. Older adults help watch out for the children and, in one case, the children helped "find" an older gentleman with dementia who had wandered away from the program.

On a more individual level, older people are a resource that can be tapped by members of younger generations. Former Representative Downey would like to see retired mathematicians and scientists involved in the school system.

Dr. Dator feels that older adults would be excellent counselors; they have lived through the challenges of childhood and adulthood and can help younger generations who are facing these challenges for the first time.

The video and text suggest that increased intergenerational interactions can help us build a better future. Without cooperation, we may find generations competing with one another. When we work together across generations, we work for a minimum level of dignity and comfort for all.

The questions become: "How can we ensure that all people, young and old, receive equitable treatment?" and "How can we make it together?" Dr. Dator reminds us that the future is not written yet; the future is an arena of possibilities and hope.

What can gerontologists do in the future? A variety of job options will be open to people who study and work in the field of aging. Read, for example, the "Implications for the Future in Chapters 4 and 9 for clues as to what careers will be in demand to meet the growing needs of older adults. These careers will be in the areas of direct service to the elderly, program planning, education and training, administration and policy, and research.

Key Terms and Concepts from the Text, Video, and *Study Guide*

Age in Place
Americans with Disabilities Act
Assistive Technology
Complementary and Alternative Medicine
Cyclical Life Plan
Ethical Dilemmas,
Family Caregiver Alliance
Feminization of Poverty
Gap Group
Gliding Out

Graying of Society
Interdependence of Generations Framework
Intergenerational Inequity Framework
Partnerships in Aging Programs
Rationing of Health Care
Senior Boom
Slippery Slope
Smart Houses
Squaring the Life Expectancy Course
Third Age

Self-Study Questions

Instructions. Fill in the blank with the appropriate word or phrase from the list of Key Terms and Concepts. Note: Only 13 of the 20 key terms and concepts can be used.

1) The _____ and the _____ are phrases that describe a trend toward more older people in society.

2) The _____ refers to the fact that most of the people living in poverty are women. This is especially true in old age because women make less than men when they work, spend fewer years in the workforce because they take on child and eldercare duties, and live longer than men.

3) People who _____ grow old in their own homes rather than relocate, even though they may have to modify their homes to compensate for physical declines that accompany aging.

4) A law that was passed that is helping make environments more accessible and "enabling" to all Americans is called the _____.

5) _____ includes tools, machines, and computer programs that help people with disabilities increase their ability to live independently.

6) The _____ is a philosophy based on the belief that the needs and contributions of different generations are so intertwined that programs benefitting one age group directly or indirectly benefit other age groups.

In contrast, the _____ is based on the belief that age-entitlement programs for older adults benefit the elderly at the expense of younger age groups.

7) In a _____, individuals may participate in the workforce, be caregivers, and attend school at any age, in any order, and as often as they like.

8) _____ includes healing techniques and traditions that are not usually considered part of western medicine.

9) _____ contain technological gadgets and computers that make living easier and/or help compensate for physical limitations.

10) Issues that raises concerns because there are no perfect solutions that are equitable to all and therefore require substantial discussion and compromise are called _____.

11) We engage in the _____ when we limit health resources to individuals or groups. This often occurs when we perceive a scarcity of resources and have to make choices about who will get which services.

Use the Glossary at the end of the Study Guide to check your answers.

124

Topics for Discussion

1) Discuss some potential outcomes of increased longevity with regard to family interactions and obligations. In what ways will changing attitudes toward divorce, remarriage, and women in the workforce affect these relationships?

2) Think of a social problem that you would like to do something about. Discuss the pros and cons of having an intergenerational alliance work on this problem.

3) Read the book, "Die Broke" by Stephen Pollan and discuss the principles advanced by Pollan as they relate to the notions of retirement, financial planning, long-term care, and that building a pile of money to give to your kids is based on the mistaken idea that money has value in and of itself... and that the last check you write is to the undertaker (and it should bounce)!

Website Challenge

Visit the following websites that can provide more information on this lesson's topics. Bookmark them for easy access in the future.

1) Generations United at http://www.gu.org

2) Canadian Association of Baby Boomers at http://www.fifty-plus.net/

3) Older Women's League at http://www.owl-national.org/

Written Assignments

Your instructor may ask you to complete one or more of the written assignments that follow.

Reaction Paper: New Knowledge and Feelings Stimulated by the Video

Write a two-page paper describing: 1) new information gained from watching the video; 2) how the experiences of the older adults in the video affected your personal view of aging; and 3) other comments to the instructor regarding this lesson or the course.

Older-Adult Interview

Interview a person who is 60 or older, asking the questions below. Write a paper about the interviewee's expectations about the future.

Interview Questions

1) How old are you now?

2) Until what age do you expect to live? What factors did you consider in estimating how long you expect to live?

3) What kinds of things are you planning to do in the future? Why are these activities important to you?

4) Think back over your parents' and grandparents' lives. Are they still alive? If so, how old are they? If not, how old were they when they died? Can you tell me three or four ways in which your life is different from their lives?

5) Think about the lives of your children and grandchildren. (If the senior has no children, ask this question about "young people today.") Until what age do you expect them to live? What kinds of options will they have when they are senior citizens? Can you tell me three or four ways in which you think their lives will be different from yours?

6) You must have seen a lot of changes over your life so far. What is the most significant change you've observed? Why? What significant changes should your children and grandchildren anticipate?

7) How should society change to assure a better life for older people in the future?

Student Questions

1) How did your interviewee's perceptions of the future compare with those discussed in the Epilogue of the text? Explain.

2) Has this interview affected in any way your personal view of aging and older adults? Explain.

Research Paper

Select one of the topics below for in-depth study. Read a book or five journal articles on the topic. A good place to start searching for reading material is in the reference section provided at the end of each text chapter. Write a five- to ten-page paper that summarizes the historical and current thinking about the topic. Identify things about the topic that are not yet resolved or may benefit from further study.

1) We have the technology to design "smart houses" which include electronic gadgets that can help disabled people compensate for their limitations. Trained monkeys and seeing-eye dogs can also increase independence among disabled people. Elaborate on some of the current and anticipated developments in this field.

2) Many health care facilities are establishing ethics committees. What are ethics committees? Who should belong to an ethics committee? What types of issues does a hospital ethics committee address? Will we see a greater need for ethics committees in the future? Why or why not?

3) Describe two programs that illustrate the concept of intergenerational collaboration. Why were these programs established? How do they operate? How do participants benefit from the programs? If programs that foster intergenerational collaboration are good, how can we develop more of them?

Future Trends

Consider the demographic trends and the concerns about the future discussed in the video and in the text. Write a two- to three-page paper in which you speculate about what you think your life will be like in your "third age."

For example, how long will you live? What will you be doing? What kinds of role options will be available to you? Will you experience physical or mental declines and, if so, how will you cope with them? What kind of relationships will you have with family and friends? Where will you live? Will you have any control over the timing and cause of your death? Explain.

If you are already in your third age, apply the above questions to someone who is young today, perhaps a grandchild. Write a paper in which you speculate about how this person will experience his/her "third age."

APPENDIX A

GLOSSARY OF KEY TERMS AND CONCEPTS

Unless otherwise noted, glossary definitions are taken from or adapted from the text,
Social Gerontology: A Multidisciplinary Perspective, by Hooyman and Kiyak.

ALS (video) - Amyotrophic Lateral Sclerosis, or Lou Gehrig's disease; a rare condition that affects the motor-neurons, which are the nerve cells that run from the brain to the muscles and control the muscles' movements. The affected muscles cannot be stimulated and the muscles waste away from disuse.

Access Services - Programs and services for older adults that provide information, referrals to other programs, case management, and transportation.

Accessibility - Absence of barriers that impede an individual's ability to use or receive services.

Accommodation - Ability of the lens of the eye to change shape from rounded to flat to see objects that are closer or farther from the lens.

Acculturation - Processes by which ethnic minorities adopt to and incorporate the behaviors and attitudes of the dominant culture within which they are living.

Active Aging – New model of viewing aging as a positive experience of continued growth and participation in family, community, and societal activities, regardless of physical and cognitive decline.

Active Life Expectancy - Number of years individuals can expect to live independently, i.e., without needing help from others with Activities of Daily Living.

Activities of Daily Living (ADL) - Personal care tasks such as bathing, dressing, grooming, using the toilet, eating, and getting in and out of bed.

Activity Theory - Social theory of aging based on the belief that: 1) active older people are more satisfied and better adjusted than those who are not active; and 2) an older person's self-concept is validated through participation in roles characteristic of middle age and older people should therefore replace lost roles with new roles to maintain their integration with society.

Acute Illness - Illness that is short-term, and one that usually allows a full recovery, for example, a common cold.

Adaptation - Adjustments that people make in response to changes in themselves and their environments to become congruent with (or fit themselves into) the new conditions.

Addison's Disease (video) - Disease caused by failure of the adrenal cortex to function, marked by a bronze-like skin pigmentation, anemia, and prostration.

Adult Day Programs - Group programs offering therapeutic exercise, socialization, activities, and meals to older adults who need stimulation and supervision. Day Care programs are for elderly people who need stimulation and supervision but little medical attention and rehabilitation. Day Health or Day Hospital programs are for elderly people who need medical attention and rehabilitation in addition to stimulation and supervision.

Advance Directives - Documents such as wills, living wills, and durable power of attorney for health care decisions that outline actions to be taken for you by others when you cannot give directions yourself, for example, in the event of death, incapacitation, or irreversible, terminal illness.

Advocacy - Lobbying for older adults, either for individuals or for the senior population as a whole, to assure receipt of services for which they are already eligible or to increase their benefits.

Aerobic Exercise - Exercise that increases the heart rate and increases oxygen consumption.

Age-Based Programs - Programs available only to people of a certain age.

Age Changes - How people normally change over time.

Age Differences - How one generation differs from another.

Age Discrimination in Employment Act - Federal law that protects workers age 45 and over from denial of employment strictly because of age.

Adult Foster Care - Live-in support of an adult by an unrelated family, usually compensated and supervised by public or private agencies. When this service is limited to older adults, it may be referred to as geriatric foster care.

Age-Graded - Adjective describing a society or system that assigns different roles, expectations, opportunities, status, and constraints to people of different ages. See also Age Stratification and Social Stratification.

Age-Heterogeneous - Including people of different ages.

Age-Homogeneous - Including people of similar ages.

Age Norm - Set of behaviors and roles normally associated with a specific age group.

Age-Segregated - Limiting membership to a certain age group.

Age Spots - Concentrations of skin pigmentation.

Age Stratification - Divisions among people based on age, with age-related boundaries and rules.

Age Stratification Theory - Theory based on the assumption that age is a universal criterion by which people's roles, rights, and privileges are distributed as they move from one stratum to the next. According to this theory, successful aging depends on being able to move smoothly into and out of a succession of age-related roles as we age.

Age Wars - Term describing intergenerational conflict over resources.

Ageism - Stereotypes and discrimination based on age.

Ageist - Adjective to describe someone or something that discriminates against people based on age or that promotes stereotypes based on age.

Aging in Place - Growing old in one's home and neighborhood, rather than relocating. For people who "age in place," home modifications are usually required to help an older person compensate for any physical declines that accompany aging.

Aging Network - System of social services for older adults funded by the Older Americans Act and other sources.

Alcoholics Anonymous - National organization that sponsors support groups to help persons addicted to alcohol become and stay sober.

Alzheimer's Disease - Brain disorder that causes irreversible dementia. In the early stages, symptoms are forgetfulness. As the disease progresses, the ability to care for oneself and to converse with others in a meaningful way are lost.

American Association of Retired Persons (AARP) - National organization open to all adults 50 and above, offering a wide range of informational materials, discounted services and products, and a powerful lobby. AARP currently has more than 35 million members.

Americans for Generational Equity (AGE) - Group that questions age-entitlement programs for older people as they reduce the amount of money available to address the needs of other generations.

American Society on Aging - Association of practitioners and researchers interested in gerontology. ASA sponsors a number of activities, including conferences, publications, and task forces on current issues.

Angina Pectoris - Shortness of breath and pain in the heart area due to reduced blood flow as atherosclerosis increases.

Anticipatory Grief - Grief for a loved one prior to his/her death, usually occurring during the time the loved one has a terminal illness.

Antiaging Medicine – New field of biological research aimed at slowing or reversing biological aging.

Anti-inflammatory Agents - Drugs that reduce swelling and pain.

Antimiscegenation - Opposition, sometimes by law, to marriage or sexual relations between a man and woman of different races.

Antioxidants - Nutrients or metabolites that can absorb the unpaired electron on free radicals and, it is speculated, delay aging. The body's naturally occurring antioxidants can be supplemented with vitamins A, C, and E and the mineral selenium.

Anxiety Disorder - Psychological disorder often triggered by external stress and accompanied by physiological reactions such as increased heart rate and sleep disturbances.

Aphasia - Inability to speak or understand speech, which is caused by strokes that affect the part of the brain that controls speech.

Apocalyptic Demography - Term suggesting that the changing age structure (to one with more older people than younger people) will have a disastrous (or apocalyptic) consequences.

Appropriate Death - Death of a person that occurs the way he/she would wish it to occur, i.e., in concert with past personality patterns.

Archetype - Term coined by Carl Jung to represent the feminine side of a man's personality (the anima) and the masculine side of a woman's personality (the animus).

Arcus Senilis - Fatty, yellow ring that forms around the cornea in some older people. It has no impact on vision.

Area Agencies on Aging (AAA) - Offices on aging at the regional and local level that develop and administer service plans to meet the needs of older adults within that locale. Established and partially funded through the Older Americans Act, about 700 AAAs operate across the U.S.

Arteriosclerosis - Loss of elasticity of the arterial walls.

Arthritis - General term to describe the 100 different conditions of inflammation and degenerative changes in bones and joints.

Assets - Individual's savings, home equity, and personal property.

Assisted Death - Deliberate help with the dying process. This can include the supplying of a dying individual with medications or other means to end his/her own life (assisted suicide) or the giving of a lethal injection.

Assisted Living - Housing model aimed at elders who need assistance with personal care, e.g., bathing and taking medication, but who are not so physically or cognitively impaired as to need 24-hour attention.

Assistive Technology - Range of electronic and computer technologies whose goal is to assist people with disabilities remain independent and perform as many ADLs as possible without assistance from other people.

Atherosclerosis - Narrowing of the passageway of the large arteries due to the development and accumulation of plaques (fatty deposits).

Attentional Control – Ability to allocate one's attention among multiple stimuli simultaneously.

Attrition - Decline in the numbers of subjects in a research study due to dropout.

Autoimmune Theory of Aging - Biological theory of aging, which suggests that as the body's immune system declines with age it becomes defective and attacks itself, resulting in frailty and death.

Autonomous - Able to and allowed to independently make decisions about health care, lifestyle, and other personal issues.

Autonomy - Self-determination.

Autopsy - Examination of the body after death, usually done to identify or validate the cause of death.

B = f(P,E) - Equation developed by psychologist Kurt Lewin that represents the statement, "behavior is a function of personal and environmental characteristics."

Baby Boomers - Nickname for the large group of individuals born between 1946 and 1964.

Baltimore Longitudinal Study of Aging - Study funded by the federal government in which a large group of healthy middle-aged and older individuals living in the community are being assessed regularly to describe normal changes that occur with aging. When the study began in 1958, it was limited to male participants; women were included in the sample in 1978.

Benign Prostatic Hypertrophy - Noncancerous enlargement of the prostate. Also known as benign hypertrophy of the prostate.

Bereavement - Suffering and deprivation after the loss of a loved one.

Bereavement Overload - Experience of older adults who are exposed to the increased frequency of family and friends' deaths and become desensitized to impact of death.

Biological Aging - Physical changes that occur with age, including the reduced efficiency of organ systems.

Bioethics - Field of study that focuses on procedural approaches to questions about death, dying, and medical decision-making.

Biomarker of Aging - Scientific measure that allows us to judge the rate at which an individual is aging.

Birth Cohort - People born within the same period of time.

Blaming the Victim - Believing that an individual is responsible for his/her own misfortunes.

Blended Families - Families whose membership consists of blood and nonblood relations through adoption, divorce, remarriage, etc.

Block Grant - Funds provided by one level of government (federal or state) to a lower level (state or local) for purposes of supporting a substantial range of benefits or services, generally at the discretion of the lower level.

Board and Care Homes - Shelters that provide room, board, assistance with Instrumental Activities of Daily Living and sometimes Activities of Daily Living to adults with varying levels of disability. As a rule, these facilities provide less intensive care than do nursing homes.

Body Composition - Proportions of lean muscle, water, and fat in the body. Humans tend to experience an increase in fat and decreases in water and lean muscle as they age.

Busy Ethic - Belief that it is good to spend one's leisure time engaged in activity (i.e., "keeping busy").

Caloric Restriction - Diet that is nutritionally adequate but low in calories. Animal studies suggest that caloric restriction may increase life span.

Cancer - Abnormal, excessive growth of cells and their spread to distant organs, which often interfere with vital organ functions.

Capitated Payments - Payments based on a fixed amount per person per day, rather than on fees for individual services provided.

Cardiopulmonary Resuscitation (CPR) - Lifesaving procedure of clearing the airway, massaging the heart, and using drugs to restore normal breathing after cardiac arrest.

Cardiovascular Diseases - Diseases, mostly chronic, of the heart and circulatory system.

Care Homes - See Board and Care Homes.

Caregiver, Family - Family member who assists an elderly family member with personal care, household and financial chores, and transportation, usually without compensation.

Caregiver, Professional - Trained person who assists an unrelated elder with nursing, personal care, and household tasks, usually for compensation.

Caregiver Burden - Personal energy, time restrictions, financial commitments, and/or psychological frustrations associated with assisting disabled persons.

Caregiving - Assisting people with personal care, household chores, transportation, and other tasks associated with daily living.

Case (or **Care**) **Management** - Obtaining and orchestrating services for disabled older adults. Such services are usually offered by a number of agencies with different eligibility criteria. Some one who provides case management is called a case manager.

Cash Substitute - Benefit given in a form other than cash, such as a voucher which may be exchanged for food, rent, medical care, etc.

Cash Transfer - Benefit paid by cash.

Cataract - Severe clouding, or opacification, of the lens of the eye, which impairs vision.

Categorical - In this context, the manner of dealing with public problems by addressing the problems of specific groups of persons rather than attempting solutions that are comprehensive or deal with problems as they affect the entire population.

Cellular Theory of Aging - Biological theory that hypothesizes that aging occurs because cells are mortal. Over the life span, they slow their number of replications and eventually die.

Centenarian - Someone age 100 or older.

Cerebral Hemorrhage - Cause of stroke, by which a weak spot in a blood vessel of the brain bursts.

Cerebral Thrombosis - Cause of stroke, by which a blood clot either diminishes or closes off the blood flow in an artery of the brain or neck.

Cerebrovascular Accident (CVA) - Also called a stroke. It occurs when a portion of the brain is completely denied blood. Aphasia, hemiplegia, and hemianopsia can result from strokes as a result of hemorrhage or thrombosis, depending on the part of the brain affected.

Cerebrovascular Disease - Impaired circulation of brain tissue due to arteriosclerotic and atherosclerotic changes in blood vessels serving the brain.

Choice in Dying - National organization supporting passive euthanasia and providing information on advance directives, now called Partnership for Caring..

Chronic Illness - Illness that lasts more than three months, is often permanent, and leaves a residual disability that may require long-term management rather than cure. Examples of chronic disease include arthritis, emphysema, hypertension, some cancers, and diabetes.

Chronic Obstructive Pulmonary Disease (COPD) - General term for diseases that damage lung tissue, such as chronic bronchitis, asthma, and emphysema.

Chronological Aging - Aging as measured by the number of years one has lived.

Cilia - Hairlike structures in the airways of the lungs and bronchia.

Circadian Rhythms - Individual's cycle of sleeping and waking within a 24-hour period.

Classic Aging Pattern - Consistent pattern of scores on the WAIS in suggests that, as we age, decline in fluid intelligence (spatial orientation, abstract reasoning, and perceptual speed) precedes decline in crystallized intelligence (verbal skills and social judgment).

Climacteric - In women, the decline in estrogen production and the loss of reproductive ability (see Menopause). In men, the decline in testosterone (see Male Menopause).

Cluttered Nest - Delayed departure or return of an adult child to parents' home.

Cognitive Appraisal - Individual's perception of an encounter with a life event or other stressor, which can minimize or magnify the extent of one's response to the stressor.

Cognitive Functioning - Intelligence, learning, memory, perception, creativity, and wisdom.

Cognitive Retraining - Teaching individuals how to use various techniques to keep their minds active and maintain good memory skills.

Cohabitation - Unmarried couples living together.

Cohort - Group of individuals of the same generation; people sharing a statistical trait such as age, socioeconomic status, or ethnicity; companions or colleagues.

Cohort Effect - In studies of age differences among generations, a cohort effect refers to differences not necessarily due to age but due to the particular cultural or historical conditions that shaped the different age groups.

Collagen - Connective tissue found in most organ systems that helps maintain elasticity.

Compadre - Close male friend and confidant.

Compassion in Dying Federation - National organization supporting the right to die, and working to educate health care providers about aggressive pain management.

Competence Model - Conception or description of the way persons perform, focusing on their abilities vis-a-vis the demands of the environment. See **Individual Competence**.

Compression of Morbidity – Given a certain length of life, a term referring to relatively long periods of healthy, active, high-quality existence and relatively short periods of illness and dependency in the last few years of life.

Compressed Mortality - Delaying death until very late life.

Congestive Heart Failure - Set of symptoms related to decreased efficiency of the pumping of the heart. Symptoms include shortness of breath, reduced blood flow to vital body parts, and edema.

Congregate Housing - Living arrangements in which communal services (such as meal preparation, social services, and/or health care) are provided to residents.

Congregate Living Facilities (video) - Group living facilities in which older people have their own rooms but share living and dining areas. Meals and transportation are provided by the facility.

Congregate Meals - See Meal Sites.

Conservatorship - Probate court appointment of a person to care for an individual's property and finances because he/she is unable to do so due to advanced age, mental weakness, or physical incapacity. See also Guardianship.

Continuity Theory - Social theory based on the belief that central personality characteristics become more pronounced with age or are retained as "life threads" with little change. People age successfully if they maintain their preferred roles and adaptation techniques throughout life.

Continuous Care Retirement Community - Multilevel facility offering a range of living arrangements, from independent living to congregate living.

Continuum of Care - Array of health services that should be available to meet the needs of older adults, including services provided in the home, community settings, and institutions to adults with all levels of health, illness, and disability.

Contractures - Freezing of joints into rigid positions due to the loss of flexibility in muscles and tendons surrounding immobilized areas.

Contributory Programs - Programs to which people contribute a portion of their income and receive an amount corresponding to their contribution. An example of a contributory program is Social Security.

Convergent Validity - Supporting a theory by several independent research efforts, which produce findings that suggest a similar conclusion.

Coping Strategies - Conscious strategies one uses to reduce or manage stress, and subsequent discomfort, from life events and chronic daily hassles. Coping can be assisted by external situations (intimate friendships, financial well-being) and one's individual values, hopes, and fears. Coping strategies can be problem-focused (to solve problems) or emotion-focused (to deal with the emotional distress that problems create). See examples of coping strategies on page 209 in the text.

Cost Containment - Effort to minimize cost without damaging effectiveness of the product or service.

Cost Effectiveness - Assessment of benefit or effect against cost used in reaching decisions about the value of programs.

Cost Efficiency - Assessment of a benefit or program based on the ratio of costs of inputs to value of outputs, with the most efficient program being one that produces the greatest benefit or output for the least cost of input.

Cost-of-Living Adjustment - Increase in salary or benefit to make up for an increase in the cost of living.

Creativity - Ability to apply unique and feasible solutions to new situations; the ability to produce original ideas or products.

Critical Theory - Perspective that genuine knowledge is based on the involvement of the "objects" of study in its definition and results in a positive vision of how things might be better rather than an understanding of how things are.

Cross-Linkage Theory of Aging - Biological theory that associates aging with the loss of collagen (connective tissue) in the skin, blood vessels, muscles, eyes, and other organs. This process makes tissue less pliable and more susceptible to damage.

Cross-Over Effect - Referring to the fact that ethnic minorities experience poorer health and higher death rates at all ages until very old age; after age 75, however, death rates for minorities are lower than for Caucasians.

Cross-Sectional Research Design - Research design in which different age groups are surveyed at a single point in time. The major drawback of this design is that differences found among age groups may be due to historical and cohort factors, rather than to aging.

Crystallized Intelligence - Knowledge and abilities that individuals acquire through education and lifelong experiences, e.g., verbal skills and social judgment.

Cued Recall - Remembering something with the help of some information. See Free Recall.

Cultural Competence - High degree of knowledge about and sensitivity to the cultural values and perceptions of the people you are working with.

Cyclical Life Plan - Life in which activities are not dictated by age. For example, in a linear life plan, individuals complete school in their youth, then raise children and have careers, then retire. In a cyclical life plan, individuals may participate in the workforce, be caregiver, and attend school at any age, in any order, and as often as they like.

Cystitis - Acute inflammation of the bladder, accompanied by pain and irritation.

Death Crisis - In the dying trajectory, an unanticipated change in the amount of time remaining to live.

Death with Dignity - Dying when one still has some independence and control over decisions about life. People concerned about dying with dignity want to be able to end their lives when they feel that their pain, suffering, and dependency outweigh the benefits of living.

Defense Mechanisms - Also called Ego Defense Mechanism. Unconscious reactions adopted by a person to defend or protect against impulses, emotions, and memories that threaten his/her identity. Primitive defense mechanisms including denying or blaming others for the problem. Mature defense mechanisms are those in which primitive instincts are expressed in socially acceptable ways. See text box on page 208 in the text.

Dehydroepiandrosterone (DHEA) - Molecule secreted by the adrenal glands. Experiments with an oral form of DHEA show that, when taken as a supplement, DHEA results in improved sleep, greater energy, and greater tolerance of stress.

Dementia - Measurable deterioration in cognitive function. Dementia can be a symptom of any number of underlying physical and psychopathologic conditions, some of which can be treated so that the dementia symptoms disappear.

Demography - Statistical study of human populations.

Dependency Ratio - In a society, the number of people who are dependent compared to the number who are employed. The ratio is calculated by dividing the number of dependents (people under age 18 plus people over age 65) by the number of workers (people between age 18 and 65). Separate ratios representing childhood dependency and elderly dependency can be calculated in the same manner.

Dependent Life Expectancy - Number of years individuals can expect to live while dependent on other people to perform Activities of Daily Living.

Depression - Psychopathology marked by depressed mood, diminished interest in activities, poor concentration, weight loss, and sleep disturbances.

Dermis - Second layer of skin, between the epidermis and the subcutaneous layers.

Developing Nations - Countries where a large portion of the economy is agricultural; these countries tend to have higher proportions of children and lower proportions of old people than do developed nations (which tend to be more urbanized and more industrial).

Diabetes Mellitus - Above-normal amounts of sugar (glucose) in the blood and urine, resulting from insufficient insulin that is necessary to process carbohydrates.

Diagnostic Related Groupings (DRG) - System of Medicare reimbursement in which hospitals are paid a fixed amount for a patient based on the diagnosis or procedure. Hospitals that spend more than that amount on the patient lose money while hospitals that spend less than that on the patient make money.

Dialectical Models of Adult Personality - Models of personality based on confrontation between changing personal needs and environmental demands. In these models, growth is defined as the resolution of these conflicts and subsequent movement to the next stage.

Differential Access - Varying levels of ability to get the services you need because services cost too much, are too far away, are provided in another language, and so forth.

Direct Benefit - Benefit given directly, in the form of a cash payment or gift of some commodity such as food or housing. (See Indirect Benefit.)

Direct Care Workers – Nurse's aides, personal assistants, and home care workers who provide hands-on care in both private homes and institutional settings.

Disability - Impairment that affects one's ability to function within normal ranges.

Discharge Planning - Arrangement of a package of home-based and community-based services required by a patient who will soon be discharged from a hospital or nursing home.

Discrimination - Judging someone on age, gender, ethnicity, or sexual orientation, rather than on individual characteristics.

Disengagement Theory - Social theory of aging based on the belief that older people, because of their inevitable decline with age, become decreasingly active with the outer world and increasingly preoccupied with their inner lives. This theory suggests that disengagement is useful for society because it facilitates an orderly transfer of power from older people to younger people.

Displaced Homemakers - Women with no history of paid work (usually because they depended on a husband's income while raising a family) and who do not qualify for credit or personal retirement benefits.

Disuse Theory - Theory suggesting that information in long-term (secondary) memory can fade away or decay unless it is exercised, as in the adage "use it or lose it."

Diverticulitis - Pouches or sacs in the intestines (which result from weakness of the intestinal wall) become inflamed and infected.

Diverticulosis - Pouches or sacs in the intestines, a common condition often without symptoms.

DSM-4 - Fourth edition of the Diagnostic and Statistical Manual, which lists the symptoms for mental disorders and other conditions that impair cognitive functioning.

Do Not Resuscitate (DNR) Order - Order given by a patient or surrogate to provide no cardio-pulmonary resuscitation (CPR). Unless this request is specified, health care personnel are obligated to save a patient who goes into cardiac arrest.

Double Decker System - In discussions of Social Security reform, this refers to an idea to split Social Security contributions into two parts, one to support a flat benefit for all those meeting eligibility requirements and another to a government-supervised retirement plan that would offer some choices about where money was invested (hopefully in funds that offer higher returns on the investment).

Double Jeopardy Hypothesis - Supposition that a person who is both old and a minority is doubly discriminated against. This term can also apply to someone who is older and female.

Dowager's Hump - Stooped look, sometimes with an outward curving of the spine between the shoulders, that results from the collapsing and compressing of vertebrae (kyphosis).

Durable Power of Attorney for Health Care Decisions - Legal document that empowers a trusted friend or family member to make decisions about the kind of health care you receive in the event of your incapacitation.

Dying Person's Bill of Rights - Set of principles stating that a person has the right to personal dignity and privacy, informed participation, and considerate, respectful, and competent care at the end of life.

Dying Process - As defined by Elisabeth Kubler-Ross, dying persons experience five stages in reaction to their death: 1) denial and isolation, 2) anger and resentment, 3) bargaining, 4) depression, and 5) acceptance.

Dying Trajectory - Perceived course of dying and expected time of death.

Earnings - Money received in payment for a job.

Echoic Memory - Auditory memory; remembering what you hear as opposed to what you see or read.

Economic Marginality - Living on an income that impoverishes, or threatens to impoverish, an individual.

Ego Integrity vs. Despair - In Erikson's model of personality development, the eigth and final stage during which older persons should strive to achieve wisdom and perspective, rather than despairing because their views of life lack meaning.

Edema - Swelling, caused by the accumulation of water or blood in body tissues.

Edentulousness - Loss of teeth.

Ejaculation - Release of semen and sperm from the penis.

Elder Mistreatment (often referred to as **Elder Abuse**) - Maltreatment of older adults, including physical abuse (assault), sexual abuse (rape), psychological abuse (verbal assault, threat, or isolation), financial exploitation (theft or misuse of money or property), and medical abuse (withholding or improper administration of medications; withholding of assistive devices such as false teeth, eye glasses, hearing aids, canes, etc.).

Elder Neglect - Deprivation of care and attention necessary to maintain physical and mental health by those trusted to provide care (neglect by others) or by the elderly person him/herself (self-neglect).

Eldercare - Services and support provided to older adults with dependencies.

Elderhostel - Program for older adults to enjoy inexpensive, short-term academic programs at colleges and universities around the world.

Elderly Support Ratio - In a society, the number of older people compared to the number who are employed. The ratio is calculated by dividing the number of people over age 65 by the number of people between age 18 and 65. The method to calculate this ratio may have to change in the future as more people over age 65 join or remain in the workforce.

Electroencephalogram (EEG) - Reading of brain wave activity.

Electroshock or Electroconvulsive Therapy
(ECT) - Treatment using electric current to
"shock" persons with major depression,
especially those who do not respond to
medications, have a high risk of suicide, have
vegetative symptoms, or severe feelings of
agitation or hopelessness.

Eligibility Criteria - Rules that govern who can
participate in a program, e.g., age as an
eligibility criterion restricts participation to people
of a certain age.

Emphysema - See Chronic Obstructive Lung
Disease.

Empty Nest Syndrome - Feelings of loneliness
and depression that may occur if a parent
cannot adjust to his/her children leaving home.

Encoding - Transferring information from short-
term (primary) memory to long-term (secondary)
memory.

Entitlement Programs - Programs available to
all people with a certain characteristic, for
example, age-entitlement programs serve
people of the certain age while need-entitlement
programs serve low-income people.

Environmental Press - Within the concept of
person-environment interaction, environmental
press refers to the demands that social and
physical environments make on the individual to
adapt, respond, or change.

Epidermis - Outer most layer of skin.

Erectile Dysfunction - In men, difficulty
attaining and/or maintaining an erection.

Erection - Swelling of the penis or clitoris in
sexual excitement.

**Erikson's Stages of Psychosocial
Development** - In contrast to Sigmund Freud,
Erik Erikson believed that individuals continue to
develop through the life cycle. He proposed
eight stages of development; each stage
presents a major crisis and one's subsequent
development is influenced by the outcome of
each crisis. See text box on page 196 in the
text.

Errors of Commission - Wrong answers.

Errors of Omission - Errors made by
neglecting to do something, e.g., answer a
question.

Estrogen - Female sex hormone produced by
the ovaries and the adrenal glands.

Estrogen Replacement Therapy - See
Hormone Replacement Therapy.

Ethics Committee - In hospitals, a group of
professionals and lay people that discusses and
makes recommendations about issues for which
no clear legal or medical standards exist, e.g.,
whether or not treatment should be continued in
hopeless cases and the right to decline or
discontinue treatment.

Ethnic Minority - Small group of people of a
particular ethnicity or culture residing within a
community dominated by a majority culture.

Ethnogerontology - Study of the causes,
processes, and consequences of ethnicity and
culture on individual and population aging.

Euthanasia - Act or practice of killing (active
euthanasia) or permitting the death of (passive
euthanasia) hopelessly sick or injured
individuals in a relatively painless way for
reasons of mercy.

External Memory Aids - Things that help
people remember things, for example,
calendars, alarms, and lists.

Extroversion - Focus on the external world; per
Jung's model of personality the ego moves from
extroversion in youth and middle age to
introversion in old age.

Familial Piety - Devotion to and reverence for
parents and family. Also called filial piety.

Feminist Perspective - The view that the
experiences of women are often ignored in
understanding and explaining the human
condition, together with efforts to attend,
critically, to those experiences.

Feminization of Poverty - A growing number of
women in poverty. Among the elderly, this is
because women make less than men when they
work, spend fewer years in the workforce
because they take on childcare and eldercare
duties, and live longer than men.

Filial Piety - Devotion to and reverence for parents and family.

Fluid Intelligence - Popularly called "native intelligence," fluid intelligence relates to the brain's organization of neurons in areas responsible for memory and associations and to the speed of processing information. Measures of fluid intelligence include spatial orientation, abstract reasoning, and perceptual speed.

Foster Care - See Adult Foster Care.

Foster Grandparent Program - Volunteer program pairing seniors with disabled children.

Fraility - Severe limitations in ADL (activities of daily living).

Free Radical Theory of Aging - Biological theory that links aging with the destructive effects of free radicals. It is hypothesized that increasing intake of antioxidants, like vitamin E and beta carotene, can inhibit free radical damage.

Free Radicals - Highly reactive chemical compounds with an unpaired electron.

Free Recall - Remembering things without using any hints or external memory aids. See Cued Recall.

Freud's Stages of Psychosexual Development - Framework for understanding human behavior proposed by Sigmund Freud (circa 1900), which suggests that one's personality achieves stability by adolescence and that little change in personality is seen subsequently in the life span.

Functional Aging - Aging as measured by the efficiency and functional abilities of an individual's organ systems and his/her physical activity levels.

Functional (or Reserve) Capacity - The ability of a given organ to perform its normal function, compared with its function under conditions of illness, disability, and aging.

Gap Group - People who are neither rich enough to pay privately for services they need nor poor enough to qualify for government assistance. Also known as "tweeners."

Gatekeepers - People in service positions who, because of regular interactions with older adults, can watch for signs indicating a need for assistance or attention.

Gay – Homosexual, especially male.

Generation X – Those born between 1965 and 1978 and who are children of the Baby Boomers.

Generational Investment - Investments made by one generation for the benefit of another, such as the payment of social security taxes by the working population for the benefit of retirees and the payment of property taxes that support public school education for children.

Generations United - Coalition of 120 organizations for different age groups working together on health and social issues.

Generativity vs. Stagnation - In Erikson's model of personality development, the seventh stage during which middle-aged and older persons become concerned about mentoring younger generations and looking toward the future, rather than stagnating in the past.

Genetic Engineering - Manipulation of genes at the somatic level to correct deficiencies or slow the aging process.

Genetic Replacement Therapy - Treatment to replace defective genes, thus prolonging quality of life and perhaps life span.

Genome Project – See Human Genome Project. Research program to identify the location and function of every gene on every chromosome.

Geriatrics - Field of medicine that focuses on how to prevent and manage the diseases of aging.

Germ Cell - Cells at the egg and sperm level.

Geronticide - The deliberate destruction of aged community members. In many societies that existed close to the edge of subsistence, this practice made sense and was often performed with great reverence or ceremony.

Gerontological Society of Aging - Association of researchers and practitioners interested in gerontology and geriatrics. GSA sponsors a number of activities, including conferences, publications, task forces on current issues, and Congressional lobbying.

Gerontology - Study of biological, psychological, and sociological aspects of aging.

Glaucoma - Eye disease with excessive production of or inefficient drainage of the aqueous humour.

Gliding Out - Phased retirement that permits a gradual shift to a part-time schedule.

Grandparents' Rights - Legal rights of grandparents to interact with grandchildren following divorce of the grandchildren's parents; liabilities of grandparents and step-grandparents as custodians of grandchildren in the absence of responsible parents.

Gray Panthers - National organization, founded by Maggie Kuhn, that encourages work on social issues through intergenerational, grass roots alliances.

Graying of Society - Trend toward more older people (supposedly with gray hair) in society.

Greedy Geezers - A pejorative name for older adults which implies that, among the generations, they are getting more than their share of resources.

Grief Process - Similar to Elisabeth Kubler-Ross's death process, grief may be experienced in three stages: shock and sorrow, questioning or searching, and recovery.

Grief Reaction - State of shock, disbelief, and depression following the death of a loved one.

Group Therapy - Psychotherapy with a group, rather than with an individual, providing participants the opportunity for peer support, social interaction, and role modeling.

Guardianship - Probate court appointment of someone to care for the individual's person, property, and finances beacuse he/she is mentally unable to care for him/herself. Also see Conservatorship.

Hassles - In contrast to life events, day-to-day activities and feelings that are chronic (long-term), for example, regrets over past decisions and concerns about one's current situations.

Health - According to the World Health Organization, health is more than the absence of disease or infirmity; it is a state of complete physical, mental, and social well-being.

Health Care Financing Administration (HCFA) - Federal agency that administers the Medicare and Medicaid programs.

Health Care Disparities – Differences in access, quality, or rate of utilization of a health care service, where ethnic minorities have a substantially lower utilization rate.

Health Disparities - Socioeconomic and racial/ethnic inequalities in health, mortality, and other adverse conditions across the life span.

Health Maintenance Organization (HMO) - Health care organization that provides a comprehensive package of care for a predetermined monthly fee. Participants pay minimal out-of-pocket expenses. The Kaiser health care system is an example of an HMO.

Health Promotion Guidelines - Specifications for good nutrition, exercise, stress control, injury prevention, and disease screening aimed at maximizing health and reducing the incidence of chronic disease.

Health Status - Individual's summary of state of disease, degree of disability, and self-perceptions of physical and mental status.

Hemianopsia - Blindness in half of a stroke victim's visual field.

Hemiplegia - Paralysis of one side of the body that can result from a stroke.

Hemlock Society - National organization that promotes the right to die for terminally ill persons, calls for legalizing assistance to people who decide to take their own lives, and publishes information on nonviolent, painless methods to commit suicide.

Heterogeneous - Different in character, not all the same.

Heterosexuality - Sexual orientation toward the opposite gender.

Home- and Community-Based Services - Services that allow older adults to continue living in the community. These include home health care, personal care services, day care, transportation programs, meals-on-wheels, foster care, and so forth.

Home-Delivered Meals - Meals, usually prepared by a church or voluntary agency, delivered to the home of an ill or disabled person.

Home Equity Conversion Mortgages - Mortgages provided by banks to older people whose houses are of value but who have little cash or income; the bank provides a monthly annuity to the home owner and, upon the home owner's death and the home's sale, receives a refund on the loan as well as a portion of the home's appreciated value.

Home Health Care - Nursing, rehabilitation, and other therapy services, as well as assistance with personal care and household maintenance, that are provided to people who are homebound and have difficulty performing ADLs.

Home Sharing Programs - Programs that assist older persons who own homes to identify live-in companions (of any age) who may pay rent, share household chores, and/or provide services (such as shopping or personal care) to the elderly home owner; the success of the program depends on the congruence of the "match" between home owners and companions in terms of their individual values, habits, needs, and abilities.

Homebound - Unable to leave the house because of illness, disability, or social isolation.

Homelessness - Living without a fixed, regular, and adequate residence.

Homeostasis - Relatively stable state of equilibrium.

Homosexuality - Sexual orientation toward the same gender.

Hormone Replacement Therapy (HRT) - In women, the prescription of hormones (primarily estrogen and progesterone) to supplement decreasing hormone levels during and/or after menopause.

Hospice - Approach to caring for the terminally ill in which the forthcoming death is accepted and palliative care is administered in the patient's home or in a homelike facility in concert with spiritual and/or psychosocial therapies.

Hot Flashes - Sudden sensation of heat in the upper body caused by vasomotor instability as nerves over-respond to decreases in hormone levels during menopause.

Human Genome Project - Research program to identify the location and function of every gene on every chromosome.

Human Growth Hormone - Hormone that stimulates growth and may help reverse aging.

Hypertension - High blood pressure, a disease associated with increased risk of heart attack, stroke, kidney problems, and premature death.

Hypoglycemia - Low blood sugar.

Hypokinesia - Degeneration and functional loss of muscle and bone due to physical inactivity.

Hypotension - Abnormally low blood pressure, characterized by dizziness and faintness from exertion after a period of inactivity, e.g., when getting out of bed quickly.

Hypothermia - Condition in which your body temperature is several degrees below normal for a prolonged period.

Hypothesis - In research, an assumption or proposition that is then tested through observation or experimentation.

Hysterectomy - Surgical removal of the uterus.

Iatrogenic Disease or Condition - Disease or condition inadvertently caused by a physician or medical treatment.

Iconic Memory - Visual memory, i.e., words, faces, and landscapes that we experience through our eyes.

Impotence - Inability to have or maintain an erection.

Income Redistribution - Transfer of funds from people with greater incomes to those with lower incomes.

Incontinence - Inability to control urine and/or feces.

Incremental - In this context, the manner of dealing with public problems by making small changes in policy rather than attempting comprehensive or major changes.

Index - In this context, steps taken to maintain the value of a benefit as the value of currency changes by increasing or decreasing the benefit in accord with the changes in the cost of living.

Indian Health Service - Federal program that provides health care for Native Americans and Alaskans of all ages through hospitals and community clinics.

Indirect Benefit - Benefit given indirectly, such as a tax deduction or exemption. (See Direct Benefit.)

Individual Competence – The theoretical upper limit of an individual's ability to function in the areas of health, social behavior, and cognition. Some of these capacities needed to adapt to environmental press include good health, effective problem-solving and learning skills, job performance, and the ability to manage activities of daily living. See **Competence Model.**

Individual Equity - Benefits received by an individual in an amount that reflects his/her actual contribution.

Inelastic Ego (video) - Being "set in one's ways" and unable to change one's personality.

Infarct - Area of tissue that dies because an obstruction has restricted or stopped the blood from reaching the area.

Information and Referral - Form of social service that assists persons by providing information and direction in finding needed services.

Information Processing Model - Conceptual model for understanding how the processes of learning and memory take place. See Figure 5.3 in the text.

Informed Consent - Principle, backed by U.S. law, that competent patients must be given information on their diagnosis, prognosis, and treatment options and that they have the right to accept or refuse medical treatment based on their understanding of its risks and benefits.

In-Home Services - Services provided to frail older adults in their homes, including homemaker assistance, respite care, friendly visits, home health services, and so forth.

Institutionalization - Placing someone in an institution; often used to mean placing an older adult in a nursing home.

Instrumental Activities of Daily Living (IADL) - Tasks such as managing money, shopping, preparing meals, keeping the house clean, doing laundry, using the telephone, and taking medications.

Instrumental Coping Strategies - Strategies that help solve the problem being confronted.

Intelligence - Range of abilities to acquire and comprehend new information, to adapt to new situations, to appreciate and create new ideas; theoretical limit of an individual's performance.

Intelligence Quotient (IQ) - Measure of one's abilities to judge well, comprehend well, and reason well, compared to others of the same chronological age.

Interactionist Perspectives - Social theories of aging that emphasize the dynamic interaction between older individuals and their social world, e.g., person-environment, symbolic interaction, labeling, and social breakdown theories.

Interdependence of Generations Framework - In contrast to the intergenerational inequity framework, an outlook based on the belief that the needs and contributions of generations are so intertwined that programs benefiting one age group directly or indirectly benefit other age groups.

Interference Theory - Theory that suggests that older people may have problems retrieving information from secondary memory because new information interferes with material already in storage.

Intergenerational Assistance - See Intergenerational Exchange.

Intergenerational Exchange - Support provided among generations within a family, for example, a niece sends money to her aunt, a grandparent baby-sits a grandchild.

Intergenerational Inequity - Inequitable distribution of scarce resources among generations.

Intergenerational Inequity Framework - In contrast to the interdependence of generations framework, an outlook based on the belief that age-entitlement programs for older adults benefit the elderly at the expense of younger age groups.

Intergenerational Living - Families living in the same household spanning two or more generations.

Intergenerational Programming - Services and programs that facilitate the interaction among age groups, for example, the Foster Grandparent Program.

Intergenerational Transfer of Knowledge - Exchange of ideas and information among generations, e.g., older members teaching younger members about family history, younger members teaching older members how to use computers.

Intergenerational Transfer of Resources - Exchange of property and finances among generations, for example: 1) older adults giving their property and finances to children and grandchildren and 2) younger members pooling money to support an older member in times of illness or inadequate income.

Interindividual Differences - Great variations observed among individuals, even among those within the same age group.

Interiority - Increasing self-awareness and appreciation for life through self-examination, life review, and/or spiritual reflection.

Intimacy - Feelings of deep mutual regard, affection, and trust, usually developed through long association.

Intimacy at a Distance - Strong emotional ties among family members even though they do not live near one another.

Intraindividual Changes - Changes that occur within an individual, for example, the graying of one's hair over the life span.

Introversion - Focus on one's inner world; per Jung's model of personality, the ego moves from extroversion in youth and middle age to introversion in old age.

Jung's Model of Personality - Theory that emphasizes life span development of consciousness and the ego from the narrow focus of the child to the otherworldliness of the older person. He also proposed that people, as they age, adopt psychological traits commonly associated with the opposite sex, i.e., men become more passive and nurturing as they age while women become more assertive and achievement-oriented.

Kinesthetic System - Body system that signals one's position in space and is important for balance.

Kyphosis - Collapsing and compressing of vertebrae in people with osteoporosis.

Labeling Theory - Theory derived from symbolic interactionism and based on the belief that people derive their self-concepts from interacting with others in their social milieu and how these people define us and react to us.

Last Acts - Coalition of 72 organizations working to improve communication and decision-making about end-of-life issues with a goal of improving care to dying people.

Leadership Council on Aging - Coalition of 41 age-related organizations working together on issues of concern to older adults.

Learning - Acquisition of a new skill or information through practice or experience.

Least Restrictive Environment - Environment that provides needed support with the most amount of freedom, enabling a disabled person to be as independent, and as little confined, as possible.

Leisure - Free time to pursue one's favorite activities.

Leisure World - Retirement community in Southern California that provides a number of services for residents, including health services, opportunities for socialization, and lifeline systems in the home.

Lesbian - Homosexual female.

Levinson's Model of Personality Development - Model outlining four "seasons" of life: pre-adulthood, early adulthood, middle adulthood, and late adulthood. Each era has specific conflicts that demand confrontation and resolution, and these conflicts stem from the individual's life structures at a particular time. See text box on page 200 in the text.

Life Change Unit - Numerical score indicating the typical level of change or stress associated with a particular event in one's life.

Life Course Capital – An expansion of the life course perspective that addresses the impact of differential acquisition of resources among different members of the cohort.

Life Course Perspective - Multidisciplinary view of human development that focuses on changes with age and life experiences.

Life Events - Internal and external stimuli (both positive and negative) that cause change in an individual's daily life, e.g., marriage, childbirth, divorce, change in financial status, and caregiving.

Life Expectancy - Average length of time members of a specific population can expect to live.

Life Review Therapy - Psychotherapeutic approach that encourages introspection through active reminiscence about past achievements and failures and that may reestablish ego integrity in depressed older persons.

Life Span - Actual number of years one lives.

Life Structures - In Levinson's theory of personality development, specific states consisting of eras and transitions.

Lifecare Communities - Retirement communities or congregate facilities that offer different intensities of service with the goal of caring for residents until the end of their lives.

Lifecare Contract - Agreement, usually with a housing project or lifecare community, for living space and services until death in exchange for an initial entry fee and fixed monthly payments.

Lifeline System - Emergency alarm system used by vulnerable older adults during periods of isolation. When activated, the alarm signals an emergency operator to send someone to check on and assist the individual.

Lipids - Fats.

Lipofuscin - Age pigment composed of fat and protein. As concentrations of lipofuscin increase (for example, in muscle fibers or in the brain), elasticity is decreased.

Liver Spots - Age spots.

Living Will - Legal document outlining one's desire that medical treatment be withheld or withdrawn if it will not provide cure and merely prolong the dying process.

Locus of Control - Where an individual feels his/her life is being controlled, externally (by fate or powerful others) or internally (by him/herself).

Long-Term Care- Medical, nursing, and social services provided to people with chronic illnesses who need daily assistance either in their home or in an institution.

Long-Term Care Insurance - Private insurance designed to cover the costs of institutional, and sometimes home-based-services, for chronically disabled people in need of daily assistance.

Longevity - Long duration of individual life; length of life.

Longitudinal Research Design - Studies in which the same people are surveyed at specified intervals over a period of months or years to measure individual changes that occur over time.

Love - Strong affection for another arising out of kinship, personal ties, common interests, and/or sexual attraction.

Lymphocytes - Cells that include the cellular mediators of immunity.

Macular Degeneration - Disease of the eye in which the macula receives less oxygen than it needs, resulting in destruction of the existing nerve endings in this region and a loss of the central visual field.

Major Depression - Depression accompanied by vegetative signs, suicidal thoughts, weight loss, and sudden mood changes.

Male Menopause - Significant change experienced by men as their production of testosterone decreases in later life. Although male fertility is maintained, some older men experience testicular atrophy, prostate enlargement, and associated psychological doubts. Most endocrinologists feel that hormonal changes experienced by aging men are not as dramatic or abrupt as the menopausal changes experienced by women, which include complete loss of fertility and depletion of estrogen.

Managed Care - Health care policy under which patients are provided health care services under the supervision of a single health professional, usually a physician. This means that in order to see a specialist, the patient must be referred by the supervising health professional.

Mandatory Retirement - Requirement to retire at a certain age.

Masked Depression - Depression denied or hidden by its manifestation as physical discomfort or memory loss rather than mood change.

Mastectomy - Surgical removal of one or both breasts, usually in treatment of breast cancer.

Mastery, Active and Passive - Referring to gaining control. A person with a passive mastery style does not feel powerful enough to directly influence his/her fate. A person with an active mastery style tends to rely more on personal abilities and less on others.

Masturbation - Erotic stimulation of the genital organs achieved by manual contact exclusive of sexual intercourse.

Maximum Life Span - The maximum number of years a given species could expect to live if environmental hazards were eliminated, about 115 to 120 years for humans.

Meal Sites - Centers at which group meals are provided to older adults.

Means-Based Entitlements - Social programs delivered to persons who meet defined criteria of eligibility based on need and ability to pay for services. See also Need-Based Programs.

Means-Tested Programs - Social programs available to persons who meet define criteria of eligibility based on need and ability to pay for services. See also Need-Based Programs.

Median Age - Age that divides a population into two groups; half the members are younger than that age and half the members are older than that age.

Mediators - Internal memory aids, both visual and mnemonic, that help file new information in long-term memory or help associate it with information that is already there.

Medicaid - Program jointly financed by federal and state government that provides coverage for health care costs of low-income people regardless of age. States have some flexibility in how Medicaid funds are spent, but most states cover hospital care, physician services, outpatient services, skilled nursing home care, and intermediate (custodial) nursing home care.

Medicaid Waiver - Exceptions to the Medicaid rules that allow states to use Medicaid dollars (usually restricted to pay for nursing home care) to pay for selected home-based long-term care services.

Medical Savings Account - Tax-exempt account into which individuals could put Medicare dollars to pay for qualified medical expenses. This would be combined with a high-deductible insurance policy to cover catastrophic injuries or illness.

Medicare - Federal health insurance program that provides partial coverage (80% of allowable charges) for medical care costs of people 65 years of age and older who contributed to the Social Security system. Part A provides partial coverage of hospital care and very limited skilled nursing home and home care. Part B provides partial coverage of physician services, outpatient services, diagnostic x-ray, and laboratory services.

Medicare Catastrophic Health Care Act - Federal law passed in 1988 that imposed an additional tax on upper-income elders so that the Medicare program could limit out-of-pocket expenses by the elderly, provide protection against spousal impoverishment, and increase coverage for skilled nursing home and home care in the event of a severe illness. It did not provide protection against costs of extended long-term care. A huge grassroots protest by older adults led to the legislation's repeal in 1989.

Medicare Plus Choices (also referred to as **Medicare + Choice**) **Plans** – Available in many parts of the country, these are plans that provide care under contract to Medicare, and allow beneficiaries more choices in where and how they obtain health care.

Medigap Insurance - Insurance that can be purchased to cover a large portion of health care expenses not covered by Medicare.

Melanin - Dark skin pigmentation produced by the body to protect it from ultraviolet rays.

Memory - Three types of memory are sensory, primary (or short-term), and secondary (or long-term). Remembering is the retrieval of information stored in primary and secondary memory.

Menopause - In women, the process of the cessation of menstruation, complete after 12 months of no menstrual flow.

Mental Health Centers - Centers providing ambulatory treatment for psychological and psychiatric disorders.

Mercy Killing - Deliberate actions taken by others to end the life of a terminally ill or chronically disabled individual without his/her permission.

Milieu Therapy - Psychotherapeutic approach conducted by providing a good, therapeutic environment that enhances a person's independence and feelings of control.

Mnemonics - Verbal riddles, rhymes, and codes associated with new information, for example, 'i' before 'e' except after 'c.'

Mobile Society - Society in which relocating from place to place is the norm, putting distance among family members; this practice limits access of older people to family caregivers.

Modernization Theory - Theory suggesting that older people lose political and social power as the society places increasing value on technology, mass education, and nuclear, rather than extended, families.

Monogamy - Having a single sexual partner.

Morbidity - Sickness or disability.

Mortality - Death.

Mourning - Culturally patterned expressions of grief.

Multigenerational Family - Three or more generations living at the same time.

Multilevel Facilities - Housing projects that offer a range from independent living to congregate living and nursing home care.

Mutuality - Sharing of sentiments.

Myocardial Infarction - Heart attack in which the heart is deprived of blood for so long that a portion of it is permanently damaged. Also called Acute Myocardial Infarction.

Myopia - Nearsightedness.

National Asian Pacific Center on Aging - National organization of professionals concerned with increasing the responsiveness of aging programs to Asian and Pacific Islander Americans.

National Association of Retired Federal Employees - National organization of adults retired from the federal government, primarily involved in political and social issues.

National Caucus for the Black Aged - National organization of professionals concerned with increasing the responsiveness of aging programs to African Americans.

National Council of Senior Citizens - Mass-membership organization involved in political action for older adults.

National Council on Aging - National organization of more than 2,000 social welfare agencies concerned with aging, primarily serving as technical consultant to groups working to address problems facing older adults.

National Family Caregiver Support Program – A federal program that works with state and area agencies on aging to provide services to support family caregivers.

National Health Care - Nationally sponsored system of providing adequate health care to all citizens regardless of their ability to pay. The U.S. and South Africa are the only developed countries in the world that do not provide their citizens with a form of national health care.

National Retired Teachers Association - Mass-membership group for older adults who have retired from careers in teaching.

Naturally Occurring Retirement Communities - Building, neighborhood, or region (such as Florida) largely occupied by older people, but not planned specifically for this population.

Natural Helpers - People who assist others because of their concern, interest, and innate understanding.

Need-Based Programs - Programs available to individuals based on need, like low income. An example of a need-based program is Supplemental Security Income.

Neurons - Nerve cells.

Nocturnal Myoclonus - Neuromuscular disturbance affecting the legs during sleep.

Nocturnal Penile Tumescence - In men, involuntary sleep-related erections.

Non-Contributory Programs - Programs providing benefits that do not require the beneficiary to contribute two ard the cost of the benefit.

Non-Events - Life events that are expected but fail to materialize.

Non-Normative Events - Events that happen off-time, i.e., at an unexpected time in life, given one's age.

Nontraditional Families - New family structures derived through gay and lesbian partnerships, communal living, cohabitation, informal adoption, etc.

Normative Events - Events that happen on-time, i.e., at the expected time in one's life.

Nursing Homes - Residential facilities where nursing staff provide 24-hour care to people with chronic illnesses who need assistance with ADL and IADL.

Nutrition Programs - Programs that deliver meals to homebound older adults or provide meals in congregate settings such as senior centers.

Observational Analysis - Method of research in which the researcher simply watches the subject(s) to describe and develop hypotheses about the observed interactions.

Off-Time Events - Events that happen at an unexpected time, e.g., having your child die before you do is an off-time event.

Older American Volunteer Program - Federally sponsored volunteer program that recruits older people to work with disadvantaged groups.

Older Americans Act (OAA) - Federal law, administered by the Administration on Aging (AoA), that establishes and funds state and local offices to plan, coordinate, provide, and contract services for older adults.

Older Women's League (OWL) - National organization concerned about issues affecting older women, especially health care and finances.

Oldest-Old - Among older adults, those 85 and older.

Old-Old - Among older adults, those 75 to 84.

Olfactory Sense - Sense of smell.

On Lok - Comprehensive program of health and social services provided to very frail adults residing in certain neighborhoods of San Francisco with a goal of preventing or delaying institutionalization by safely maintaining these adults in their homes.

On-Time Events - Events that happen at an expected time, e.g., retiring at age 65 would be an on-time event because it is expected that most people retire around age 65.

Opportunity Structures - Social arrangements, formal and informal, that limit or advance options available to peple based on such features as social class, age, ethnicity, and sex.

Orgasm - Climax of sexual excitement.

Osteoarthritis - Gradual degeneration of the joints most subject to stress, i.e., hands, knees, hips, and shoulders.

Osteopenia - Significant loss of calcium and reduced bone density not associated with increased risk of fractures.

Osteoporosis - Loss of bone that results in decreased bone strength, diminished height, and increased bone brittleness.

Outreach - Social service that endeavors to locate those in need of services with a goal of explaining possible benefits, facilitating their enrollment in entitlement programs, and encouraging their receipt of needed services.

Ovariectomy - Surgical removal of both ovaries.

PACE - Fifteen-site federal demonstration program that replicates the On Lok model of single access to and coordinated payment of a comprehensive package of preventive, acute, and long-term care services to allow frail elders to live as independently as possible. PACE stands for Program for the All-inclusive Care for the Elderly.

Palliative Treatment - Treatment designed to relieve pain provided to a person with a terminal illness for whom death is imminent.

Paranoia - Irrational suspicion of other people.

Paraphrenia - Late-onset schizophrenia with paranoid features.

Partnership in Caring – National organization supporting passive euthanasia and providing information on advance directives (formerly known as Choice in Dying).

Patient Self-Determination Act - Federal law requiring that health care facilities inform their patients about their rights to decide how they want to live or die, for example, by providing them information on refusing treatment and on filing advance directives.

Payroll Taxes - Taxes calculated as a percentage of an organizations payroll or of an individual's income. For example, individual payments to Social Security are based on one's income.

Peace Corps - Voluntary agency that supports U.S. citizens of all ages to work in developing countries, usually on projects related to health care, education, and economic development.

Peers - Friends and confidants selected because of similarities in age, sex, marital status, psycho-economic status, or other characteristics.

Penile Implant - Devices surgically implanted in the penis to reverse impotence and allow an erection.

Pensions - Retirement plans sponsored by government or business. Many older adults receive income from pensions as well as from Social Security.

Perception - Function in which the information received through the senses is processed in the brain.

Period Effect - In studies of age differences among generations, referring to differences not necessarily due to age but due to the particular historical conditions that shaped the different age groups.

Periodontitis - Gum disease.

Peritonitis - Inflammation of the membrane that lines the cavity of the abdomen.

Person-Environment Interaction - Dynamic process in which an individual's needs change over time and in which the individual constantly interacts with, adapts to, and changes the environment to meet these needs.

Person-Environment Fit or **Person-Environment Congruence** - Concept that describes a good match between an individual's needs and the environment.

Person-Environment Perspective - Model for understanding the behavior of people based on the idea that persons are affected by personal characteristics such as health, attitudes, and beliefs as they interact with and are affected by the characteristics of the cultural, social, political, and economic environment.

Personal Care Aide - Caregiver specially trained to assist disabled adults with bathing, dressing, and grooming.

Personal Support Services - Programs that provide workers who can clean the home, assist with ADL and IADL, and phone or visit regularly.

Personality - Set of innate and learned traits that influence how each person responds and interacts with the environment.

Pharmacotherapy - Therapy using medication.

Pig in a Python - Analogy describing the large, demographic bulge caused by the movement of the Baby Boomers through time (see Figure 1.8 in the text).

Planned Housing - Housing projects developed with religious or government funds, either as subsidized housing for low-income elderly or age-segregated housing for middle-income and upper-income elderly.

Policy - Principles that govern action directed toward specific ends, designed to identify and ameliorate problems and implying changes in situations, systems, practices, beliefs, and/or behaviors.

Political Economy of Aging - Theory based on the belief that social class is a structural barrier to older people's access to resources and that dominant groups within society try to sustain their own interests by perpetuating class inequities.

Politics of Entitlement - In contrast to the politics of productivity, a philosophy that casts older adults as a group deserving of public support regardless of need.

Politics of Productivity - In contrast to the politics of entitlement, a philosophy that sees older adults as increasingly diverse and contributing to society to the extent of their abilities.

Polygamy - Having more than one spouse at a time.

Polypharmacy - Taking multiple medications, including prescription drugs and over-the-counter medicines and supplements, which could cause unwanted and unnecessary side effects.

Population Pyramid - Graphic representation of the proportions of young and old persons in a population (see Figure 1.8 in the text).

Positivism - Perspective that knowledge is based solely on observable facts and their relationship to one another (cause and effect or correlation) and rejects the search for ultimate origins.

Postmenopause - In women, the period of life after menopause.

Postmodern Theory - Critique of language, discourse, and research practices that constrict knowledge.

Poverty Level - Fixed dollar amount of income determined by the federal government; if a household makes less than this dollar amount, it is deemed poor.

Preferred Provider Organization - A network of independent physicians, hospitals, and other helath care providers who contract with an insurance entity to provide are at discounted rates.

Premenopause - In middle-aged women, the period between reproduction and nonreproduction marked by a decline in ovarian function, estrogen, and regularity of menstrual flow.

Preorgasmic Plateau Phase - In men and women, the phase of lovemaking prior to orgasm in which sexual tension is at its height.

Presbycusis - Age-related hearing loss.

Primary Memory - Temporary holding and organizing of information in short-term memory, which has limited capacity. This capacity does not change with age.

Primogeniture, Law of - Exclusive right of the eldest son to inherit his father's estate.

Progeria - Rare condition in which aging is accelerated and death may occur by age 15 or 20.

Progesterone - Female sex hormone produced by the ovaries.

Proprietary - Privately owned and operated, in contrast to government owned and operated.

Prospective Payment System - System of reimbursing hospitals and physicians a lump-sum based on the patient's diagnosis, rather than for the cost of each individual service provided.

Prostate, Enlargement of - Growth of the prostate, due to changes in prostatic cells with age, which can result in pain and difficulties urinating. Also known as benign prostatic hypertrophy.

Pseudo-Dementia - Depression in older adults that manifests itself as loss of memory and problem-solving skills rather than mood changes.

Psychodynamic Group Therapy - Using psychoanalytic concepts such as insight, transference, and the unconscious to review symptoms of depression and to prevent its recurrence by understanding why the individual behaves in self-defeating ways.

Psychological Aging - Changes that occur in perceptual processes, mental functioning, personality, and coping.

Psychopathology - Personality disorders, psychiatric disorders, and cognitive impairment.

Psychotherapy - Treatment for psychological or psychiatric disorders.

Radical Prostatectomy - Surgical removal of the prostate, usually in treatment for prostate cancer.

Range-of-Motion Exercises - Exercises that help stretch and keep limber the arms, legs, hands, and other parts of the body through their full range of movement.

Rational Suicide - Ending one's life for good and valid reasons.

Rationing Health Care - Restricting access to health care in order to save money. For example, by not allowing Medicaid coverage of expensive procedures like organ transplants, we would have more money to cover custodial care services.

Reactive Depression - Depression in response to specific distress such as illness or the death of a spouse.

Reality Orientation - Psychotherapeutic approach in which confused and disoriented persons are reminded of person, place, and time.

Recall - Searching through and retrieving information from the vast store of information in secondary memory. Essay exams test our recall abilities.

Reciprocal Relationships - Sharing of resources and privileges among people; mutual dependence and support.

Recognition - Matching information in secondary memory with stimulus information. Multiple-choice exams test our recognition abilities.

Recognition Threshold - Intensity of a stimulus needed in order for an individual to identify or recognize it.

Rectangularization of the Survival Curve - Survival of all individuals to their maximum life span (see Figure 1.4 in the text).

Refractory Period - In men, the time between ejaculation and another erection.

Rehabilitation - Health services designed to improve physical functioning following an accident, such as a fall resulting in a hip fracture, or illness, such as a stroke.

Relocation - Moving from one living situation to another, which can be traumatic for older adults if they are not prepared for or in agreement with the move.

Reminiscence Therapy - Psychotherapy used with depressed, anxious, and sometimes confused older adults, in which the older person is asked to remember and think about successful coping experiences and positive events in the past.

Remotivation Therapy - Psychotherapeutic approach in which groups of people who have withdrawn from social activities are guided through group discussion by encouraging each participant to share his/her feelings or experiences with the subject matter.

Representativeness of the Sample - In research, the small group of people you are studying is like the larger population you want to learn something about. In other words, your small group "represents" the large group.

Residual Role of Government - Based on values commonly held by Americans of individual freedom, individual rights, self-determination, privacy, and personal responsibility, the belief that government should serve only a backup role in providing benefits, e.g., government should respond to crises rather than attempting to prevent problems or attack underlying causes of problems.

Resilience – The ability to thrive under adversity or multiple challenges by taking life's ups and downs in stride.

Respite Care - Care to temporarily relieve family caregivers of their duties so that they can rest or run errands. Respite care can be provided at home, in the community, or in institutions for a few hours to a few months.

Retired Senior Volunteer Program (RSVP) - Federally sponsored program in which older adults volunteer in schools, hospitals, and other social agencies.

Retirement - Period of life, usually starting at age 65, during which an individual stops working in the paid labor force.

Retirement Communities - Communities in which older adults live in their own houses or apartments but share recreational, social, and/or health facilities.

Reverse Mortgages - See Home Equity Conversion Mortgages.

Rheumatoid Arthritis - Chronic inflammation of the membranes lining joints and tendons.

Right-to-Die - Right of an individual to hasten or cause his/her own death.

Right-to-Know - Right of an individual to understand his/her diagnosis and prognosis so as to make decisions about further care.

Robust Aging - Broader concept than successful aging, which includes exceptional functioning on measures of physical health, cognitive abilities, emotional well-being, and social involvement.

Role - Behavior expected of a person who occupies a particular position, for example, in society, in the family, at work, etc.

Role Change - Change in the set of behaviors of a person.

Role Continuity - Idea that role behaviors learned early in life remain useful at later stages of life, even though exact roles may change. For example, a teacher can continue using teaching skills as a volunteer after retirement.

Role Development - Evolution or changes within existing roles over time, for example, within a marriage or as a parent.

Role Dilemma - Conflicts or confusion associated with gaining, losing, competing for, or changing roles.

Role Discontinuity - Behaviors learned at early in life may become useless or conflicting at a later stage of life. For example, people who have worked long hours throughout their lives may be uncomfortable with the expectation to relax after retirement.

Role Gain - Addition of a function or position, for example, the role of grandparent is gained when one's children have children.

Role Loss - Loss of a function or position, for example, a widow loses the role of spouse, a retiree loses the role of employee.

Role Model - Clear guide to the behaviors of a certain role, usually in the form of a person who has distinguished him/herself in the role.

Role Theory - Social theory based on the belief that roles (student, parent, business person, homemaker) define us and our self-concept. Age is associated with the types of roles people are expected to fill and how they play these roles.

Rolelessness - State of being without a specified set of standards to guide behavior.

Rural Elderly Enhancement Program - Program in Alabama that helps keep people in their own homes and improves their nutritional status through the use of home visitors who shop and help prepare meals.

Safety Net - Minimum level of support provided by the government to citizens that keeps them from poverty. While the U.S. government sponsors many programs for low-income citizens, evidence exists that these programs, in fact, do not provide a safety net and that many subgroups of Americans do live in poverty.

Samurai - Japanese warrior, known for his stoicism.

Sandwich Generation - Referring to middle-aged people most likely to have caregiving demands from aged parents as well as from spouses and children.

Schizophrenia - Psychotic disorder characterized by lack of contact with reality and disintegration of personality.

Seattle Longitudinal Study - A long-term study that began in 1956 to collect data on mental abilities (intelligence, learning, and memory).

Sebaceous Glands - Glands that produce oil, for example, in the skin.

Secondary Memory - Long-term memory, which has an unlimited capacity that does not change with age.

Selective Benefits - Benefits available based on individually-determined needs. See Means-Based Entitlements.

Selective Dropout - People who drop out of a longitudinal study due to poor health or another characteristic (other than participation) that distinguishes them from people who continue in a study. See **Selective Survival**.

Selective Survival – A problem in aging research resulting when those who remain in a study sample no longer are representative of the original cohort, thereby skewing study results. Frequently those who were healthiest at birth and maintain good health throughout their lives are those who enjoy higher socio-economic status. See **Selective Dropout**.

Self-Concept - Cognitive image of self and identity. The maintenance of a "good" self-concept is achieved by assimilating new experiences into one's self-concept and/or accommodating one's self-concept to fit the new reality. As this is often dependent on an individual's roles (child, parent, teacher, volunteer), successful aging includes being able to satisfactorily redefine self-concept in the face of role change.

Self-Efficacy - Feeling of confidence in one's ability to deal with challenges and new situations.

Self-Esteem - One's emotional assessment of self. As with self-concept, older people who successfully maintain self-esteem are able to satisfactorily redefine the meaning of self, accept the aging process, objectively review life and learn from it, and refocus goals and expectations.

Self-Fulfilling Prophecy - Performance influenced by pre-performance expectations, for example, people who are told that their age may keep them from performing well often perform poorly.

Self-Paced Tests - Exams in which the subject can control the amount of time spent on each item.

Senecide - Deliberate destruction of aged community members. In many societies that existed close to the edge of subsistence, this practice made sense and was often performed with great reverence or ceremony.

Senescence – Biological aging. The gradual accumulation of irreversible functional losses to which the average person tries to accommodate in some socially acceptable way.

Senior Boom - Large number and proportion of older adults expected early in the 21st century when the Baby Boomers pass age 65.

Senior Center Programs - Centers in which seniors can congregate to share a meal and engage in social, physical, educational, recreational, and cultural programs.

Senior Citizen - Nickname used for individuals 65 years of age and older.

Senior Companion Program - Vounteer program in which able-bodied seniors help disabled older people.

Senior Employment Programs - Programs sponsored by government or business that encourage the employment of older workers.

Senior Learning Programs - Academic programs specially designed for older adults, or programs of tuition waivers that allow older adults to take college courses at no cost.

Senior Net - National educational program that teaches computer skills and provides opportunities for older people to communicate with one another through online computer networks.

Senior Power - Political power that can be leveraged by older adults in efforts to change public policy.

Sensation - Process of taking in information through the sense organs.

Sensory Discrimination - Minimum difference necessary between two or more stimuli for a person to distinguish between them.

Sensory Memory - Reception of information through the sense organs, stored for a few tenths of a second, after which it is passed on to primary and secondary memory or forgotten.

Sensory Threshold - Minimum intensity of a stimulus that a person requires to detect the stimulus.

Sequential Research Design - Research design concurrently using cross-sectional and longitudinal methods to overcome some of the problems encountered in using those designs.

Serial Monogamy - Engaged in monogamous relationships, one following another.

Serial Retirement - Moving in and out of the workforce, perhaps retiring at age 50 from a first career, retiring again at age 65 from a second career, and perhaps retiring from a third career at age 80.

Service Corps of Retired Executives - Program that links retired executives as technical and financial consultants with companies in the United States and abroad that ask for assistance.

Sex - In its most narrow sense, a biological function involving genital intercourse or orgasm. In a broader sense, expressing oneself in an intimate way through a wide-ranging language of love and pleasure in relationships.

Sexual Dysfunction - In men or women, difficulties engaging in sexual intercourse. Causes may be physical, psychological, or social.

Sexuality - Feelings of sexual desire, sexual expression, sexual activity.

Shared Housing - Two or more unrelated people living in the same house; usually each has a private bedroom, but all use the same kitchen and living areas.

Silver-Haired Legislatures - Organizations modeled after state legislatures in which seniors are elected to "office" and learn lobbying and policy making skills.

Single Room Occupancy (SRO) Hotels - Older buildings in urban centers that have been converted to low-cost apartments. Often these are single rooms with minimal cooking facilities and shared bathrooms.

Sinusitis - Inflammation of a sinus.

Sleep Apnea - Five to ten second cessation of breathing during sleep.

Smart Houses - Houses containing technological gadgets and computers that make living easier and/or help compensate for physical limitations. An example is a house with voice-activated computers that can write letters and turn off the lights on command.

Social Adequacy - Shared societal responsibility to provide a basic standard of living for all potential beneficiaries (sometimes called a "safety net") regardless of the size of their economic contribution.

Social Aging - Changes in social roles and relationships over the life course.

Social Gerontology - Area of gerontology concerned with the impact of social and socio-cultural conditions on the process of aging and with the social consequences of this process.

Social Exchange Theory - Theory based in the belief that an individual's status is defined by the balance between his/her contributions to society, which are determined by his/her control of resources, and the cost of supporting him/her.

Social Expectations - Behaviors and actions that society expects people in a certain role or certain group to perform.

Social Health Maintenance Organization (SHMO) - Prepaid health plans that provide both acute and long-term care to voluntarily enrolled Medicare beneficiaries.

Social Insurance - Benefits paid to persons based upon contingencies to which all people are exposed, including such factors as age, disability, sickness, and unemployment.

Social Policy - Principles that govern actions about a social concern.

Social Program - Programs that address the specific social concerns.

Social Security - Federal program into which workers contribute a portion of their income during adulthood and then, beginning sometime between ages 62 and 67, receive a monthly check based on the amount they earned.

Social Services Block Grant - Block of federal money provided to states to pay for services to low-income citizens of any age. Under the Block Grant system, states decide which programs to fund and which citizens are eligible for them.

Social Stratification - Divisions among people, e.g., by age or ethnic group, for purposes of maintaining distinctions among various strata by significant characteristics of those strata.

Social Support - Interactions among family, friends, neighbors, and programs that sustain, maintain, and inspire us daily and especially during hard times.

Social Support, Formal - Programs and services that assist older adults.

Social Support, Informal - Family, friends, and neighbors who assist older adults.

Social Theories - Plausible, general principles that provide frameworks within which to understand human behavior. In gerontology, social theories try to explain changes in social relationships that occur in late adulthood and suggest how older people can best relate to their environments.

Socialization - Lifelong process by which individuals learn how to perform new roles, adjust to changing roles, relinquish old ones, and thereby become integrated into society.

Socio-Economic Status (SES) - Measure of how "well off" someone is, based on income and occupation.

Somatic Cells - Cells that compose tissue and organs.

Somesthetic - Sensitivity of touch.

Spatial Memory - Ability to recall where objects are in relationship to one another in space.

Spending Down - Spending one's savings until they are low enough to meet the low-income criteria for assistance from Medicaid.

Spiritual Well-Being - Well-being that manifests as self-determined wisdom, self-transcendence, achievement of meaning and purpose for one's continued existence, and acceptance of the wholeness of life.

Spousal Impoverishment Plan - Amendment to the Medicaid program that allows the spouse of an institutionalized person supported by Medicaid to retain a relatively generous amount of income and assets, rather than spend down to poverty as previously required.

Squaring the Life Expectancy Course - Trend toward a square-shaped "curve" describing a population in which each person lived a long-healthy life, and then died suddenly.

Stage Theories of Personality - Theories that an individual develops though various stages, each one necessary for adaptation and psychological adjustment. Erikson's theory of personality development is an example of this.

State Units on Aging (SUA) - State offices that engage in statewide planning and advocacy on behalf of older adults in the state. SUAs were established and are partially funded through the Older Americans Act.

Stereotypes - Standardized mental picture that is held in common by members of a group and represents an oversimplified opinion, affective attitude, or uncritical judgment.

Stress - Physical, social, and psychological stimuli that can have positive or negative effects on health and behavior. Some forms of stress positively increase productivity. Too much stress can increase anxiety or even produce physiological responses, such as increased heart rate, muscle tension, and rapid breathing.

Stress Responses - Physiological or psychological adaptations made in response to internal or external stimuli that cause a state of imbalance. Stress responses can be produced by major life events, role change, chronic daily "hassles," and so forth.

Stressors - Stimuli that cause stress.

Stroke - See Cerebrovascular Accident.

Structural Lag - Inability of social structures (patterns of behavior, attitude, ideas, policies, etc.) to adapt to changes in population and individual lives.

Subculture Theory - Belief that older people maintain their self-concepts and social identities through their membership in a subculture.

Subcutaneous - Deepest layers of skin, under the dermis and epidermis.

Successful Aging - Combination of physical and functional health, high cognitive functioning, and active involvement with society. See Figure 6.1 in the text.

Suicide - Taking one's own life.

Surrogate Decision Maker - Someone appointed to make decisions for an individual who is not capable of making them for him/herself, perhaps because the person has dementia or is in a coma.

Surrogate Family - Family consisting of unrelated individuals, usually formed to substitute for missing and distant blood-related family members.

Superwoman Squeeze - Increasing demands on women to perform well in the workforce and complete household chores while providing quality care to dependent children and parents.

Supplemental Security Income - A federal program established in 1974 to provide a minimal income for older individuals living on the margin of poverty.

Symbolic Interactionism - Belief that the interactions of such factors as the environment, individuals, and their encounters in it can significantly affect one's behavior and thoughts, including the aging process.

Synapse - The junction between any two neurons.

Telomerase – The enzyme responsible for rebuilding telomeres.

Terminal Decline Hypothesis – The hypothesis that persons who are close to death decline in their cognitive abilities.

Test Anxiety - Nervousness about taking an exam, which may result in poor performance.

Testosterone - Male sex hormone.

Third Age - Last third of life, starting from about age 55 or 60.

Tinnitus - Noise or ringing in the ears, which can be due to a buildup of wax, a punctured tympanic membrane, or excessive exposure to noise in the environment.

Tip-of-the-Tongue States – Difficulty retrieving names from secondary memory but often spontaneously recalled later.

Title XX - Provision of the Social Security Act that funds social services to low-income citizens regardless of age. Examples of services for older adults funded by Title XX include homemaker and chore services, home-delivered meals, adult protective services, adult day care, foster care, and residential care.

Top Heavy Families - Families in which the number of adults (parents, grandparents, and great-grandparents) is disproportionately greater than the number of children.

Trait Theory of Personality - Personality theories that describe individuals in terms of characteristic of "typical" attributes that remain relatively stable with age.

Tweeners - People who are neither rich enough to pay privately for services they need nor poor enough to qualify for government assistance. Also known as the gap group.

Two-Stage Orgasm - Experienced by younger males, the sense of ejaculation inevitably followed by actual semen expulsion.

Two-Tier System of Health Care - Two levels of care, depending on ability to pay. For example, some health care providers refuse to treat Medicaid and/or poorer Medicare patients because the reimbursement is too low. Thus, poor people have fewer options for care or may not have access to care at all.

If a person has Medigap insurance or can pay out-of-pocket, he/she can go to any health care provider for care.

Unemployment Rate - Number of people without jobs compared to the total population within a specific age group.

Universal Benefits - Benefits available on the basis of social right to all persons belonging to a designated group.

Universal Eligibility - Program for which everyone is eligible, regardless of income, age, ethnicity, and so forth.

Urogenital Atrophy - Reduction in the elasticity and lubricating abilities of the vagina approximately five years after menopause.

Vesting of Pension Benefits - Amount of time a person must work on a job in order to be eligible for pension payments upon retirement.

Veterans Administration (VA) - Government program that provides health care for war veterans through more than 170 VA hospitals, more than 100 VA nursing homes, and contracts with community facilities.

Viropause - Male menopause or the male climacteric.

Vital Capacity - Maximum amount of oxygen that can be brought into the lungs with a deep breath.

Visual Mediators – The method of locations; memorizing by linking each item with a specific location in space.

Wear and Tear Theory of Aging - Biological theory of aging that each species ages at a genetically-determined rate within a genetically determined life span. This, compounded by environmental stress and poor lifestyle, leads to the deterioration of cells, and to frailty and death.

Wechsler Adult Intelligence Scale (WAIS) - Instrument used to measure adult intelligence, which consists of eleven subtests: six Verbal Scales measuring mostly crystallized intelligence and five Performance Scales measuring mostly fluid intelligence.

White House Conference on Aging - Large conference sponsored by the U.S. president in 1961, 1971, and 1981 to examine policy issues affecting older adults. The Conference scheduled for 1991 was held in 1995.

Widow(er) Syndrome - Term coined by Masters and Johnson describing sexual dysfunction following a long period of abstinence due to a spouse's illness and/or death.

Wisdom - Integration of experience, introspection, reflection, intuition, empathy, intelligence, and memory into matured vision and matured interaction with the environment.

Women in the Middle - Women who have competing demands from aged parents, spouses, children, and employment.

Workaholic - Someone who works compulsively and has few interests outside of work.

Work Ethic - Feeling that work is valuable and that nonproductive use of time is wasteful and suspect.

Working (Primary) Memory – The active process of holding newly acquired information in storage; a maximum of 7±2 stimuli before they are processed into secondary memory or discarded.

Young-Old - Among older adults, those 65 to 74.

PARTICIPANTS IN THE VIDEO

Experts

The Honorable Neil Abercrombie
U.S. House of Representatives
Washington, DC

William H. Adler, M.D.
National Institute on Aging
Rockville, MD

Marie Louise Ansak, M.S.W.
On Lok Senior Health Service
San Francisco, CA

Robert Atchley, Ph.D.
Scripps Gerontology Center
Miami University
Athens, OH

Vern Bengtson, Ph.D.
Andrus Gerontology Center
University of Southern California
Los Angeles, CA

Herbert Benson, M.D.
New England Deaconess Hospital
Boston, MA

James E. Birren, Ph.D
Borun Center for Gerontological Research
University of California at Los Angeles
Los Angeles, CA

Colette Browne, Dr.P.H.
School of Social Work
University of Hawaii at Manoa
Honolulu, HI

Kenneth Brummel-Smith, M.D.
Oregon Health Sciences University
Portland VA Medical Center
Portland, OR

Robert Clark, Ph.D.
Department of Economics and Business
North Carolina State University
Raleigh, NC

Gene D. Cohen, M.D., Ph.D.
National Institute on Aging
Washington, DC

Paul T. Costa, Ph.D.
National Institute on Aging
Rockville, MD

Michael Crow, Ph.D.
National Institute on Aging
Rockville, MD

Betty Crowder, M.S.W.
Episcopal Sanctuary
San Francisco, CA

James Allen Dator, Ph.D.
Department of Political Science
University of Hawaii at Manoa
Honolulu, HI

Vincent J. DeFeo, Ph.D.
Department of Anatomy and
  Reproductive Biology
University of Hawaii at Manoa
Honolulu, HI

Former Congressman Thomas Downey
New York, NY

Rev. Monsignor Charles J. Fahey
Third Age Center
Fordham University
New York, NY

Herman Feifel, Ph.D.
Psychological Services, VA Outpatient Clinic
Los Angeles, CA

Jerome Fleg, Ph.D.
National Institute on Aging
Washington, DC

Lou Glasse, M.S.W.
Older Women's League
Washington, DC

Harvey L. Gochros, D.S.W.
School of Social Work
University of Hawaii at Manoa
Honolulu, HI

Madeleine J. Goodman, Ph.D.
Office of Vice President for Academic Affairs
University of Hawaii at Manoa
Honolulu, HI

Rabbi Earl Grollman, Ph.D.
Belmont, MA

Melinda J. Grooms, R.N.
Home Health Services
Portland, OR

Robert Harootyan, M.S., M.A.
Forecasting and Environmental
  Scanning Department
American Association of Retired Persons
Washington, DC

Leonard Hayflick, Ph.D.
School of Medicine
University of California at San Francisco
San Francisco, CA

Nancy R. Hooyman, Ph.D.
School of Social Work
University of Washington
Seattle, WA
William Hoyer, Ph.D.

Department of Psychology
Syracuse University
Syracuse, NY

Michael Kaplan, Ph.D.
National Institute on Aging
Rockville, MD

Jack Kevorkian, M.D.
Royal Oak, MI

Douglas Kimmel, Ph.D.
Clinical Psychologist
Hancock, ME

H. Asuman Kiyak, Ph.D.
Geriatric Dentistry Program
University of Washington
Seattle, WA

Theodore Koff, Ed.D.
Arizona Long-Term Care Gerontology Center
University of Arizona
Tucson, AZ

Edward Lakatta, Ph.D.
National Institute on Aging
Rockville, MD

Thomas Lapine, M.D.
Danvers, MA

George R. Martin, Ph.D.
National Institute on Aging
Rockville, MD

Linda Martin, Ph.D.
Population Institute
East-West Center
Honolulu, HI

E. Jeffrey Metter, M.D.
National Institute on Aging
Rockville, MD

Meredith Minkler, Dr.P.H.
School of Public Health
University of California at Berkeley
Berkeley, CA

William Narang, M.S.W.
Leisure World
Sepulveda, CA

Marita Nelson, Ph.D.
Department of Anatomy and
  Reproductive Biology
University of Hawaii at Manoa
Honolulu, HI

Antonino Passaniti, Ph.D.
National Institute on Aging
Rockville, MD

Barbara Payne, Ph.D.
Decatur, GA

K. Warner Schaie, Ph.D.
Gerontology Center
Pennsylvania State University
University Park, PA

Edwin S. Shneidman, Ph.D.
Neuropsychiatric Institute
University of California at Los Angeles
Los Angeles, CA

Ruth Sifton, M.P.H.
Oahu Central Day Care Center
Wahiawa, HI

Samuel Simmons, Ph.D. Hon.
The National Caucus and Center on Black Aged
Washington, DC

Marta Sotomayor, Ph.D.
National Hispanic Council on Aging
Washington, DC

Richard Sprott, Ph.D.
University Center on Aging
San Diego State University
San Diego, CA

E. Percil Stanford, Ph.D.
University Center on Aging
San Diego State University
San Diego, CA

Mary Alice Stevenson, M.S.W.
Downtown Branch Director
San Francisco Senior Center
San Francisco, CA

Robyn Stone, Dr.P.H.
The Project Hope, Center for Health Affairs
Washington, DC

Richard Suzman, Ph.D.
National Institute on Aging
Rockville, MD

Jeanette C. Takamura, Ph.D.
Executive Office on Aging, State of Hawaii
Honolulu, HI

Joseph Jay Tobin, Ph.D.
Family Studies, University of New Hampshire
Durham, NH

Susan Tolle, M.D.
Portland, OR

Fernando Torres-Gil, Ph.D.
Commissioner on Aging
Washington, DC

George Z. Williams, M.D., D.Sci.
Medical Research Institute
Pacific Medical Center
San Francisco, CA

Sherry Willis, Ph.D.
Gerontology Center
Pennsylvania State University
University Park, PA

Steven Zarit, Ph.D.
Gerontology Center
Pennsylvania State University
University Park, PA

Other Participants

Janet Adkins
Ronald Adkins
Elizabeth Allen
Florence Austin
Doris Birchander
Eric Birchander
Tanya L. Bloom
Arthur Boudreault
Robert M. Brown
Thac Do Bui
Buster Capone
Pasquale Capone
Raymond Capone
Frank Catanzaro
Abby K. Chang
Charlie Chao
Charles M. Clark
William Bert Cline
Lawrence Collins
Catherine Conroy
Ethel Cooper
Marian Cowan
Faye L. Cruse

Ilse Darling
Sylvia Davis
Louise Di Virgilio
Ruth Dow
Celestine Eggleston
Oliver Francisco
John Franggos
Mary Franggos
Mary Goodman
Dean Gotham
Bert Higert
Suzanne Higert
Beverly E. Ickes
Jean Jaworski
Hayward King
Haruko Kiyabu
Kevin Mack
Hatcher Matosian
Donald McClure
Mabel McConnell
Walter Morris
Pat Nickerson
Ivy Nip

Jeanann Nye
Marguerite Ogawa
Tatsuno Ogawa
Robert Okura
Michael J. Orlando
Mollie Pier
Kristin Pollard
Jane Potter
David Reese
Eleanor Reese
Jack Rice
Nancy Rice
Josephine H.
Rosen
Mary Saladino
Leo Salazar
Lillian Salazar
Darith Seng
Joseph Serrao
Dorothy Sharp
Wilf Sharp
Robert Shaw
Viola M. Smith

Samuel Stephens
Charles Stump
Helen Sunahara
Lois B. Swift
Ben Tamashiro
Gloria Tamashiro
James Tate
Alice Tateishi
Allen Tateishi
Virginia Templeton
Meryl Thulean
M. Henrietta
Towsley
June Troxell
Betty Tuff
Lindsey Tuff
Mildred Tuttle
Mary Wonson
Roger Wonson
Blanche D.
Woodbury
Jovita Zimmerman

GROWING OLD IN A NEW AGE is an introductory gerontology telecourse and video series. It includes 13 one-hour television programs, a text, a *Study Guide*, and this *Faculty Guide*.

GROWING OLD IN A NEW AGE examines the biological, psychological, and sociological aspects of aging and considers what it means to be an older person in contemporary society.

The coordinated text for the telecourse, *Social Gerontology: A Multidisciplinary Perspective (Seventh Edition)* by Nancy R. Hooyman and H. Asuman Kiyak, also stands alone as an interdisciplinary introduction to the field of aging. The text and *Study Guide* are available from Allyn & Bacon. The *Faculty Guide* is available free to institutions licensing the telecourse.

The GROWING OLD IN A NEW AGE telecourse was developed by the Center on Aging at the University of Hawaii and is part of the Annenberg/CPB Collection.

For further information about licensing the telecourse, contact the PBS Adult Learning Service at http://www.pbs.org/als/growing_old/ or 1-800-257-2578.

For other information about *Social Gerontology: A Multidisciplinary Perspective (Seventh Edition)*, the *Study Guide*, and this *Faculty Guide*, write to:

Allyn and Bacon
75 Arlington Street
Suite 300
Boston, MA 02116

NOTES

NOTES

NOTES

NOTES

NOTES

NOTES

NOTES

NOTES